COLOR ATLAS OF
Forensic Toolmark Identification

COLOR ATLAS OF
Forensic Toolmark Identification

Nicholas Petraco

CRC Press
Taylor & Francis Group
Boca Raton   London   New York

CRC Press is an imprint of the
Taylor & Francis Group, an **informa** business

CRC Press
Taylor & Francis Group
6000 Broken Sound Parkway NW, Suite 300
Boca Raton, FL 33487-2742

© 2011 by Taylor and Francis Group, LLC
CRC Press is an imprint of Taylor & Francis Group, an Informa business

---

Library of Congress Cataloging-in-Publication Data

Petraco, Nicholas.
    Color atlas of forensic toolmark identification / Nicholas Petraco.
        p. cm.
    Includes bibliographical references and index.
    ISBN 978-1-4200-4392-1 (alk. paper)
    1. Machine tools--Identification--Atlases. 2. Machine tools--Identification--Handbooks, manuals, etc. 3. Evidence, Criminal--Handbooks, manuals, etc. 4. Forensic sciences--Handbooks, manuals, etc. I. Title.

HV8077.5.T66P48 2010
363.25'62--dc22   2009049902

Visit the Taylor & Francis Web site at
http://www.taylorandfrancis.com

and the CRC Press Web site at
http://www.crcpress.com

Dedication

The author dedicates this work to the memory of his close friend and brother in life, FDNY Fire Captain Kevin Cassidy (A/K/A Number 2). Kevin was a Vietnam veteran and veteran of the 9/11 attack on the World Trade Center. He is one more of America's heroes who will not be memorialized by the country and city he loved and selflessly served throughout his short life. Kevin died from an illness contracted at the World Trade Center while ignoring his own safety in order to save the lives of injured strangers and searching for the remains of the victims of this evil attack. May Kevin rest in peace forever in the arms of the God of our Universe.

Contents

Foreword

After studying, researching, teaching, and working as a forensic scientist for nearly forty years, I have come to believe that the credo for every forensic scientist should be:

> To labor to seek out the truth, the whole truth, and nothing but the truth, to the best that is humanly possible, using accepted scientific principle and practice, and to report and testify to that truth, freely and honestly, to all concerned parties, without any human bias or influence from any monetary, personal, career, or societal gain, or pressure from any person, individual, group, agency, institution, organization, or corporate, social, political, governmental, or religious interests or agendas.

Nicholas Petraco, Criminalist, D-ABC

Acknowledgments

The author would like to thank his mentor, Dr. Peter R. DeForest, D. Crim., for teaching him how to think as a forensic scientist. He would also like to thank Assistant Commissioner Dr. Peter A. Pizzola, NYPD Police Laboratory Director, and all the members of the Forensic Investigations Division for their encouragement, help, and support—without it, this work would not have been possible.

Mary Eng, BS, Managerial Criminalist, NYPD Forensic Investigations Division Police Laboratory, edited the full text and added constructive comments and important ideas to the entire work.

Lisa Faber, MSFS, Criminalist IV, Supervising Criminalist, NYPD Police Laboratory, edited and added valuable comments and ideas to the text.

Dr. Nicholas D. K. Petraco earned a BS in chemistry from Colgate University, Hamilton, New York in 1998 and a DSC in quantum chemistry from the University of Georgia, Athens, Georgia in 2002. He was a postdoctoral fellow in applied mathematics at the University of Waterloo in Ontario, Canada from 2002 to 2004 after which he was appointed to the faculty of the John Jay College of Criminal Justice and The Graduate Center, City University of New York. His current research interests focus on the application of statistical pattern recognition methods to physical evidence, specifically as applied to ballistics and toolmarks. Dr. Petraco researched and authored Chapter 8 of this text as well as editing the entire text.

Hal Sherman, Detective 1st Grade, NYPD Crime Scene Unit (Retd.) and coauthor of *Illustrated Guide to Crime Scene Investigation* (CRC Press, 2006) edited, made prolific comments, and shared valuable ideas to the portions of this work relating to the recognition, documentation, and collection of toolmark evidence at crime scenes.

Jane Moira Taupin, MS, an internationally known, Australian-born forensic scientist and widely published researcher and author, recently coauthored with Chesterene Cwiklik *Forensic Examination of Clothing: Protocols in Forensic Science* (CRC Press, July 2010). Ms. Taupin provided valuable comments and insights in those portions of this work concerned with the forensic examination of damaged textiles.

About the Author

Nicholas Petraco earned a BS in chemistry and an MS in forensic science from John Jay College of Criminal Justice, the City University of New York. He served as a detective/criminalist at New York City's Police Laboratory from 1968 to 1990 and held the position of senior forensic microscopist of the laboratory's trace section between 1982 and 1990, when he became a private forensic consultant. Mr. Petraco has helped educate thousands of forensic scientists, worked on more than 5,000 death investigations on behalf of prosecution and defense attorneys, and testified as an expert in more than 500 trials conducted in local, state, and federal criminal and civil courts.

Introduction

When an item like a tool comes into contact with a soft surface, it imparts a negative image or imprint onto that softer surface. The resulting imprint may depict any or all of the tool's physical structure, i.e., class characteristics, wear patterns, damage patterns, and microscopic striations. The same phenomenon occurs when an item of footwear or a tire or any object comes into contact with a soft surface. Collectively, this type of physical evidence is classified as impression evidence. Forensic scientists routinely encounter various forms of impression evidence at scenes of crime. Impression evidence and its analysis can be very important to an investigation.

Most forms of impression evidence can be considered in a general sense as either two- or three-dimensional marks. The majority of these marks or impressions fit into one of several primary categories:

- Plastic fingerprints
- Latent or patent prints
- Textile impressions
- Imprints made by footwear
- Imprints made by tires
- Bite marks
- Obliteration of stamped numbers
- Marks made by firearm mechanisms
- Marks made by power tools
- Marks made by hand tools
- Outlines made by puncturing tools

This work will be primarily concerned with the latter two categories. The results of this effort may also be applicable to other categories of impression evidence, e.g., firearms.

A *tool* is defined in *Webster's Encyclopedic Unabridged Dictionary of the English Language* as "an implement, esp. one held in the hand, for performing or facilitating mechanical operation, as a hammer, saw, file, etc. Synonyms: 1. Tool, implement, instruments, utensil refer to contrivances for doing work."[1]

In practice, a tool can be any device, appliance, apparatus, utensil, instrument, or machine designed to perform or do, by either manual or powered means, mechanical work.

When tools are used or misused, they often leave marks or holes on or in the surfaces to which they are applied. These marks can manifest as any manner of cut, pinch, snip, score, notch, gash, hack, slash, nick, impression, depression, indentation, dent, hole, serration, dimple, hollow, bump, burrow, tunnel, punch, puncture, bend, or striations (fine scratches, grooves, or channel). Collectively, these marks are known as toolmarks.

Toolmarks are normally subdivided into a variety of classifications depending on the class characteristics they exhibit. In its simplest form, a class characteristic is a mark or configuration of marks that is attributable to a particular type or class of tool or device based on its apparent shape, outline, or silhouette. In situations where a series of class characteristics mimics a tool's working surface morphology, the author prefers to use the term *class characteristic pattern* in place of class characteristics. The reason for this preference in terminology is that rarely does a single mark, caused by one class characteristic, enable an examiner to determine a tool's class. Rather, a pattern or configuration of marks allows an examiner to determine the type or class of tool that made the questioned mark. Figures 1 to 5 help to demonstrate this concept.

Class characteristics are the result of deliberate design features, intentionally imparted to a tool during the manufacturing process. All the individual tools being manufactured during a given run will have the same class characteristics. Primarily, these class features include the same component parts, the shape and size of the tool, and its overall morphology. However, they will also include the striations, flaws, and imperfections peculiar to the tools and dies used in the tool's manufacturing process.

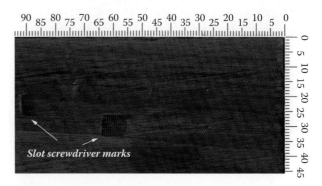

Figure 1 The impressions present in the wood suggest a ¼-inch slot-bladed screwdriver with parallel lines was utilized in this case.

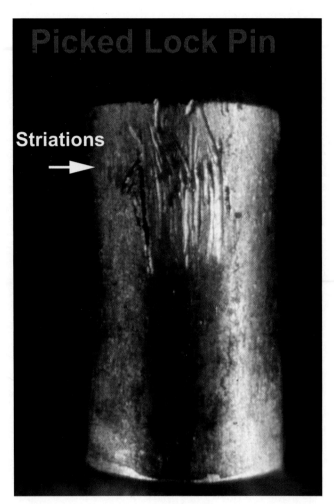

Figure 2 Pick marks on a tumbler pin removed from a lock cylinder. These marks suggest professional lock picks were used and not some makeshift device such as a paper clip.

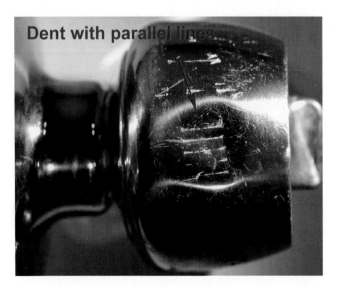

Figure 3 The dent containing well-defined and spaced parallel lines suggests that large channel-lock pliers or a vise grip was used to produce this mark.

Figure 4 The morphology of the cut marks present on the end of the lock's shackle indicates that a shearing type bolt cutter was used to cut the shackle.

Figure 5 The pattern or overall morphology (class characteristic pattern) of the puncture marks on this can's top instantly tells one that a beer can type can opener is responsible for the holes.

These idiosyncrasies are often termed subclass characteristics. These features will only be found on the tools they produced during a particular manufacturing run and, as such, can be quite useful in establishing the common origin of a questioned toolmark.

Class characteristics are subdivided into a variety of genera:

Toolmark Examination

I

Basic Geometric Optics for Toolmark Examiners

1

Before one can discuss the use of lenses and microscopes to form images of toolmarks on wood, metal, and other materials and surfaces, one must have at least a rudimentary understanding of the nature of light and how it interacts with matter. The *Merriam-Webster Dictionary* defines *light* simply as "something that makes vision possible."[1] This definition implies that light must be present for vision to take place. In other words, if there is no light, there is no vision. This simple statement is easily tested. Go outside on a dark, winter, moonless night, in an area where there is no artificial light, and place one of your hands directly in front of your face. You might sense your hand in front of you, but I guarantee you will not see it. Why? No visible light is being reflected from your hand onto the retinas of your eyes.

What is light? Light is electromagnetic radiation of any wavelength. Visible light is that part of the electromagnetic radiation spectrum given off by stars that is detectable by the eye. What is electromagnetic radiation? Electromagnetic radiation is the spectrum of energy given off by active stars. Electromagnetic radiation consists of a series of electromagnetic waves that travel at

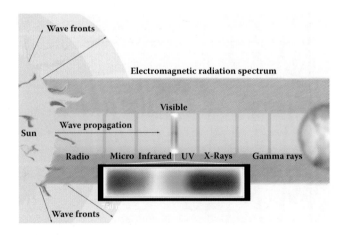

Figure 1.1 The electromagnetic radiation spectrum (EMRS) is emitted by the chromosphere of the sun. The visible light portion of the EMRS is of primary importance in the study of geometric optics. The visible spectrum that the human eye typically responds to is 700 to 400 nm, while its maximum sensitivity is normally 550 nm, or green light. Visible light is composed of all the colors of the rainbow, in spite of its composition; humans see visible light as white light.

the speed of light, 3.0×10^{10} cm/s, and have both electric and magnetic fields associated with them. Largely, our sun, a star, is a glowing mass of hydrogen plasma at temperatures greater than 6,000°C. At these severe temperatures, hydrogen plasma fuses to form helium nuclei in a process known as nuclear fusion. This process is the source of all radiant energy given off by our sun (a small star) and is the primary source of the electromagnetic radiation that is sent vibrating in all directions from the sun's surface. A portion of that radiation travels 93 million miles to reach the earth's surface. That part of the sun's electromagnetic radiation spectrum that can stimulate the retina of the human eye is visible light. Modern physics affirms that light has a dual nature. Light sometimes behaves as if it is a wave and at other times as if it is a particle. The theories that establish the dual nature of light are out of the scope of this text. In this work, we will treat light as if it behaves as a wave.

Energy can transfer from one point to another by two methods. One method involves the movement of matter to transport energy; the other method involves the movement of waves to transport energy. An example of the former method is a hammer used to drive a nail into wood. An example of the latter is light moving through space, a vacuum, void of matter. Figure 1.1 depicts the electromagnetic radiation produced and emitted by our sun.

There are two basic types of waves: transverse waves that require no matter or material to transport their energy, and mechanical waves that require matter to transfer their energy. Electromagnetic waves are transverse waves; they travel from the sun through space, which is void of matter (see Figure 1.1). Figure 1.2 shows the transfer of energy through water by longitudinal wave motion.

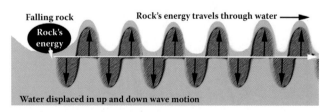

Figure 1.2 A cross section of the transfer of energy from a falling rock by the displacement of matter in a medium (water) by a longitudinal wave. The energy actually travels in a circular motion in all directions away from the rock.

Wave Characteristics and Nomenclature

All types of waves have universal characteristics, and therefore follow the same general rules.

In geometric optics, we are only concerned with the transverse waves in the form of light. The linear distance between two equivalent points on successive waves is termed a wavelength, which is designated lambda (λ). The highest portion of a wave is known as the crest, while the lowest portion of a wave is called the trough. The maximum displacement of a wave is known as its amplitude. The frequency (f) of a wave is the number of wavelengths that travel a given linear distance per unit of time. Frequency is measured in hertz (Hz). One hertz is equal to one wave per second. If one knows the frequency and wavelength of a wave, the velocity (v) of that wave can be precisely determined (see Equation 1.1). Wave characteristics and nomenclature are shown in Figure 1.3.

$$v = f\lambda \qquad (1.1)$$

The quantity of energy a wave contains is relative to its displacement from its rest position and is characterized by its amplitude. Two waves traveling in phase in the same medium can interact with one another.

This phenomenon is termed interference. Interference can be constructive (additive), which results in the final wave's amplitude increasing in size, or destructive (subtractive), which results in the final wave's amplitude decreasing in size. Figure 1.4 illustrates aspects of wave interference.

As a wave travels through the same medium, its speed remains constant and is solely dependent on the properties of that medium. When waves travel from one medium into another medium, e.g., from air into glass, their speed changes. If the wave passes from a less optically dense medium into a more optically dense medium, the wave will slow down. Conversely, if the wave passes from a more optically dense medium into a less optically dense medium, the wave will speed up. Figure 1.5 demonstrates what happens when a series of electromagnetic waves traveling in air enters a transparent block of glass at 90 degrees incident to the surface of the glass block.

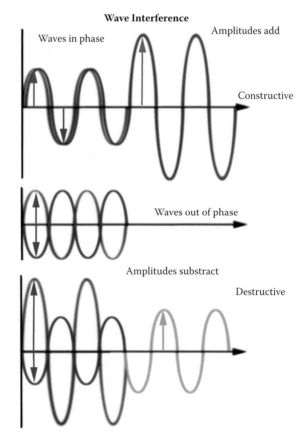

Figure 1.4 The interference of waves traveling in the same phase (in the same plane) in a medium can be either constructive or destructive. In constructive interference, their energy displacement from the rest position (amplitude) is additive and results in a larger amplitude; in destructive interference, their energy displacement from the rest position is subtractive and results in a smaller amplitude. In the case of the central waves there is no resulting wave because the two interfering waves nullify each other.

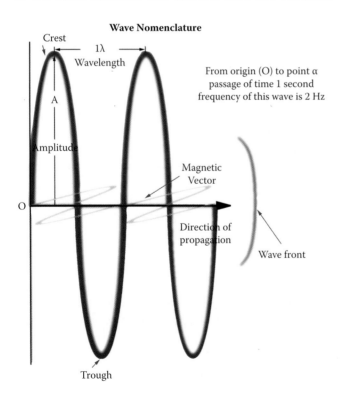

Figure 1.3 A series of two electromagnetic waves. Electromagnetic waves have both electric and magnetic components. In geometric optics we are concerned primarily with the electric properties.

When waves traveling through a medium approach a reflective object's outer surface, they are reflected from that surface at the same angle they approached the object. This is in accordance with the law of reflection: the angle of incidence is equal to the angle of reflection. The angles of incidence and reflection are both measured from a normal line (perpendicular) drawn to the object's surface at the site of incidence.

Snell's Law

Light rays emitted from the sun or other primary sources are normally diffuse, and thus travel in all directions. If incident light rays are reflected from a surface, the reflected rays of light become polarized. Polarized light waves differ from diffused light in that they vibrate in only one direction or plane (see Figures 1.6, 1.7). When waves of light approach the interface of two different transparent media at an acute angle, their direction will change. Some of the diffused incident light will be reflected, while some of the diffused light will be refracted. Both the reflected and refracted light waves are polarized, and vibrate in opposite planes. Figure 1.7 depicts what takes place when light waves are incident upon a more optically dense, transparent surface, at an angle other than 90 degrees.

When waves of light travel from medium *a* into medium *b*, more optically dense light rays are refracted toward the normal. **Snell's law** states that a ray of light bends in such a way that the ratio of the sine of the angle of incidence (*i*) to the sine of the angle of refraction (*r*) is a constant. For a light ray traveling from medium *a* into any medium *b*, this constant, the ratio between the sines of both angles, is called the index of refraction (*n*) (see Equation 1.2). In this equation, *i* is the angle of incidence, *r* is the angle of refraction, n_1 is the refractive index for medium *a*, and n_2 is the refractive index of medium *b*.

$$n_1 \sin i = n_2 \sin r \qquad (1.2)$$

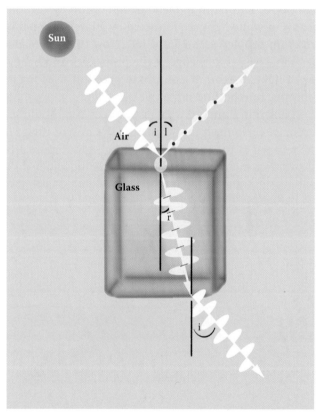

Figure 1.7 Snell's law states that a ray of light bends in such a way that the ratio of the sine of the angle of incidence (*i*) to the sine of the angle of refraction (*r*) is a constant. Illustrated is what occurs when diffused light waves are incident on a transparent surface at an angle other than 90 degrees to the incident surface. The reflected and refracted light waves are both polarized and vibrate perpendicular to each other. The angle of reflection (l) is equal to the angle of refraction. The reflected light vibrates in a plane perpendicular to that of the page you are reading, while the refracted light, also polarized, is vibrating in the plane of the paper.

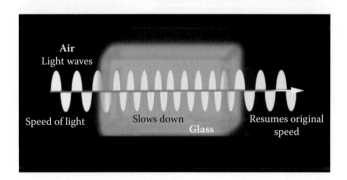

Figure 1.5 Light waves slow down as they travel from air into an optically denser, transparent medium at 90 degrees. Conversely, light waves speed up as they reenter the less optically dense medium.

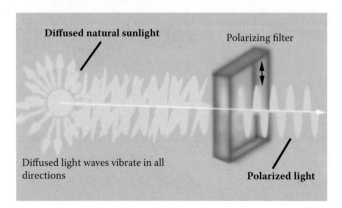

Figure 1.6 Diffused light from the sun or an incandescent light bulb vibrates in all directions, while polarized light vibrates in only one plane or preferred direction.

Dispersion of Light

When rays of light from the sun or an artificial white light source fall on the surface of a glass prism, the light is refracted and is thereby dispersed into its component colors. All electromagnetic waves travel through space at the speed of light, 3.0×10^{10} cm/s. However, in all other media, these waves travel more slowly, and waves of different frequencies travel at somewhat different speeds. As a result, the index of refraction is a little different for each wavelength comprising white light. Therefore, when white light falls on a prism, the waves of each color bend, or refract, by different amounts and the light disperses, or separates, into its component wavelengths (see Figure 1.8). [2-7]

The arrangement of the different colors that emerge from a glass prism is called a spectrum. Spectra of white light are normally seen after a rainstorm in the form of a rainbow. This natural phenomenon occurs when sunbeams of white light are refracted by a large number of tiny rain droplets (see Figure 1.9). Now that the reader has some basic knowledge of the properties and behavior of light, we can discuss some practical uses for its reflective mirrors and refractive behavior.

Look into a mirror; what do you see? You should see an image of yourself in the mirror. The mirror image is the reversal of the subject from left to right. Figure 1.10 illustrates a mirror image of a photographic folder.

Lenses

Lenses are a necessary part of eyeglasses, telescopes, cameras, and microscopes. Lenses are typically made from glass; however, they can be constructed from plastic as well as minerals such as fluorite. There are two main types of lenses: **converging** and **diverging**.

A converging lens can be thought of as two triangular-shaped prisms stacked on their bases, one on top of the other, as demonstrated in Figure 1.11. If one

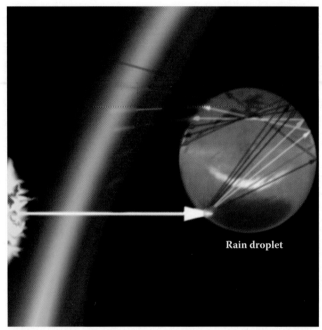

Figure 1.9 Rainbows form when white light from the sun is dispersed into its spectral components by refraction and reflection by large numbers of minute water droplets.

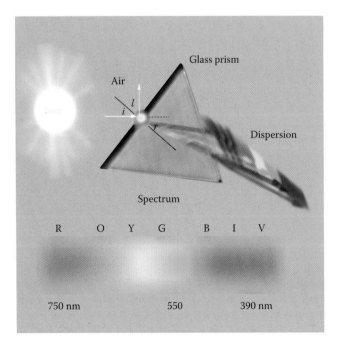

Figure 1.8 Depicted above is the dispersion of the visible or white light portion of the EMRS into its component colors or wavelengths. The scientific name for white light is polychromatic light, or light of many (poly) colors (chromatic).

Figure 1.10 A red photograph holder. The front view of the folder is marked A; the back of the folder, B, contains the same information as A; and C is the mirror image of B. Note that the mirror image is a reversal of B and is set back into the mirror. This image is known as a virtual image because it appears to be behind the mirror. Virtual images cannot be shone upon a screen.

cements their bases together and rounds off their thick central edges by grinding, a converging, or **convex**, lens is formed.

A converging lens causes light waves from infinity to refract and come together to a sharp focus at a point some distance from the lens' optic axis. This point is the focal point, while the distance from the lens' optic axis to its focal point is the focal length. The principal axis of any lens is a line drawn perpendicular to the plane of the lens through its midpoint. A lens' optic axis is a line drawn from top to bottom through its midpoint (see Figure 1.12).

The second type of lens, called diverging, causes light waves from infinity to refract and diverge apart (see Figure 1.13). Diverging lenses are normally termed concave lenses. All images formed by concave lenses are virtual and erect, as demonstrated in Figure 1.14.

Examples of the six standard shapes of lenses are shown in Figure 1.15. The behavior of a simple lens can be expressed by Equation 1.3, often called the lens maker's formula. In this equation, fl is the focal length, p is the object distance from the lens' principal axis, and q is the image distance from the lens' principal axis:

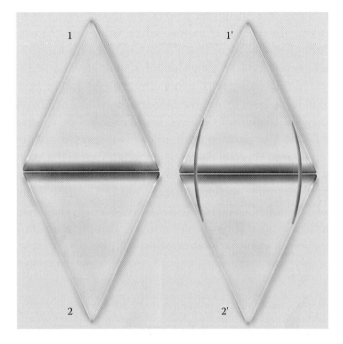

Figure 1.11 Two triangular-shaped glass prisms stacked on their bases, prism 1 on top of prism 2. If one cements their bases together and rounds off their thick central edges by grinding, a converging lens is formed.

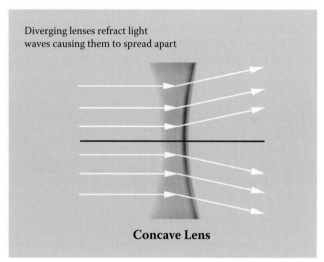

Figure 1.13 Diverging lenses cause light waves from infinity to refract and diverge apart. Concave is the common name for diverging lenses.

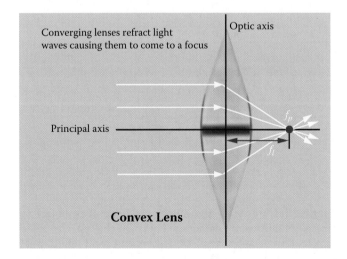

Figure 1.12 A converging lens causes light waves from infinity to refract and come together to a sharp focus along the lens' principal axis. Converging lenses are known as convex lenses. The focal point is designated (f_p) and the focal length is designated (f_l).

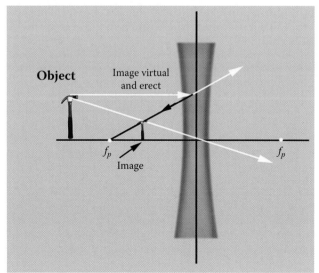

Figure 1.14 The formation of an image of a hammer by a concave lens. Note the image is erect and virtual (not focusable on a screen).

$$\frac{1}{fl} = \frac{1}{p} + \frac{1}{q} \qquad (1.3)$$

A significant location along the principal axis of a lens is twice its focal length. In Figure 1.16 an object is placed at a distance greater than two focal lengths along the lens' principal axis; in this position, the image that is formed is inverted, real, and reduced in size. Four common image formations with converging lenses showing the object-to-image relationships are depicted in Figures 1.17 and 1.18. In Figure 1.17, at the top, the object is placed in between the first and second focal length positions, along the lens' principal axis. This setup produces an image of the object that is real, inverted, and enlarged in size. At the bottom, the object is placed at the second focal length position, along the lens' principal axis. This setup produces an image of the object that is real, inverted, and the same size as the object. In Figure 1.18, at the top, the object is placed at the first focal length position, along the lens' principal axis. This setup produces no image. At the bottom, the object is placed between the lens and first focal length position producing a virtual and erect image.

Several problems arise when one is imaging objects using white (polychromatic) light and curved lenses. Image distortion, such as coma, pincushion, and barrel, is but one of the minor problems that have plagued lens makers. However, the major distortion problems that arise are chromatic aberration and spherical aberration. As discussed earlier, when white light travels through a glass lens, each wavelength composing the light is refracted at a slightly different angle, and is dispersed into its various colors. Thus, if white light from an object passes through a glass lens, it will form a fuzzy image of the object that will be surrounded by colored halos. White light entering a lens is dispersed or broken up into spectral colors, from red to violet. The short wavelengths, i.e., violet and blue, are refracted more than the longer wavelengths, i.e., red and orange. Thus, each color has a different focus. Consequently, the image of the object will have color fringes. This phenomenon, known as **chromatic aberration**, can be corrected by

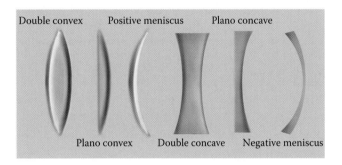

Figure 1.15 The six standard shapes of lenses used in the making of a variety of optical devices such as eyeglasses, cameras, telescopes, and microscopes. From left to right: double convex, plano convex, positive meniscus (thicker in the center, thinner at the ends), double concave, plano concave, and negative meniscus (thinner in the center, thicker at the ends).

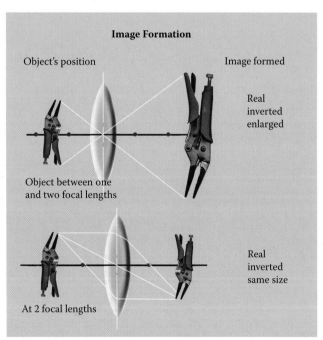

Figure 1.17 Two of the common single lens object-to-image situations are depicted above. On the top, the object is placed in between the first and second focal length positions along the lens' principal axis. This setup produces an image of the object that is real, inverted, and enlarged in size. On the bottom, the object is placed at the second focal length position, along the lens' principal axis. This setup produces an image of the object that is real, inverted, and the same size as the object.

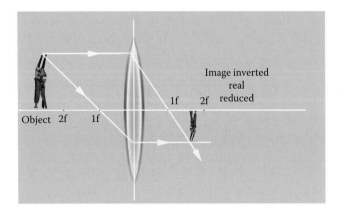

Figure 1.16 An object is placed at a distance greater than two focal lengths away from the lens along its principal axis. In this position, the image that is formed is inverted, real, and reduced in size.

combining different lenses that will cancel this effect. Typically, in a doublet composed of a converging lens made from crown glass and a diverging lens made from flint glass, the lenses are cemented together to form an achromatic lens system. Figures 1.19 to 1.22 demonstrate the problem and how lenses are used to eliminate chromatic aberration.

Spherical aberration is the next major lens distortion. The light rays entering a lens at its outer edges are refracted more than the rays entering the lens near its center. Thus, the resulting image of the object will be fuzzy, and slightly out of focus (see Figure 1.23). This problem can be reduced and a sharp image can be attained with a simple lens by placing a diaphragm along the lens' principal axis so that only the central rays form the image. Figure 1.24 illustrates how spherical aberration is corrected by placing a diaphragm between the object and the lens forming the image.

Common geometric distortions are aberrations commonly seen in stereomicroscopy. These distortions are observed as changes in shape of an image. Figure 1.25 shows two common types of geometric distortions: pincushion and barrel.

The lens in the human eye forms images in much the same manner as a convex lens. Many of the problems with lens distortions can also be compensated for by adding

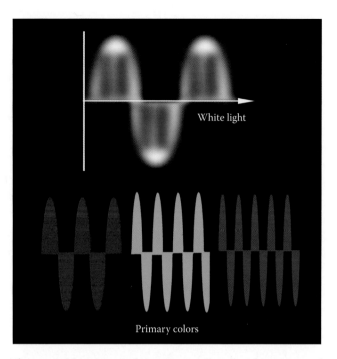

Figure 1.19 White light is depicted with its primary colors. Note that there are a different number of wavelengths for each primary color for the passage of 1 second of time. Thus, the frequency of each primary color is different.

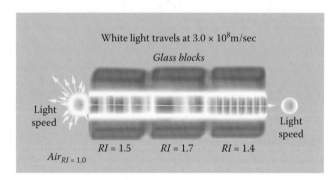

Figure 1.20 As white light travels from air through glass blocks with different refractive indices, it changes speed.

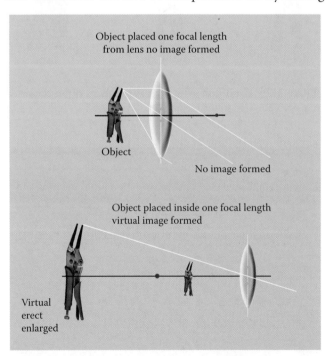

Figure 1.18 Two of the common single lens object-to-image situations. At the top, the object is placed at the first focal length position, along the lens' principal axis; this setup produces no image. At the bottom, the object is placed between the lens and the first focal length position, along the lens' principal axis; this setup produces an image of the object that is virtual, erect, and enlarged.

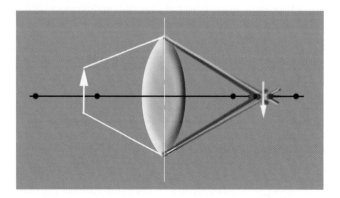

Figure 1.21 White light entering a lens is dispersed or broken up into its spectral colors, from red to violet. The short wavelengths, i.e., violet and blue, are refracted more than the longer wavelengths, i.e., red and orange. Thus, each color has a different focus. Consequently, the image of the object will have color fringes.

various lenses to correct for the existing distortion(s). Figure 1.26 shows how the human eye forms an image. The image projected onto the retina is sent to the brain via the optic nerve. The process of image formation by the human brain is still not fully understood.

When light rays approach a convex lens parallel to its principal axis they interact with the tiny space between the minute structures composing matter. The phenomenon is known as diffraction. Diffraction is the bending of waves around a physical barrier placed directly in their path. A diffraction pattern is formed when a grating, composed of a transparent film that has closely spaced, fine lines drawn on its surface, is placed in the path of a beam of light. Figure 1.27 depicts the interaction of a laser beam with a line grating. Diffraction is important to study in this context

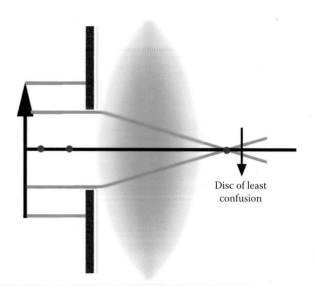

Figure 1.24 Spherical aberration is corrected for a single lens by placing a diaphragm between the object and the lens forming the image.

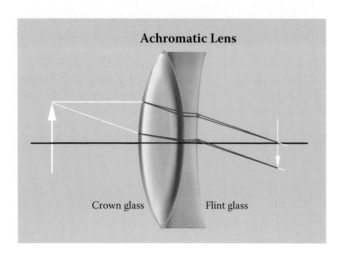

Figure 1.22 A doublet composed of a double convex lens made from crown glass and a double concave lens made from flint glass; the lenses are cemented together to form an achromatic lens system to correct the condition for the red and blue wavelengths of light.

Figure 1.25 Common geometric distortions often observed in less expensive macroscopic lens systems.

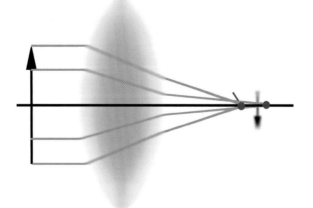

Figure 1.23 The light rays entering a lens at its outer edges are refracted more than the rays entering the lens near its center, thus forming a fuzzy image of the object.

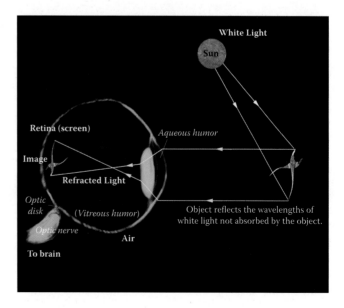

Figure 1.26 A cross section of the human eye showing how an image is formed on the retina.

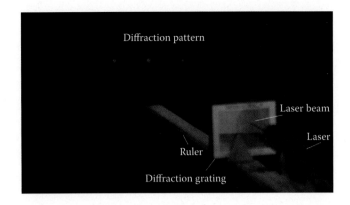

Figure 1.27 Diffraction of monochromatic laser light as it interferes with the grooves of a diffraction grating. Prof. Ernst Abbey showed that this phenomenon is responsible for the formation of an image by the microscope.

because it has been proven that the interference of diffracted and undiffracted light rays from the specimen forms the image produced by the compound light microscope.

References

1. *The Merriam-Webster dictionary*, F. C. Mish, ed., 429. 1997. Springfield: MA.
2. Chamot, E. M., and Mason, C. W. 1930. *Handbook of chemical microscopy*, 4–50. Vol. I. New York: John Wiley & Sons.
3. Shillaber, C. P. 1944. *Photomicrography in theory and practice*, 198–99. New York: John Wiley & Sons.
4. Needham, G. H. 1958. *The practical use of the microscope*, 225–29. Springfield, IL: Charles C. Thomas.
5. Zieler, H. W. 1974. *The optical performance of the light microscope part I, 1972 and part II*. Chicago: Microscope Publications Ltd.
6. DeForest, P. R. 1982. Foundations of forensic microscopy. In *Forensic science handbook*, ed. R. Saferstein, 416–528. Vol. 1. Englewood Cliffs, NJ: Regents/Prentice Hall.
7. Petraco, N., and Kubic, T. 2004. *Microscopy for criminalists, chemists, and conservators*. Boca Raton, FL: CRC Press.

Basic Microscopy for Toolmark Examiners $\mathcal{2}$

The microscope is the most important scientific tool available to a forensic toolmark examiner. Without it, the study, examination, identification, individualization, and comparison of questioned toolmarks recovered from crime scenes would not be possible.

The simplest microscope is a hand magnifier that consists of either one lens or two to three lenses cemented together. Simple microscopes produce magnified images on the order of two to twenty times a specimen's actual size. They provide their user a macroscopic view of the study specimen, thus enabling the viewer to see minute detail not achievable with the unaided eye (see Figure 2.1).

Compound microscopes are different from simple microscopes in that their images are formed by two lens systems, the objective lens and the ocular, or eyepiece. The stereomicroscope and the comparison microscope are the two types of compound microscopes most often used by toolmark examiners. Although the theory and nomenclature discussed herein apply to any type of compound microscope, this work will concentrate on the stereomicroscope and the comparison microscope.[3-12]

In its simplest sense, a compound microscope is an amalgamation of two lens systems and a source of illumination. The first lens, known as the objective lens, forms the **primary image** of the specimen. The ocular then **magnifies** the primary image and projects it to the eye-point (or Ramsden circle), which is the area above the field lens of the ocular at which the pupil is positioned. Figure 2.2 is a simple diagram of a rudimentary compound microscope used by toolmark examiners. In Figure 2.2 a source of illumination is directed toward the specimen at an oblique angle. The light interferes with the specimen. The specimen, a metallic surface, reflects the light toward the objective lens, which collects the light and forms a primary image of the specimen. The primary image is then magnified by the ocular or eyepiece and presented to the eye-point, or Ramsden circle. There are two types of compound microscopes used by toolmark examiners in their daily work: the stereomicroscope and the comparison microscope. The parts and adjustments of each type, as well as important aspects of image formation, are presented in this chapter.

Compound microscopes are all composed of the same basic elements. To begin with, an optical bench in the form of a stand with a pillar or arm and steadying base is necessary to hold all the microscope's components. Normally the pillar is attached directly to a sturdy base, which allows for vibration-free operation

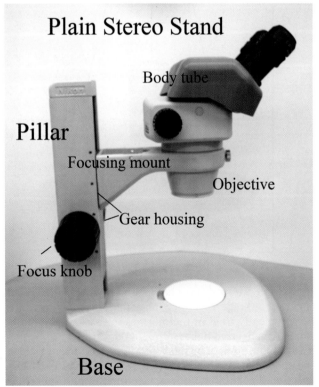

Figure 2.2 Example of a typical stereomicroscope base and pillar configuration.

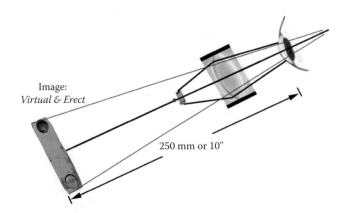

Figure 2.1 The object (lock) is within the focal point (*fp*) of a simple magnifier, and the eye is close to the lens. Under these conditions, a virtual, erect image is perceived at 25cm (10 inches) away for the eye.

of the imaging system. Built into or attached to the pillar is usually a rack and pinion focusing mechanism that allows for the coarse and fine adjustment to focus the final image. In general, with stereomicroscopes the objective and body tube are moved during the focusing

process, while with comparison microscopes the stage is either raised or lowered to adjust the focus of the final image. Examples of common types of stands used for stereomicroscopes and comparison microscopes are shown in Figures 2.2 to 2.4.

Next, a body tube with a nosepiece at its lower end houses the objective lenses, and the upper end houses the ocular. In the recent past microscope makers manufactured their objectives for body tubes with a mechanical tube length of 160 mm, as the specimen at focus was slightly above the objective's focal point (see Figure 2.2). In Figure 2.3, the stage, objective lenses, body tube, head, and eyepieces are all aligned along the microscope's optic axis.

Since the onset of the new millennium, microscope manufacturers are designing their objective lenses with infinity correction. In this design, the specimen is placed at the front focal plane of the objective lens. Consequently, the rays leaving the objective are projected to infinity. In this arrangement, a tube lens must be inserted into the body tube so the projected rays converge at the ocular's diaphragm (see Figure 2.5). These systems allow for the insertion of accessories within the microscope's optical

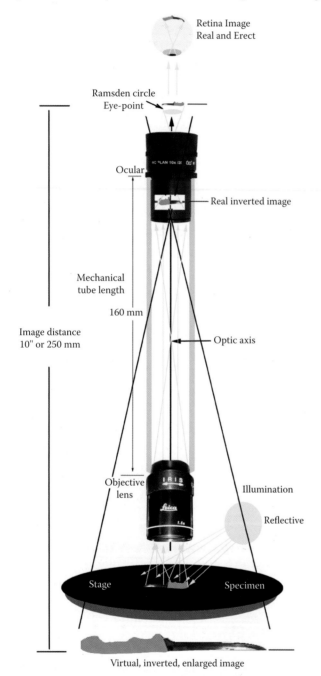

Figure 2.3 Rudimentary compound microscope diagram showing the stage, specimen, objective and ocular arrangement typically used in toolmark examination. A daylight source of reflective light is directed towards the specimen at an oblique angle. The light interferes with the specimen. The specimen, a metallic surface, reflects the light to the objective lens, which collects the light, and forms a primary image of the specimen. The primary image is than magnified by the ocular or eyepiece and presented to the eye-point or Ramsden circle.

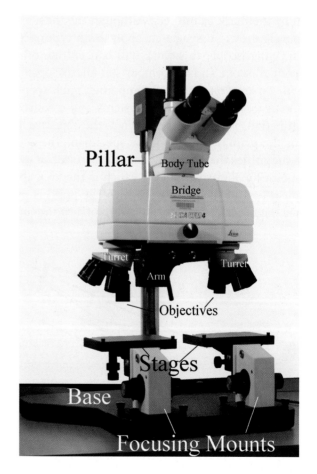

Figure 2.4 Example of a typical comparison microscope base and pillar configuration.

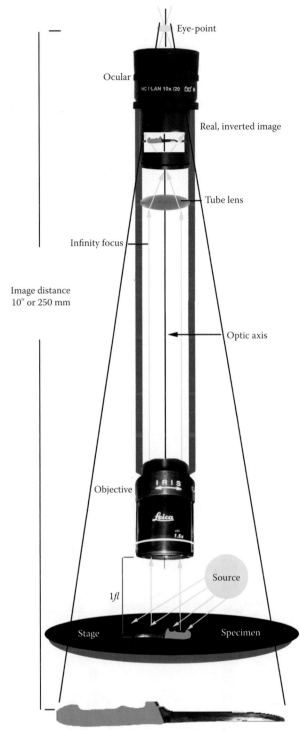

Eye-point

Ocular

Real, inverted image

Tube lens

Infinity focus

Image distance
10" or 250 mm

Optic axis

Objective

Source

1*fl*

Stage

Specimen

Virtual, inverted, enlarged image

Figure 2.5 In the infinity focus design, the specimen is placed at one focal length (at the front focal plane) from the objective lens. Consequently, the rays leaving the objective are projected to infinity. In this arrangement, a tube lens must be inserted into the body tube in order for the projected rays to converge at the oculars diaphragm. This system allows for the insertion of accessories within the microscope's optical path without the danger of producing ghost images or increasing over magnification. Objectives made for infinity focus systems would have an infinity symbol (∞) placed on their outer covers.

path without the danger of producing ghost images or increasing the system's overall magnification.

An archetypal body tube used in modern stereomicroscopes is depicted in Figure 2.6; note the presence of a tube lens at the base of this unit. Parallel rays exiting the objective or an intermediate optical device (zoom body) will be focused by the tube lens into an image at the intermediate plane of the eyepiece.

The stage is an integral component of any contemporary microscope. The stage provides the platform onto which the specimen is placed and manipulated. While there are many types of stages available, the most versatile stage for toolmark examination is often just a large flat surface onto which the specimen can be placed and easily maneuvered in front of the objective lens. Most new comparison microscopes have stages attached directly to focusing mounts that are, in turn, attached to the microscope's base. Figures 2.7 and 2.8 illustrate the stage configurations present on two modern comparison microscopes. In Figure 2.7, each stage is attached to its own focusing mount, which in turn is attached to the base. In Figure 2.8, the stages are attached to focusing mounts that are built into the base and are controlled independently by coarse and fine adjustment knobs.

The stages used in the manufacture of modern stereomicroscopes are also available in a wide variety of shapes and sizes. A large flat surface that allows for easy maneuvering of the specimen in front of the objective

Body Tube

Ocular's intermediate
image plane

Tube lens

Parallel rays
from objective

Zoom body

Objective

Figure 2.6 An archetypal body tube used in modern stereomicroscopes is depicted; note the presence of a tube lens at the base of the unit. Parallel rays exiting the objective or an intermediate optical device (zoom body) will be focused by the tube lens at the ocular's intermediate image plane.

lens is still most desirable for use in toolmark examinations. To this end, some stereomicroscopes come with no stage at all; instead, the table or bench top upon which the microscope sits serves as its stage. Figure 2.9 shows one low-end and one high-end stereomicroscope, both with large flat stages built into their bases. Figure 2.10 depicts a stereomicroscope that has no stage. This stereomicroscope has a large free-standing table

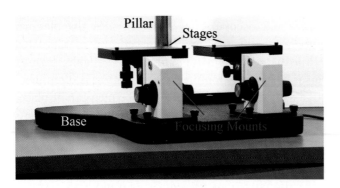

Figure 2.7 Comparison microscope base with two independently focusable square stages each attached to focusing mounts controlled by separate coarse adjustment knobs.

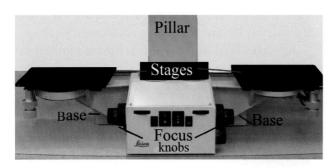

Figure 2.8 Comparison microscope base with two independently focusable rectangular stages attached to focusing mounts controlled by separate coarse and fine adjustment knobs.

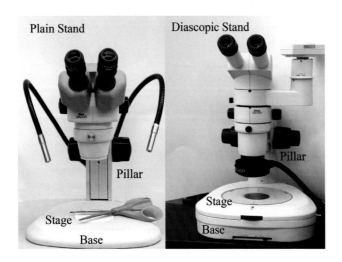

Figure 2.9 Two zoom stereomicroscopes with large flat stages built into their bases.

stand, composed of a pillar, an adjustable arm, and a very heavy base for stability. The stereomicroscope body, which contains the eyepiece tube, oculars, zoom body, and objective, is attached to the boom or table stand by a focusing mount.

The most important component of any microscope system is the objective lens because it is primarily responsible for the resolution achieved in the image it forms of the specimen under investigation. Resolution is the ability of a lens to separate two closely spaced physical points in an object into an image in which they appear to be two distinct, separate individual points. The front lens of an objective collects the light that interferes with the specimen. The quantity of image-forming light collected by the objective is related to the focal length of the objective, the refractive index (n) of the medium between the specimen and the objective's front lens, and the numerical aperture (NA) of the objective. Figure 2.11 demonstrates the many factors influencing an objective's NA. The numerical aperture is defined mathematically as

$$NA = n \sin \tfrac{1}{2}AA \text{ or } (\mu)$$

The angle aperture (AA) varies with the focal length of the objective lens system. Both the light-gathering capacity of an objective and its ability to resolve fine detail in a specimen are directly related to the AA of an objective. The resolving power of a compound microscope is also dependent on the condenser's NA. Consequently, the

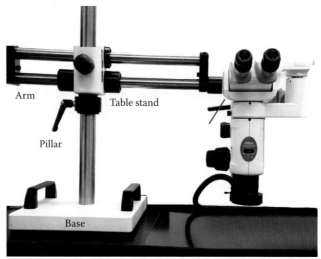

Figure 2.10 Depicted above is a stereomicroscope without a stage. This stereomicroscope has a large free standing table stand composed of a pillar, an adjustable arm, and a very heavy base for stability. The stereomicroscope body, which contains the eyepiece tube, oculars, zoom body and objective, is attached to the boom or table stand by a focusing mount.

approximate resolving power (*R*) of a microscope can be defined mathematically as

$$R = \frac{\lambda}{(\text{NA objective} + \text{NA condenser})}$$

where *R* is the smallest distance between two distinct side-by-side structural details in a specimen and λ is the size of the wavelength of the interfering light. In systems with no condenser (most reflected light systems), the approximate resolving power (*R*) of a microscope can be defined mathematically as

$$R = \frac{\lambda}{\text{NA objective}}$$

Typically, the higher the useful NA of an objective lens system, the greater is its resolving power.

Over the past century, toolmark examiners have utilized various types of objective lenses in their examination protocols. In the early part of the twentieth century, low-power, fixed-magnification, fixed numerical aperture, and achromatic lenses were employed by toolmark examiners. These systems normally had an aperture iris placed above the lens portion to control the intensity of the illumination in the primary image (see Figure 2.12).

Toward the middle of the century, two categories of achromatic objective lenses were manufactured for toolmark examinations. Since the usual specimen examined by toolmark examiners is an opaque, metal surface, some manufacturers utilized metallurgy objective lenses in the construction of comparison microscopes. Leitz used Ultropak objective lenses and Ultropak illumination systems for the illumination of opaque specimens. Figure 2.13 depicts an example of a low-power Leitz Ultropak objective lens.

In addition, Leitz provided several types of lenses primarily designed for scientific macro photography as reflected light objectives in their comparison microscopes. Leitz utilized Summar®, Photar®, and Makro® lenses for this purpose. Examples of some Makro and Photar lenses are given in Figures 2.14 and 2.15.

These typically low-power camera/objective macro lenses have adjustable iris diaphragms with corresponding *f*-stop positions (to control depth of field) indicated on their outside barrels. A common array of *f*-stop sizes is from 4.0 to 16. However, a full range of *f*-stops, from 2.5 to 44, is available to the user. Figure 2.16 shows a Photar 1:4.580mm lens at various *f*-stop settings.

Near the end of the century, two categories of objective lenses found favor and were commonly used for toolmark examinations: the zoom magnification macro lens and the fixed-magnification, fixed-NA objective lens. Now most lens systems produced by high-end microscope manufacturers are of high quality, and are corrected for most types of lens aberrations and distortion. Whether one chooses achromatic (corrected for two colors

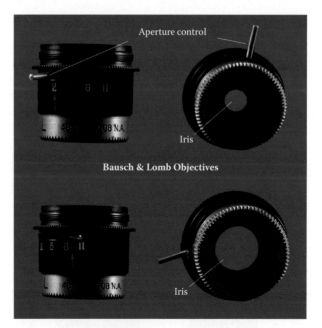

Figure 2.12 Old style objectives produced by an early manufacturer of comparison microscopes. The lens has a magnification of 2.5× and an NA of 0.08. The aperture numbers seen on this objective **do not** follow the convention associated with f-stops. In this instance the smaller number has a smaller aperture, while the larger number has a larger aperture.

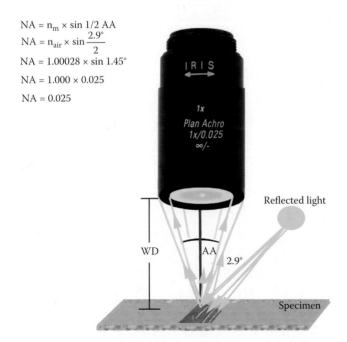

NA = n_m × sin 1/2 AA
NA = n_{air} × sin $\frac{2.9°}{2}$
NA = 1.00028 × sin 1.45°
NA = 1.000 × 0.025
NA = 0.025

Figure 2.11 Shown above is a modern style objective lens commonly used by a toolmark examiner, and the many factors used in the computation of the objective's NA.

chromatically and the color green spherically) or apochromatic (corrected for up to five colors chromatically and three colors spherically) objectives is now primarily a function of budget rather than need. When choosing objectives for toolmark examination, one must remember that the ideal magnification range is still between 8× and 30×, as reported by Hatcher et al.[1] Thus, the advantage gained in toolmark examinations by using such highly corrected apochromatic objective lens systems is almost

negligible. Therefore, modern achromatic objectives function estimably for toolmark examinations. Examples of the two categories of modern objective lenses are demonstrated in Figures 2.17 and 2.18.

Although the choice of objective lens used is normally a matter of personal preference on the part of any examiner, there are distinct differences between these

Figure 2.13 Low power Leitz® Ultropak objective lens. The outer ring of lens sections (C) surrounding a central objective lens (O), act as a condenser, condensing the light coming from an attached illuminator. The center lens objective O collects the reflected light that illuminated the specimen and forms an image of the specimen. This method of illumination will be discussed in more detail in another portion of this chapter.

Figure 2.15 Three Leitz Photar® macro lenses provided with RMS screw tread for use in photomicrography and with comparison microscopy. The range of magnification of these three lenses is ideal for use in toolmark comparisons.

Figure 2.14 Two Leitz Makro® macro lenses provided with RMS screw tread for use in photomicrography and with comparison microscopy

Figure 2.16 A Leitz Photar® lens showing 4 common f-stop aperture settings.

two types of objectives. Many examiners find using a zoom-style objective lens somewhat easier. Once they set the specimen up and focus it at the lowest power settings, to achieve a larger image of the specimen, they simply zoom up to a higher magnification. A severe disadvantage to the zooming method is the decrease in illumination due to extending the bellows; this often results in a less resolved final image. Another disadvantage of the zoom lens system is that it is much harder to determine the final magnification of the specimen. This author prefers the fixed-magnification, fixed-NA objective lenses. To begin with, each lens is inscribed with all of its vital information (see Figure 2.19). Next, a large selection of different fixed-magnification objectives can be placed on the same nosepiece, allowing for effortless changing of objectives by simply rotating the nosepiece or turret. In addition, since the objectives are manufactured as a set, all are designed to project an image of the portion of the specimen being viewed to the center of the ocular's preset diaphragm. A set of matched objectives, like the one shown in Figure 2.18, is designated as being parfocal and parcentric (once one lens is in focus and centered on the specimen, any one of the lenses on the same turret will be in focus and centered on that specimen when rotated into position).

Finally, fixed lens systems produce sharper, more detailed, finely resolved images than do zoom lens systems.

There are two primary types of stereomicroscopes, the Greenough and the common main objective. The Greenough was the first practical, fully functional stereomicroscope. Produced in the late nineteenth century, Greenough stereomicroscopes are composed of two separate objective lenses, each paired with one eyepiece or ocular. This configuration provides a

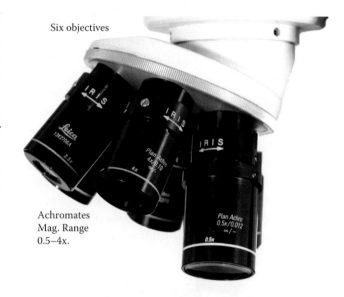

Figure 2.18 A set of Leica plan achromatic objective lenses. Each has a fixed NA, a fixed magnification and a built in iris diaphragm. The range of magnification with a 10× eyepiece is 5.0 to 40×. The author prefers the use of fixed magnification objective lenses over the zoom type lens.

Figure 2.17 Shown is a Leica Makrozoom® achromatic objective lens used on many of Leica's modern comparison microscopes. This lens has a magnification range from 0.8 to 8.0×. The iris diaphragm is placed at the top portion of the lens and is used to control the intensity of the illumination and the depth of focus achieved in the final image.

Figure 2.19 Above is shown a Leica® plan achromatic, fixed magnification, fixed NA objective lens.

compound microscope for each eye and, as a result, produces two different images of the specimen. The common main objective type stereomicroscope is the more modern form of stereomicroscopy. This style of stereomicroscopy has one main objective lens mounted just underneath two Galilean type telescopes. Typically, an erecting prism, tube lens, and ocular are positioned above each telescope. This configuration also provides two different images of the same specimen. Both types of stereomicroscopes produce three-dimensional images because they provide two different angles of view of the same specimen, thereby producing somewhat different images for each eye, thus resulting in stereoscopic vision. Figure 2.20 depicts a schematic of a Greenough type stereomicroscope, which is the earlier form of stereomicroscope. Figure 2.21 shows a diagram of a common main objective type stereomicroscope.

Although modern stereomicroscopes are designed to magnify specimens up to 400 diameters, toolmark examiners rarely, if ever, exceed 50 power. The SM was developed to allow the user to observe objects in three dimensions, as they normally see with their unaided eyes. As one increases the magnification of a specimen, the depth of field (3D appearance) of the specimen tends to decrease, thereby causing the final image to appear more and more two-dimensional. This nullifies

the purpose of the stereomicroscope's design, which is primarily to make specimen manipulation and the macroscopic observation of a specimen's physical structure and properties easier by providing the viewer with a three-dimensional macroscopic image. Figure 2.22 illustrates a very versatile stereomicroscope mounted on a boom stand. The range of magnification of this zoom stereomicroscope equipped with a 0.5× objective and a set of 10× oculars is from 5.0× to 31.5×. The boom stand allows for the easy positioning and observation of large bulky specimens.

A full line of dedicated common microscope objective lenses are available for stereomicroscopes. Plan achromatic, single common lenses with magnifications ranging from 0.5× to 2.0× are available from all major microscope manufacturers and are more than adequate

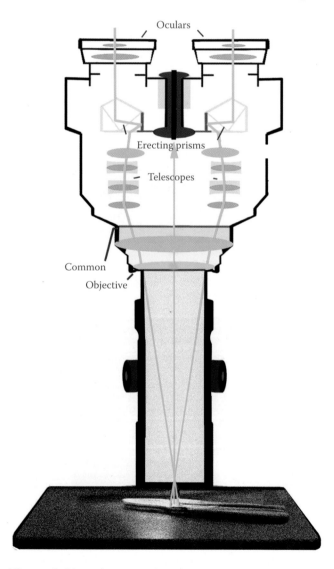

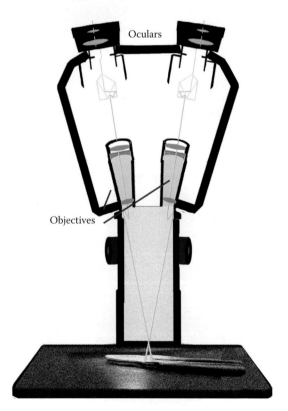

Figure 2.20 Shown is a schematic of a Greenough type stereomicroscope. Note the two objectives each aligned with one ocular or eyepiece.

Figure 2.21 A diagram of a common main objective stereomicroscope. Note the position of the main objective lens, telescopes, relay lenses, erecting prisms and the two oculars (OC).

for use in toolmark examination. However, more highly corrected objectives, with magnifications such as 0.3×, 0.5×, 0.75×, 1.0×, 1.5×, 1.6×, and 2.0×, having numerical apertures ranging from 0.023 to 0.131, are also available, though at a substantially higher cost than achromatic lenses.[2] Figures 2.23 and 2.24 show an array of some common stereo microscope objectives available today.

Shown in Figure 2.23 are two stereomicroscope achromatic common microscope objectives (corrected for two colors chromatically and the color green spherically) and one stereomicroscope plan apochromatic common lens objective (corrected for four or five colors chromatically and three or four colors spherically). Figure 2.24 depicts two stereomicroscope plan semiapochromatic common microscope objectives, corrected for flatness of field, two to four colors chromatically, and three or four colors spherically, made from extra-low-dispersion glass, which has properties similar to those of the mineral fluorite.

Another important lens system in any microscope is its eyepiece, or ocular. An eyepiece functions as a magnifier; its sole purpose is to magnify the intermediate image formed by the objective lens. There are two primary categories of eyepieces: the negative or Huygenian eyepiece, which has a diaphragm positioned at the intermediate image plane between the eye and field lenses, and the positive or Ramsden eyepiece, which has a diaphragm positioned at the intermediate image plane below the eye and field lenses. Modern eyepieces are produced to work with specific objective lens systems. It is imperative that one use the matching eyepiece made for use with a highly corrected objective lens in order to compensate for the chromatic aberrations that are inherent in most highly corrected objective systems. Therefore, it is always recommended that one use the oculars designed for use with a particular manufactured objective. Examples of both categories of eyepieces are shown in Figure 2.25.

A vital aspect of any type of optical image system is the lighting technique used to illuminate the subject

Figure 2.23 Shown above are two stereomicroscope plan achromatic common microscope objectives (corrected for flatness of field, 2 colors chromatically, and the color green spherically) and one stereomicroscope plan apochromatic common microscope objective (corrected for flatness of field, 4–5 colors chromatically, and 3–4 colors spherically).

Stereomicroscope

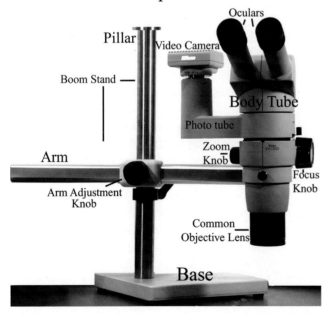

Figure 2.22 Illustrated above is a very versatile stereomicroscope mounted on a boom stand. The range of magnification of this zoom stereomicroscope equipped with a 0.5× objective and a set of 10× oculars is from 5.0× to 31.5×. The boom stand allows for the easy positioning and observation of large bulky specimens.

Figure 2.24 Shown above are two stereomicroscope plan semi-apochromatic common microscope objectives made from extra low dispersion glass, which has similar properties to the mineral fluorite.

matter. In toolmark examination, the moderate size and opaque nature of the typical specimen dictate the use of various incident light techniques to illuminate the sample. In addition, the relatively low magnification ranges employed in both stereomicroscopy (5× to 100×) and comparison microscopy (4× to 50×) allow for the incorporation of conventional macro photography and its well-established lighting techniques. Filters have also

Eyepieces

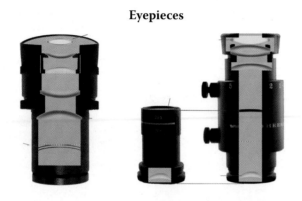

Figure 2.25 Illustrated are the two most common types of eyepieces or oculars: the Huygenian and the Ramsden.

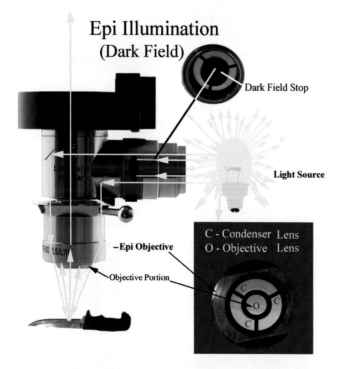

Figure 2.26 Depicted above is an Ultropak epi-illumination device formerly made by Leitz®. Light rays from the attached light source are reflected by the mirror straight down into the condensing lens system which surrounds the objective. The reflected light rays are focused onto the specimen's opaque surface by the condensing lens system, whereupon they interact with the specimen. Some of the light rays are reflected back to the objective lens, which collects them and forms an intermediate image of the specimen.

been used to augment the illumination used in stereomicroscopy and reflected light comparison microscopy to maximize image formation. In particular, polarized light filters are used to reduce glare from metallic surfaces, while daylight filters (6,000 K) are used to control color balance. Improvements in optical and illumination systems used in these macroscopic methods have resulted in maximizing the useful numerical aperture of these systems, thereby resulting in clearer, higher-quality images with superior rendering of surface details.

The simplest method used to illuminate opaque specimens has been, and still is, an incandescent, tungsten light source with a focusable double-convex lens built in. The beam of light from the light source is focused at an oblique angle onto the specimen's surface by adjusting the lens' focus. The angle of the incident beam is changed while the specimen is being observed with a camera or microscope in order to achieve the optimum contrast within the final image. This type of lighting device is all but obsolete.

Various forms of fiber optic lighting fixtures, as well as white LED lighting devices have all but replaced the older style reflected light illuminators. In comparison microscopy, the fiber optic light source comes paired with two cables connected to one power supply, which controls the current directed to the source to attain improved color balanced illumination for both questioned and known specimens. Light-emitting diode (LED) array light sources, although separate, are also powered by one power supply. Newer LED illuminators are now available that emit white light, eliminating the need for daylight filtration.

In order to obtain the optimum angle of the oblique illumination for each opaque specimen, the angle of the incident beam striking the specimen is varied while the specimen is being observed, until the optimum image is achieved for each specimen. This empirical process is carried out for each new specimen.

Opaque specimens are normally best observed by utilizing vertical illumination to image their outer surfaces. Microscopes designed for vertical illumination can have various arrays of condensing lenses, filters, and mirrors incorporated into the optical train between the objective lens and the body tube. Figure 2.26 illustrates an Ultropak epi illumination device, formerly made by Leitz. Light rays from the attached source are reflected by the mirrors straight down into the condensing lens system, which surrounds the objective. The reflected light rays are focused onto the specimen's opaque surface by the condensing lens system, whereupon they interact with the specimen. Some of the light rays are reflected back to the objective lens, which collects them and forms an intermediate image of the specimen. This system produces a very high quality image of the questioned (Q) and known (K) specimens (see Figure 2.27). It is important to note that all objectives intended for use with vertical illumination are corrected for use without a cover glass. Modern versions of vertical illumination systems are available today and are primarily used with Nomarski differential interference contrast (DIC) microscopy in the semiconductor industry for quality assurance purposes. Figure 2.28 illustrates a Nomarski DIC reflected light illumination system that has been used by the author in toolmark examinations involving small objects, narrow gauge wires, and stamping dies for coins or postage stamps. Figure 2.29 shows two photographs taken of the specimen shown in Figure 2.28. The photograph on the left was taken with normal reflected light, while the photograph on the right shows results obtained with Nomarski DIC reflected light illumination. Note the enhanced three-dimensional image obtained with the Nomarski DIC system. A concise explanation of this technique can be found in the literature.[13]

Stereomicroscopes frequently come fitted with reflected light ring illuminators to obtain shadow-free, soft, evenly diffused, near-vertical illumination. In the not so distant past, fluorescent ring illuminators were typically used for this purpose. Recently, ring lights,

constructed from large numbers of white light-emitting diodes, have been replacing these older types of ring illuminators, especially for use in low-power macroscopic methods. Figures 2.30 to 2.32 show several types of fiber optic and LED illuminators that are currently in use with both stereomicroscopes and comparison microscopes. While illumination from these types of devices is of high quality, vertical epi illumination still remains the standard by which all other forms of reflected light illumination are measured.

Although comparison microscopes have been used in toolmark examinations for nearly a century, their basic configuration has not changed. Typically two identical

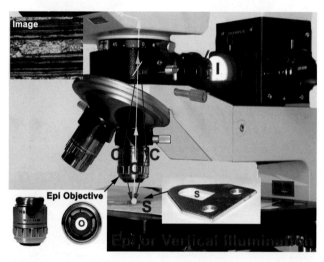

Figure 2.28 Illustrated is a Nomarski DIC reflected light illumination system that has been used by the author in toolmark examinations involving small objects, narrow gauge wire, and stamping dies for coins or postage stamps. Inset on left is a Neo S Plan, 5×, 0.13 NA, infinity corrected objective; Inset on right shows the specimen's position.

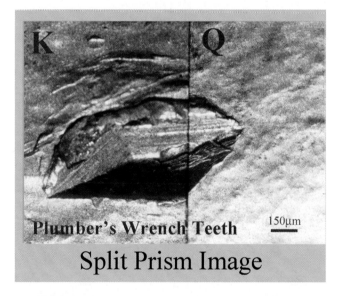

Figure 2.27 Shown above is an image of a comparison made between a questioned and known toolmark. The questioned impression (Q) was found in a pipe at the scene of a homicide in which the pipe had been loosened to allow gas to escape. The known impression (K) was produced in a piece of lead with the suspected wrench obtained from the landlord. The photograph was taken on an early version of a Leitz® comparison microscope equipped with two epi-illumination systems and two 11× Ultropak objective lenses. Note the high quality detailed image achieved by this classic system.

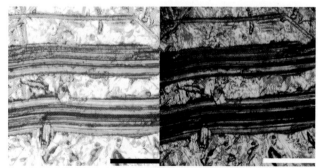

Figure 2.29 Here two photographs have been taken of the specimen shown in Figure 2.28. The left photograph is taken with reflected light while the right photograph shows results obtained with Nomarski DIC reflected light illumination. A Neo S Plan 5× 0.13 NA objective lens was used to take both photomicrographs. Note the enhanced three-dimensional appearance of the Nomarski DIC image as compared to the brightfield image. The black and white bars are equal to 0.5mm.

light microscopes with set(s) of paired objectives are optically bridged together with a special optical device designed specifically for this purpose. The device, which has become commonly known as a bridge, contains an array of prisms and lenses that transfer the intermediate image formed by each objective to a centrally located

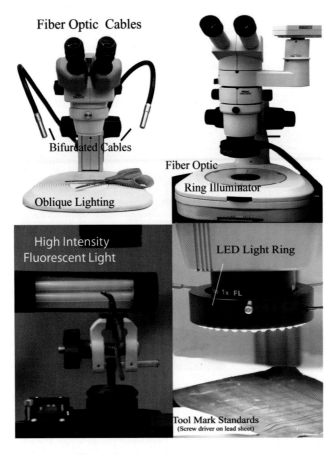

Figure 2.30 Various illuminators used in toolmark examination.

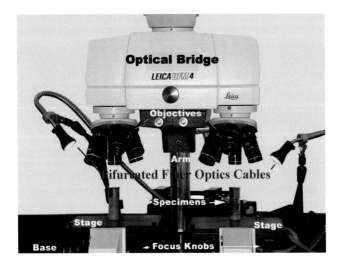

Figure 2.31 Shown is a comparison microscope with a bifurcated fiber optics illuminator outfitted with diffusing daylight filters, powered by a single power supply.

split prism. Half of each image is then directed toward the focusable eyepiece(s), which magnifies both images. The dividing line in the split prism can be sharply focused with the ocular's focusing collar. Fine corrections to the focus of each image are made by adjusting the microscope's fine focus knobs. Figure 2.33 depicts an early comparison microscope showing its primary optical components: a matched pair of 2× (Spencer) objectives with iris controls, right and left body tubes, optical bridge, and focusable 10× eyepiece. Figure 2.34 shows the internal optical components of this early comparison microscope bridge. In contrast, Figure 2.35 depicts the internal optical components of a mid to late twentieth-century comparison microscope bridge. A study of these two comparison bridges clearly illustrates that optical microscope bridges made for toolmark examination have changed little over the past century.

Even though the physical appearance and ergonomics of toolmark and firearm comparison microscopes have changed over the years, their basic optical design has not. G. A. Needham points out in his classical text *Practical Use of the Microscope*, published in 1958, that the original ballistics comparison microscope and accessories produced in 1925 by two ballistics experts, Waite and Goddard, and two microscopists, Gravell and Fischer, were so well designed that only minor changes and improvements had to be implemented since its introduction.[6]

The choice of which comparison microscope to use is usually a matter of personal preference on the part of a toolmark examiner. However, there are some common issues that must be addressed. A study by the

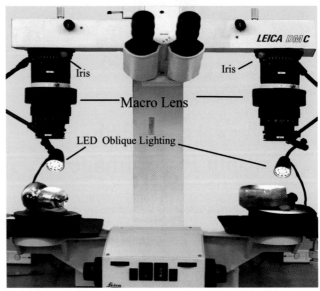

Figure 2.32 Depicted above is a comparison microscope with a light emitting diode illumination system providing oblique illumination to both the known and questioned specimens, while being powered by a single power supply.

author of the popular comparison microscopes used from the mid-1920s to the present day indicates that a comparison microscope used in toolmark examination should have, at a minimum, the following equipment and capabilities:

1. A range of magnification from 5× to 80×

2. At least one pair of matched plan achromatic objective lenses with fixed or variable (zoom) magnification range from 0.5× to at least 8.0×

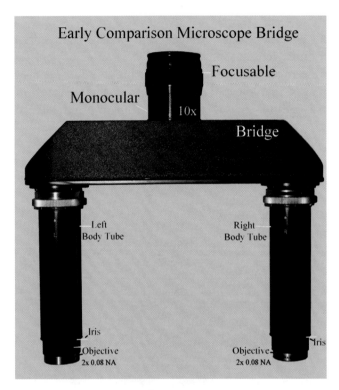

Figure 2.33 Depicted above is an early comparison microscope's optical components. The matched pair of 2× objectives with iris controls, right and left body tubes, optical bridge and focusable 10× eyepiece are identified.

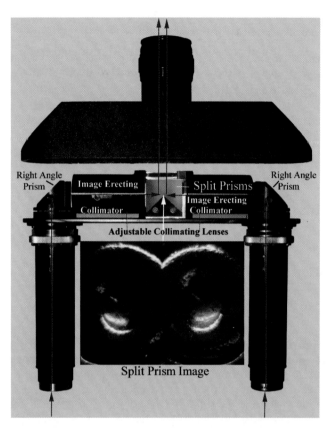

Figure 2.34 Illustrated above are all the internal optical components of an early comparison bridge along with a simple sketch of the light ray path (indicated by red arrows). The split image shown below the bridge was taken over 20 years ago by the author with this vintage comparison microscope.

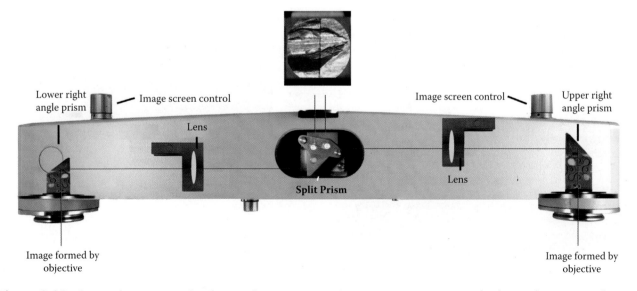

Figure 2.35 Shown above is a mid to late 20th century Leitz® comparison microscope bridge with its internal optical components exposed, and a trace of its light ray path.

3. An internal iris diaphragm for adjusting the size of the aperture
4. A matched pair of 10× compensating oculars specifically manufactured for use with the supplied objectives
5. An optical bridge that allows for the side-by-side comparison of two evenly illuminated erect images, with each image projected on the same side as the object it represents

6. Two large, flat platform stages mounted on movable ball-and-socket joints, which allow for the simple and effortless positioning of the questioned and known specimens
7. Two matched, very bright, near-daylight balanced light sources working off the same power supply, and capable of both direct and oblique reflected light illumination

Whether one chooses the fixed-magnification or zoom lens system is normally a matter of personal preference. Both systems provide highly resolved, clear images that meet the needs of any toolmark examiner. Figures 2.36 through 2.44 show a progression of

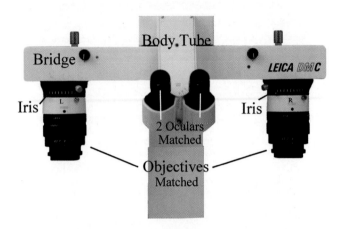

Figure 2.36 Depicts a modern comparison microscope showing its primary optical components: a matched pair of Leitz Makro® macro objective lenses (each with an iris diaphragm placed directly above each objective) an optical bridge with left and right matched objectives attached, and body tube with focusable 10× eyepieces.

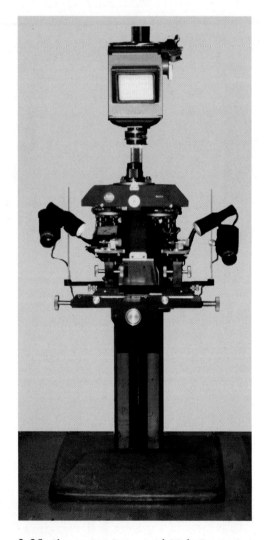

Figure 2.38 Shown is a Leitz mid 20th Century comparison microscope used by the author primarily for toolmark examinations. This unit was outfitted with two sets of Photar® objectives 1.2×, 3.6×, and 8× as well as 3 different focusable oculars, the largest one having a magnification of 10×. Some of these later units had a binocular head with a set of 10× periplan Leitz oculars. In addition, the unit came with 2 sets of Ultropak® objectives having a range of magnification of 1.5× to 11×.

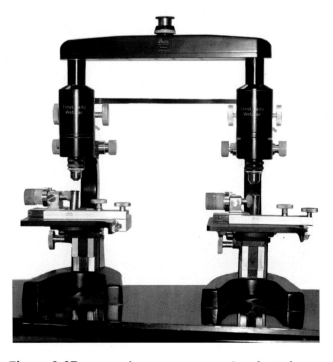

Figure 2.37 Depicted is a vintage Leitz® early 20th century comparison microscope. This unit has a pair of 2× objectives and a 10× focusable eyepiece.

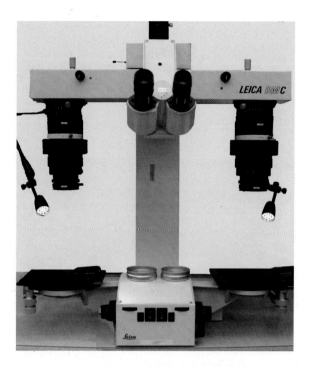

Figure 2.41 A late 20th century Leica Makrozoom® comparison microscope with a magnification range of 8× to 80×, when combined with 10× oculars and LED illumination.

Figure 2.39 An American Optical (AO) comparison microscope used from the 1970s to the 1990s.

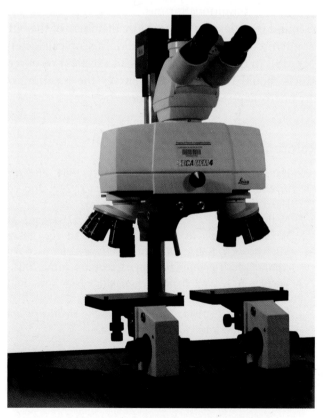

Figure 2.40 A late to mid century Leitz® comparison microscope, arguably the work horse in firearms and toolmark laboratories across the United States in the mid to late 20th century.

Figure 2.42 A modern 21st century Leica® comparison microscope outfitted with 2 sets of 0.5×, 1.0×, 1.5×, 2.0×, 2.5× and 4.0× objectives of matching 10× eyepieces. Additional objective lenses are available (i.e., lower power plan apochromates).

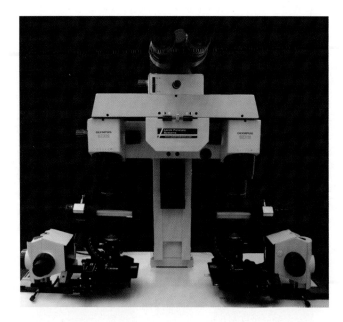

Figure 2.43 A modern 21st Century comparison microscope in which two high quality stereo zoom microscopes are optically bridged together to produce a very fine, easy to use, low power comparison microscope.

the development of the ballistics/toolmark comparison microscope over the past century.

Finally, definitions for most microscope terms can be found in a glossary prepared by members of the oldest microscope society (New York Microscopical Society (NYMS)) in the Clifton, U.S. It is an excellent resource, which should be consulted whenever the meaning of any microscope term is in question.[14]

References

1. Hatcher, J. S., Jury, F. J., and Weller, J. 1954. *Firearms investigation, identification and evidence*, 242. 2nd ed. Harrisburg, PA: The Stackpole Company.
2. Nothnagle, P. E., Chambers, W., and Davidson, M. W. *Introduction to stereomicroscopy*, 10–12. Nikon MicroscopyU. Retrieved from http://www.microscopyu.com/articles/stereomicroscopy/stereointro. html, 2008.
3. Wagner, A. F. 1929. *Experimental optics*. New York: John Wiley & Sons.
4. Shillaber, C. P. 1944. *Photomicrography in theory and practice*. New York: John Wiley & Sons.

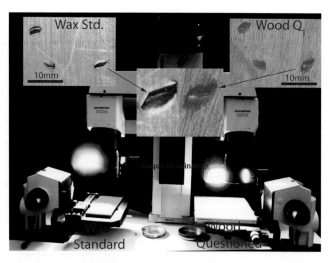

Figure 2.44 A Leeds® comparison microscope bridging two Olympus® SZX12 stereo zoom microscopes together to produce a very fine, easy to use, low power comparison microscope outfitted with several different stage configurations for toolmark examinations. Several of these stages will be seen throughout this text.

5. Kirk, P. 1953. *Crime investigation*. New York: John Wiley & Sons.
6. Needham, G. H. 1958. *The practical use of the microscope, including photomicrography*. Springfield, IL: Charles C. Thomas.
7. Zieler, H. W. 1972. *The optical performance of the light microscope: Part 1*. London: Microscope Publications Ltd.
8. Zieler, H. W. 1972. *The optical performance of the light microscope: Part 2*. London: Microscope Publications Ltd.
9. Delly, J. G. 1980. *Photography through the microscope*. 8th ed. New York: Eastman Kodak Co.
10. DeForest, P. R. 1982. Foundations of forensic microscopy. In *Forensic science handbook*, ed. R. Saferstein, 417–528. Vol. I. Englewood Cliffs, NJ: Regents/Prentice Hall.
11. Abramowitz, M. 1988. *Microscope basics and beyond*. Vol. 1. Melville, NY: Olympus America.
12. McCrone, W. C., McCrone, L. B., and Delly, J. G. 1978. *Polarized light microscopy*. Ann Arbor, MI: Ann Arbor Science.
13. Abramowitz, M. 1990. *Reflected light microscopy: An overview*. Vol. 3. Melville, NY: Olympus America.
14. Aschoff, W. W., Kobilinsky, L., Loveland, R. P., McCrone, W. C., and Rochow, T. G. 1989. *Glossary of microscopical terms and definitions*. Chicago: McCrone Research Institute.

Precision Measurement for Toolmark Examination

3

To transform toolmark examinations and comparisons from an art to a science, one must study questioned marks before preparing test marks with exemplar tools. The fine nature and microstructure of questioned toolmarks dictates the necessity for utilizing high-precision measuring equipment in the study. The use of accurate measuring instruments and gauges is essential to the scientific study of questioned toolmarks, and the reproduction of meaningful, precise test toolmarks to be used in the comparison process. Typically, the unit of measure employed in the U.S. conventional system is millionths of an inch or 0.000001 in. or microinch, and in the SI metric system, millionths of a meter or 0.000001 m or micrometer (μm). Angles are measured in degrees and minutes (60 min per degree) in both systems. Notably, metric measuring tools are frequently easier to use and read than U.S. measuring tools. Thus, one *should not* avoid using metric-based measuring devices when available.

Prior to making extremely precise measurements of questioned toolmarks, one must first become familiar with these devices and their proper use. The first instrument we will study is the steel rule.

The steel rule is the least complicated measuring device available to the toolmark examiner. Steel rulers or straightedges are divided into fractions of inches, in units of tens or decimal inches, and metric units (i.e., meters, decimeters, centimeters, and millimeters). Figure 3.1

shows three steel rules; one has fractional inch units, the other has metric unit divisions, and the third has both. In scientific measurements, acquiring accurate linear dimensions of an object is based on the use of scientifically recognized calibrated **rules or calibration standards**, which are traceable back to a recognized source, i.e., the National Institute of Standards and Technology (NIST). NIST-traceable gauge block standard as well as NIST-traceable Starrett® rules were used to calibrate all of the measuring devices used in this work.

In order to learn how to read a rule, carefully study the rules shown in Figure 3.1 and the enlarged portion of a rule depicted in Figure 3.2. Practice making measurements with a variety of steel rules on known NIST

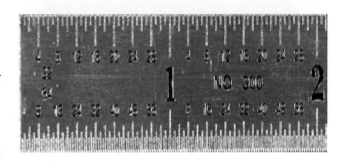

Figure 3.2 An enlarged portion of a steel ruler showing ⅟₃₂ and ⅟₆₄ in. divisions.

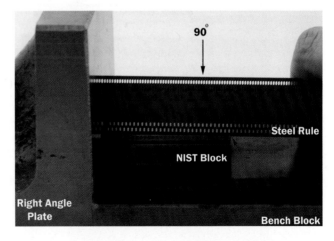

Figure 3.3 A NIST 2 in. gauge block standard being measured with a steel rule. The workpiece or NIST block is placed on top of a flat metal bench block, and both the steel rule and NIST block are butted against a right-angle plate. The rule is held at a right angle to the surface of the workpiece and the measurement is noted.

US Conventional System
Based on inches and feet
Each division equal to 1/32nd or 1/64th

Metric System
Based on international system of units (SI)
Each division is equal to 1 mm or 1/2 mm

Hybrid Metric and US Conventional

Figure 3.1 Steel rulers with both fractional inches units and metric units.

standard blocks (see Figures 3.3 and 3.4) until you become proficient. Figure 3.5 shows a NIST-traceable gauge block standard with its serial number and certified dimension marked on its front surface. The use of the NIST-traceable standard blocks and rules also serves to calibrate the accuracy of the rulers being used to make the measurements.

Start by measuring larger fractional inch divisions like ¼ and ⅛ in., and then gradually work your way down to smaller fractional inch divisions, e.g., ⅟₃₂ and ⅟₆₄ in. Practice until you are able to make quick and

accurate measurements with each type of ruler. If precision is important, the steel rule should never be used as shown in Figure 3.6. In Figure 3.6 the rule is placed in a flat orientation directly on top of the pipe, and across the pipe's opening. The positioning of this rule makes it difficult to accurately align and read the rule's gradations.

After you become proficient at using the steel ruler, practice making measurements on items you may encounter in toolmark casework, e.g., pieces of wood, lengths of pipes, tool working surfaces. Figure 3.6 illustrates two incorrect methods of measuring the diameter of a pipe with a steel rule. At the top of Figure 3.6, the positioning of the rule in a flat horizontal posture, directly on top of the pipe's opening, makes it nearly impossible to accurately align and read the rule's gradations. On the bottom of Figure 3.6, aligning the end of the steel rule with the workpiece can lead to error because the steel rule's endpoint might be worn, rounded, or even crushed. Figure 3.7 illustrates a correct method for measuring toolmarks on an item with a steel rule. The workpiece and rule are butted against a right-angle plate or knee, while the rule is held at an angle to the surface of the workpiece.

Figure 3.4 A calibrated set of NIST-traceable gauge blocks with certificate. Each gauge block is serial numbered and has its calibrated value marked on its front surface.

Figure 3.6 Two incorrect ways of measuring with a steel rule. Top: The positioning of the rule in a flat horizontal posture, directly on top of the pipe's opening, makes it nearly impossible to accurately align and read the rule's gradations. Bottom: Aligning the end of the rule with the workpiece can lead to error because the rule's endpoint might be worn, rounded, or even crushed.

Figure 3.5 A NIST-traceable gauge block standard with its serial number and certified dimension marked on its front surface.

To this point, all of the measurements have been made by the direct comparison of an established standard with the workpiece. Along with the direct method of making measurements there are indirect methods for making precise measurements. Indirect methods involve using devices such as calipers and dividers (see Figure 3.8) to evaluate the portion of the workpiece to be measured, and then comparing the caliper assessment to a known external standard, as seen in Figures 3.9 and 3.10. Calipers and dividers are useful devices for assessing dimensions. These implements are normally used with steel rules to make accurate measurements within 1/64 in. In Figure 3.9, a divider is used to measure the linear distance between two impressions of wrench tooth marks found on a cast iron gas pipe's surface. The

divider is then transferred to a steel rule to determine the measurement's value.

In Figure 3.10 a caliper is being used to measure the outside diameter of a section of gas pipe. The caliper is then transferred to a square to determine the measurement's value.

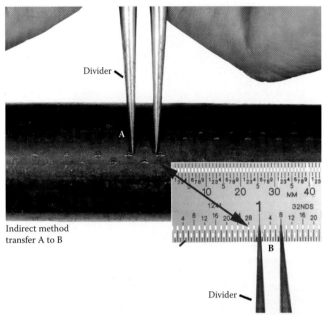

Figure 3.9 A divider (A) is used to measure the linear distance between two impressions of a wrench's tooth marks found on a cast iron gas pipe's surface. The divider is then transferred to a steel rule (B) to determine the measurement's value. Caution must be used to avoid marking the surface being measured.

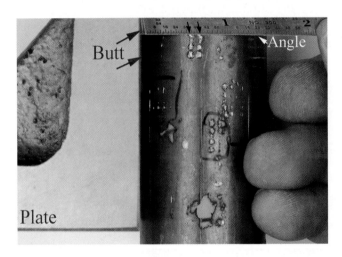

Figure 3.7 A correct method for measuring toolmarks on an item with a steel rule is demonstrated. The workpiece and rule are butted against a right-angle plate or knee, while the rule is held at an acute angle to the surface of the workpiece. The rule's gradations are aligned with the toolmarks being measured, and the size of the measurement is noted.

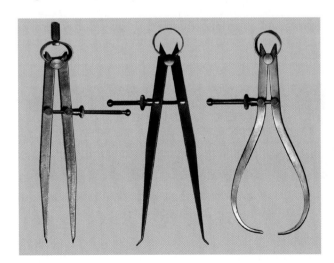

Figure 3.8 From left to right: Spring joint dividers, spring joint inside calipers, and spring joint outside calipers.

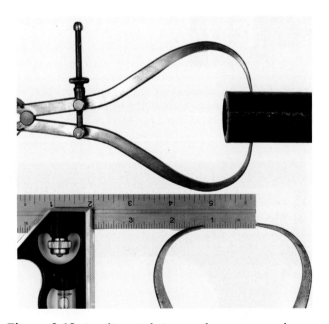

Figure 3.10 A caliper is being used to measure the outside diameter of a section of gas pipe. The caliper is then transferred to a square or rule to determine the value of the measurements.

When making indirect measurements one must be certain that the caliper being used is being properly applied to the workpiece. Figure 3.11 illustrates the improper positioning of a caliper's legs within a

Figure 3.11 The tilted position of the shown caliper will result in an incorrect assessment of the workpiece's diameter.

Figure 3.12 The position of the pictured caliper will result in a correct assessment of the workpiece's diameter. The caliper is then transferred to a steel rule and the value is noted.

workpiece to determine its true diameter. The caliper should be moved and adjusted until it is aligned with the true diameter of the workpiece (see Figure 3.12). Using calipers and dividers to make accurate and precise measurements requires practice to become proficient. Although calipers are normally used to obtain inside and outside diameter measurements, they are also used to measure thickness, with depth and angularity. The serious reader is encouraged to practice making all types of measurements with calipers to become competent using these instruments.

Today, direct measurement calipers are readily available. These devices are simply a combination of both caliper and rule merged together into one instrument capable of making direct measurements. Two common direct measurement calipers are depicted in Figures 3.13 and 3.14; both have graduated lines engraved or printed on their sleeves, and measurements are made by simply reading the gradations directly from the sleeve. The caliper in Figure 3.13 is primarily used for the acquisition of inside and outside diameters. The caliper in Figure 3.14 is used for thickness measurements.

Figure 3.14 A caliper that is used to directly measure the thickness of an object, e.g., sheet metal stock, plastic sheeting.

Figure 3.13 A common slide caliper, which allows for the acquisition of direct inside and outside linear measurements.

Mechanically measuring calipers are the most common of all handheld calipers used today for making direct measurement. Dial calipers as well as digital and electrical calipers are capable of four-decimal-place accuracy (0.0001 in.) and are used to take all kinds of physical measurements (see Figures 3.15 and 3.16).

The development of the modern micrometer caliper in France in the mid nineteenth century made the taking of direct measurements quick and accurate, without the need for calculations. In Figure 3.17 a modern handheld micrometer caliper is illustrated. This micrometer is based on the original design of the first micrometer caliper developed in France, with

the addition of a Vernier scale. Micrometers employ a precisely made screw thread that rotates within a stationary nut to produce measurements to 0.0001 in. or 0.001 mm.

When one rotates the thimble of the style of micrometer shown in Figure 3.18 in a counterclockwise (CCW) direction, the thimble retreats across the micrometer's graduated sleeve from the 0.0 position away from the anvil. As the thimble retreats, its rim exposes graduated divisions marked on the sleeve (Figure 3.18). Rotation of the thimble, which is divided into twenty-five equal divisions around its circumference, each equal to 0.0001 in., exposes gradations marked on the micrometer's sleeve, which is divided into 1/10 in., and each one-tenth division is subdivided into four equal portions, each equal to 0.025 in. The Vernier scale, on the left side of the sleeve, is divided into eleven equally spaced parallel

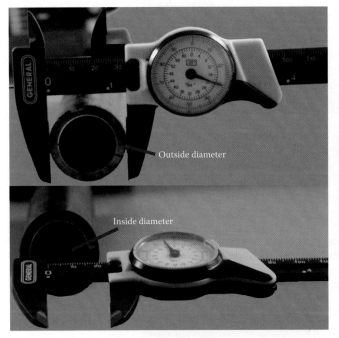

Figure 3.15 A dial caliper being used to measure the outside (top) and inside (bottom) diameters of a gas pipe.

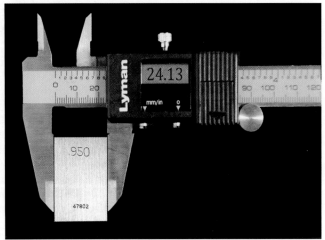

Figure 3.16 A digital caliper being used to measure the outside of a NIST-traceable gauge block standard in millimeters (mm).

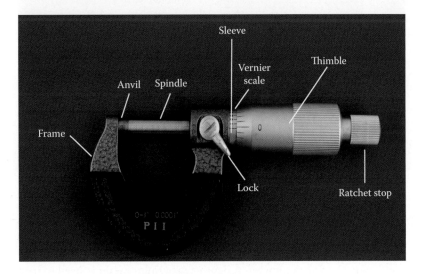

Figure 3.17 A modern micrometer showing all of its major components.

lines. These lines occupy the same quantity of space as the ten lines on the micrometer's thimble. Each division in the Vernier scale is thus equal to 0.0001 in.

When making a measurement on the Vernier scale with a micrometer, first read and record the highest number exposed on the sleeve. In Figure 3.18 this number

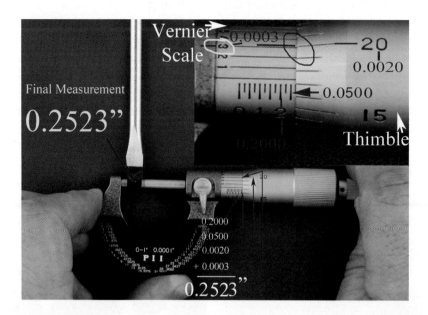

Figure 3.18 The blade of a standard slot screwdriver is being measured with a micrometer. When one rotates the thimble of the style of micrometer shown in a counterclockwise (CCW) direction, the thimble retreats across the micrometer's graduated sleeve from the 0.0 position away from the anvil. As the thimble retreats, its rim exposes graduated divisions marked on the sleeve, as seen. Rotation of the thimble, which is divided into twenty-five equal divisions around its circumference, each equal to 0.0001 in., exposes graduated marks on the micrometer's sleeve, which is divided into ¹/₁₀ in., and each one-tenth division is subdivided into four equal portions, each equal to 0.025 in. The Vernier scale, on the left side of the sleeve, is divided into eleven equally spaced parallel lines. These lines occupy the same quantity of space as the ten lines on the micrometer's thimble. Each division is thus equal to 0.0001 in. To start making a measurement, first read the highest number on the sleeve and record. Add to this number 0.005, the number of vertical lines between the highest sleeve number and the thimble's rim. Finally, find the line on the thimble that lines up exactly with the line on the Vernier scale. Add both numbers to the sum of the first two numbers to determine the final measurement's value.

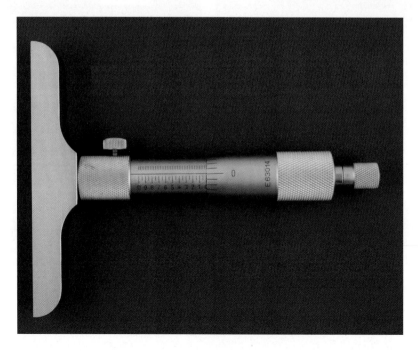

Figure 3.19 A modern depth gauge hand micrometer. A depth gauge micrometer is used to measure the depths of holes, slots, and projections. The measuring range can be increased by changing to longer spindles.

is 0.2000 in. Next, count the number of vertical lines between the highest sleeve number and the thimble's rim. In Figure 3.18 this number is 2. Next, multiply the 2 × 0.025 in. and add the result to the first number (0.2000 + 0.0500 = 0.2500 in.). Finally, find the line on the thimble that lines up exactly with the line on the Vernier scale. In Figure 3.18 the line on the thimble is marked 0.0020 in., and on the Vernier scale it is marked 0.0003 in. Add both of these numbers to the sum of the first two numbers, as seen in Figure 3.18 (0.2500 + 0.0020 + 0.0003 in.).

A large variety of micrometers designed for different applications are readily available. Many are equipped with a digital display to simplify the measuring process and provide highly precise readings. Some of the most commonly used micrometers are depicted

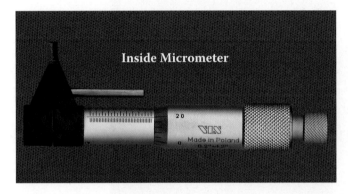

Figure 3.20 A modern inside micrometer. An inside micrometer measures internal diameters and is used for many applications. It can be used to measure the internal diameters of pipes, holes, and rings; the widths of slots; and so on. The micrometer scale is read from right to left, and the thimble is rotated in a clockwise (CW) direction.

in Figures 3.19 to 3.22. In Figure 3.23 a depth gauge micrometer is being used to measure the depth of a drill hole in wood.

Many other measuring tools and gauges, such as wire gauges, protractors, hooked rules, drill gauges, height gauges, drill point gauges, screw pitch gauges, radius gauges, feeler gauges, small holes gauge, and so on, can be used in the assessment of questioned toolmarks. A few of the common gauges and tools are shown in Figures 3.24 through Figure 3.29. Other tools and gauges will be demonstrated throughout this text. Depicted in these figures are several gauges that can be used to study questioned toolmarks in order to postulate how they were made. These data are then used to accurately replicate the questioned toolmarks in the form of known standards prepared for use in comparison studies.

The proper use of two common gauges is illustrated in Figures 3.25 and 3.26. In Figure 3.25 a wire gauge is used to determine the gauge of a wire cut during the disabling of a production machine in a manufacturing plant. The wire is placed into the various size gauge openings until a snug fit is achieved. In Figure 3.26 a screw recovered from a broken lock in a burglary is examined to determine its thread size.

Figure 3.27 depicts a portion of a brass-plated door lock plate with several lever action (screwdriver) toolmarks scratched into its brass-plated surface. In Figure 3.28 the width of the major toolmark present on the door lock plate is being measured directly with a steel rule and a right angle block, while in Figure 3.29, two different angles, angle 1 and angle 2, manifested

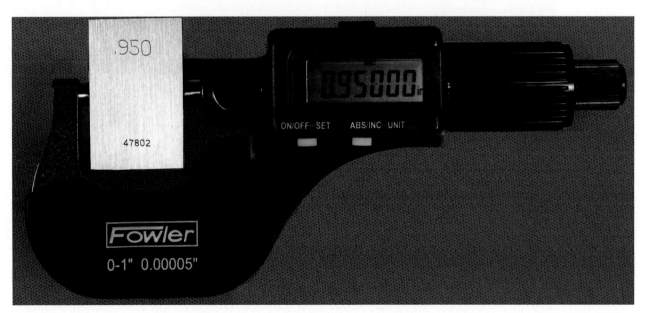

Figure 3.21 A modern digital micrometer capable of measuring in both inches and millimeters. A NIST-traceable gauge block standard is being used to test the accuracy of the micrometer.

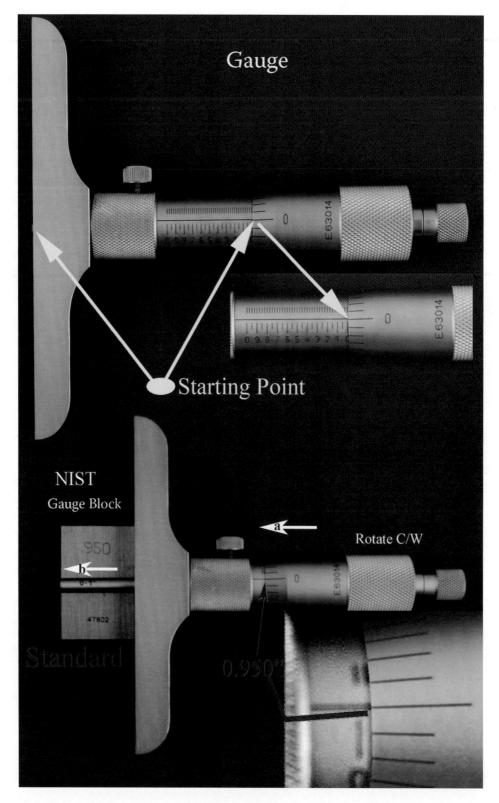

Figure 3.22 A modern depth gauge hand micrometer measuring a NIST-traceable gauge block standard is being used to test the accuracy of the micrometer. The arrow marked (a) shows the movement of the thimble as it is being rotated in a CW direction, while the arrow marked (b) shows the movement of the 0–1 in. rod. The micrometer scale is read from right to left along the sleeve, and the thimble is rotated in a clockwise (CW) direction.

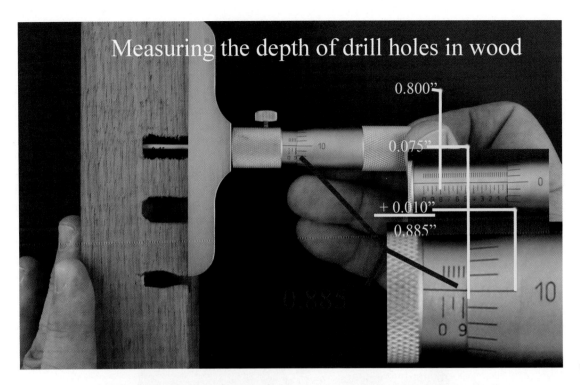

Figure 3.23 A modern depth gauge hand micrometer measuring a drill hole in a block of wood. The micrometer scale is read from right to left along the sleeve, and the thimble is rotated in a clockwise (CW) direction.

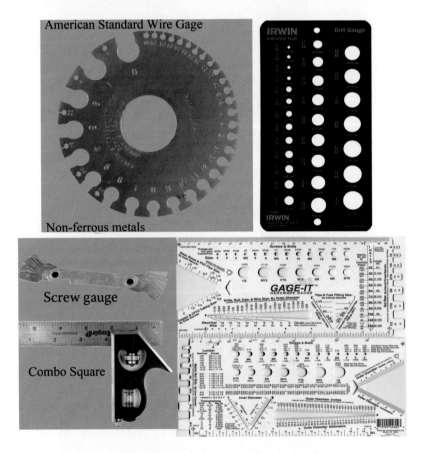

Figure 3.24 Readily available gauges and tools that can be used in the study of toolmarks. Top left: Standard wire gauge. Top right: Drill gauge. Bottom left: Screw thread gauge. Bottom left: Combination square. Bottom right: A GAGE-IT hardware gauge is capable of making an enormous array of different measurements.

within this toolmark are being measured with two different styles of protractors.

Now that you have started to acquire a basic knowledge of how to make accurate and precise measurements of tools and toolmarks on a macroscopic scale, Chapter 4 will cover measurement of tools and toolmarks with the microscope and ocular micrometers.

References

1. O'Hara, C. E., and Osterburg, J. W. 1952. Criminalistics: The application of the physical sciences to the detection of crime. In *Measuring instruments*, 54–67. 2nd ed. New York: The MacMillan Co.

2. Davis, J. E. 1958. *An introduction to toolmarks, firearms and the striagraph*. Springfield, IL: Charles C. Thomas.

3. Feirer, J. L., and Tatro, E. E. 1961. *Machine tool metal-working principles and practice*. New York: McGraw-Hill Co.

4. Johnson, H. V. 1968. *Technical metals*. Peoria, IL: Chas. A. Bennett Co.

5. Kennedy, C. W., Hoffman, E. G., and Bond, S. D. 1987. *Inspection and gaging*. 6th ed. New York: Industrial Press.

6. Walker, J. R. 2000. *Modern metalworking*. Tinley Park, IL: The Goodheart-Willcox.

Figure 3.25 The test wire is placed into appropriate size gauge opening slots until a snug fit is achieved.

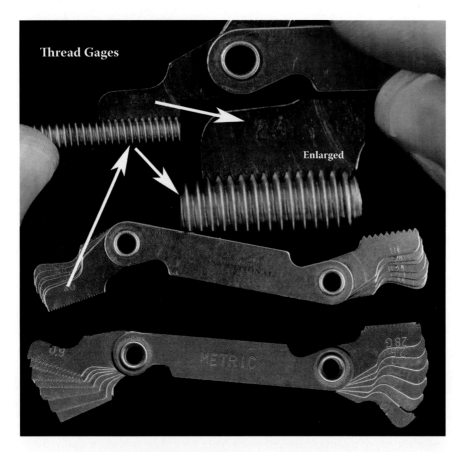

Figure 3.26 A screw is examined to determine its thread size.

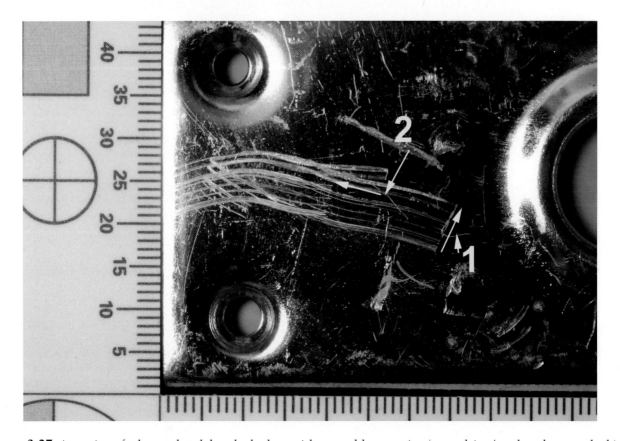

Figure 3.27 A portion of a brass-plated door lock plate with several lever action (screwdriver) toolmarks scratched into its surface. Two angles manifested in this toolmark are measured in Figure 3.29.

Figure 3.28 The width of the major toolmark present on the door lock plate is being measured directly with a steel rule and a right angle block.

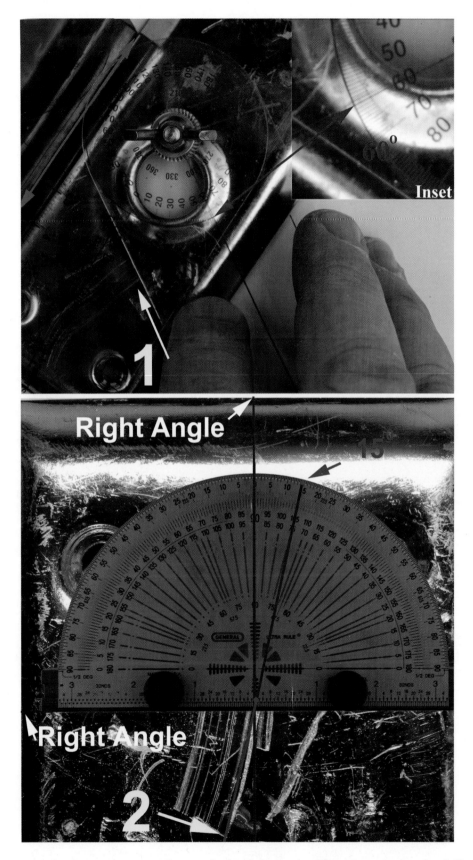

Figure 3.29 Measurement of two primary angles, marked 1 and 2. Each is being measured with a different style protractor. The first angle (1) is being measured with a ruler style protractor, while the second angle is being measured with a steel protractor. Angle 1 measures 60 degrees and angle 2 measures 15 degrees.

Measurement with the Microscope for Toolmark Examination

4

Measurement of small linear distances, angles, volumes, and areas with a compound light microscope is known as micrometry. Quantitative measurement with a microscope involves the use of various types of ocular and stage micrometer scales, a few of which are shown in Figures 4.1 to 4.3. In scientific measurements, acquiring accurate linear dimensions of an object is based on the use of standard, calibrated **rules**, which are traceable back to a recognized source, i.e., National Institute of Standards and Technology (NIST). Normally, the length, depth, and width of an object are determined by placing a ruler in direct contact with the object being examined and comparing the numerical gradations present on the ruler directly with the portion of the object being studied. Making measurements at various magnifications with a compound microscope is achieved with the use of calibrated ocular micrometer rulers in conjunction with stage micrometers. The resolving power of the light microscope is equal to one-half the wavelength of green light (546 nm), or approximately 273 nm or 0.273 µm. Linear distances smaller than 0.273 µm cannot be

resolved with light microscopy. In toolmark examinations this is of little consequence because the linear distances normally measured are much larger than the resolving limits of the microscope.

The same rationale used to obtain the linear dimensions of an object based on the use of standard calibrated rules can be applied directly to the measurement of the dimensions of the minute specimens being observed with a compound light microscope. Length and width dimensions of microscopic-sized specimens can be obtained with an ocular micrometer that has been calibrated with a stage micrometer. Figure 4.4 shows the placement of a micrometer at the ocular's intermediate image plane. Next, values are assigned to the ocular's equally spaced, arbitrary divisions, by calibration with a standard stage micrometer.

In Figure 4.5, a stage micrometer (SM), which contains a 1 mm ruler, etched into a highly polished metal surface and divided into one hundred equal divisions, each equal to 10 µm, is being imaged with a stereomicroscope. At

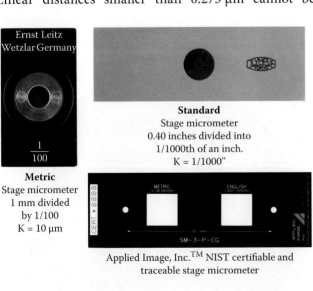

Figure 4.1 Three reflected light stage micrometers. At the top left is a Leitz metric stage micrometer, 1 mm divided into 1/100 mm; each division is equal to 10 µm. At the top right is an Olympus stage micrometer, 0.4 in. divided into forty equal divisions, each equal to 0.001 in. The accuracy of the metric and standard stage micrometers was calibrated with an Applied Image™, Inc., NIST-certifiable and -traceable number SM-3-P-OP microstage micrometer.

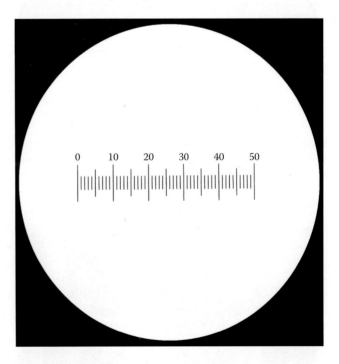

Figure 4.2 An ocular micrometer with fifty equally spaced divisions. The value of one ocular micrometer division is calibrated with one of the stage micrometers for each objective lens present on a reflected light microscope or each zoom position on a stereomicroscope.

the top-middle portion of this figure is an eyepiece that contains an ocular scale whose arbitrary divisions will be assigned values by calibration with the stage micrometer shown at the bottom. On the right of Figure 4.5 are shown enlargements of the stage micrometer, and images of both the stage and ocular micrometers. Shown in Figure 4.6 is the alignment of the image of the stage micrometer's lines with the ocular micrometer's lines. After aligning these lines as one would align a vernier scale, one counts the number of ocular micrometer divisions that align with a number of staged micrometer lines.

To determine the micrometer ($1 \, \mu m = 1 \times 10^{-6}$ m) value of each ocular micrometer division (OMD), the equation shown in Figure 4.7 is solved for one OMD. This process is repeated for each zoom setting on your

stereomicroscope, and each objective on your reflected light compound stereomicroscope, as seen in Figure 4.8.

The measurement of the diameter of a piece of thin copper wire is illustrated in Figure 4.9. First the image of the calibrated ocular micrometer is superimposed over the

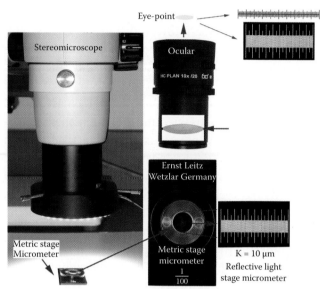

Figure 4.5 A stage micrometer (SM) that contains a 1 mm ruler, etched into a highly polished metal surface and divided into one hundred equal divisions, each equal to 10 μm, is being imaged with a stereomicroscope. At the top-middle portion of this figure is an eyepiece that contains an ocular scale whose arbitrary divisions will be assigned values by calibration with the stage micrometer shown at the bottom. On the right are enlargements of the stage micrometer and images of both the stage and ocular micrometers.

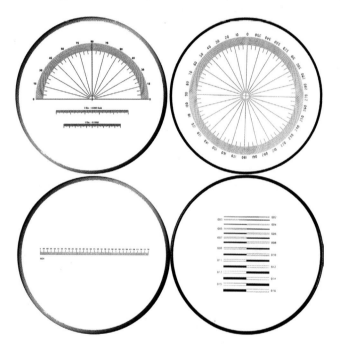

Figure 4.3 Four different ocular micrometers: top left, a protractor and two known linear distances; top right, a circular protractor; bottom left, a linear distance; and bottom right, known linear thickness in the form of a solid bar or two lines. These ocular micrometers do not have to be calibrated.

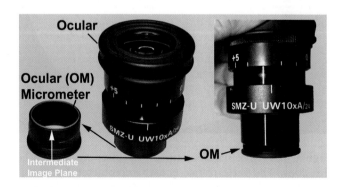

Figure 4.4 The placement of an ocular scale at the intermediate image plane of the eyepiece.

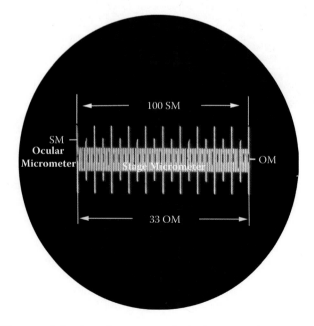

Figure 4.6 The alignment of the image of the stage micrometer (100) with that of the ocular micrometer (33).

image of the specimen with the stereomicroscope's zoom knob set to position 5. The number of ocular micrometer divisions aligned with the edges of the copper wire are counted and then multiplied by the calibrated value of one OMD with the microscope set to the five zoom position (see Figure 4.8) to determine the wire's diameter (1,308 μm or 1.31 mm). The approximate accuracy of this method is between 2 and 8 μm, depending on the quality of the optical components employed, the magnification

$$1 \text{ OMD} = \frac{\#\text{SMD} \times 10 \text{ μm}}{\#\text{OMD}} =$$

$$1 \text{ OMD} = \frac{100 \times 10 \text{ μm}}{33} =$$

$$1 \text{ OMD} = \frac{1000 \text{ μm}}{33} =$$

$$1 \text{ OMD} = 30.3 \text{ μm}$$

Thus, one ocular micrometer division (OMD) equals 30.0 μm for this particular zoom setting for this stereomicroscope.

Figure 4.7 The computation of the micrometer value for each ocular micrometer division.

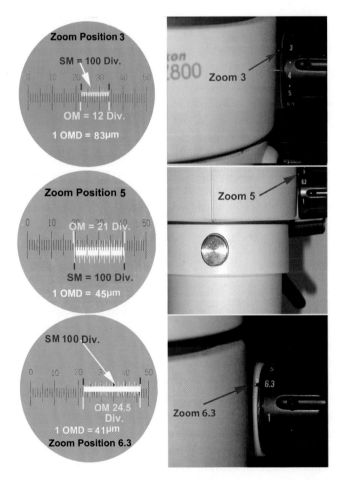

Figure 4.8 The computation of the micrometer (μm) value for several zoom settings (3, 5, and 6.3) for this stereomicroscope. As the magnification increases, the value for each ocular micrometer division decreases.

used, the resolution and quality of the stage and ocular micrometers, as well as the skill of the examiner calibrating the system. In Figures 4.10 and 4.11 ocular micrometers are used to measure the angle and width of striations made by a screwdriver on a piece of metal.

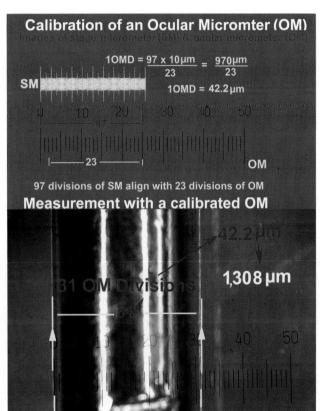

Figure 4.9 Measurement of the diameter of a copper wire. The image of the calibrated ocular micrometer is superimposed over the image of the specimen with the stereomicroscope's zoom knob set to position 5. The number of ocular micrometer divisions aligned with the edges of the copper wire are counted and then multiplied by the calibrated value of one OMD with the microscope set to the 5 zoom position to determine the wire's diameter (1,308 μm or 1.31 mm).

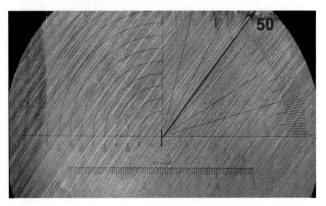

Figure 4.10 A protractor ocular micrometer is used to measure the angle of striations made by a screwdriver on a piece of metal.

A Filar micrometer is a specialized eyepiece with a movable line set and a fixed vernier scale in the form of a graduated ocular scale typically divided into one hundred divisions. The movable line set and the fixed graduated ocular scale are housed in a drum-shaped eyepiece fitted with a graduated, rotatable micrometer knob. The micrometer screw is also divided into one hundred

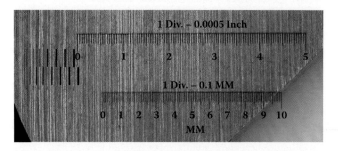

Figure 4.11 Shown are three ocular micrometers that can be used to measure the width of striations made by a screwdriver on a piece of metal.

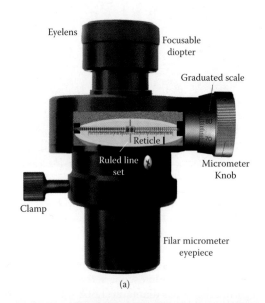

(a)

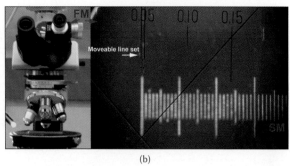

(b)

Figure 4.12 (Top) A Filar eyepiece micrometer with its primary component parts. (Bottom) A conventional Filar micrometer eyepiece mounted in the right ocular tube of the microscope. The image on the right depicts the movable line set (white arrow) and the Filar micrometer (blue arrow) aligned with the stage micrometer (red arrow).

intervals, so that one division corresponds to 0.1 interval of the eyepiece scale. One full rotation of the micrometer knob moves the measuring rule (line) across one interval of the eyepiece scale. An adjustable diopter is available to obtain a clear image of the movable line set and graduated scale. Filar micrometers are engineered to obtain precise measurements (see Figure 4.12).

To make a measurement, a reference line on the movable line set is aligned to the edge of the specimen; next, a reading of the knob is noted. The drum is then rotated to move the reference line across the specimen feature, and a second reading is taken on the drum scale. The difference between the two readings yields an apparent linear dimension of the specimen feature measured, and when calibrated with a stage micrometer, enables an absolute determination of the feature size. Figure 4.13a shows a Filar micrometer attached to a metering system to the desired magnification range (5×), and Figure 4.13b illustrates the parts and calibration check of a Filar micrometer outfitted with a digital metering system. First, the metering system is set to the desired magnification range (5×) and the units of measurement (inches). Next, the desired zoom value is set, and the microscope is focused until a sharp image of the stage micrometer is obtained. Next, the movable line set is aligned with the first division of the stage micrometer. The meter should now read +000.0. Next, the drum knob is rotated; this action causes the movable line to travel from left to right across the image of the stage micrometer. Finally, stop at the desired stage micrometer division and take a meter reading. In the example shown in Figure 4.13b, the movable line set traversed twenty stage micrometer divisions, or twenty thousandths of an inch, the exact value covered on the stage micrometer and recorded on the meter. After calibration this unit can be used to make extremely accurate and precise measurements of linear distances.

The toolmaker's microscope is capable of viewing and measuring linear distances, diameters of holes, thread angles, thread pitch, tool edges, tool wear surfaces, and much more. The toolmaker's microscope acquires its name from its main function of measuring and viewing the edges of tools and worn surfaces in the tool and die maker's industry. However, these microscopes are great for doing general micromeasurements. They have x-y stage micrometers that allow for precise measurement of linear distances and circles. The crosshair scale in the eyepiece gives a precise point of reference as the microscope's stage is moved, and the stage micrometers are used to provide readouts for the distance traversed.

Precise measurement of lengths, diameters, and distances is important for many applications in industry as well as in toolmark examination. Common tools and equipment are measuring microscopes and vernier calipers. The two major measurement standards are the English system and metric system. A manual or digital vernier caliper is able to give basic measurements. The English measuring system unit of precise measurement is 1/1,000 in., while the metric unit of measurement is

Metered Filar Micrometer

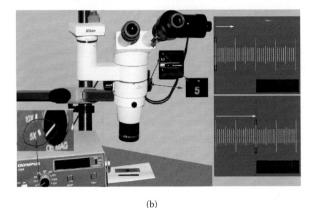

(a)

(b)

Figure 4.13 (a) A Filar micrometer attached to an electronic, digital metering system. (b) A calibration check of a digital Filar micrometer set at the 5× metering position, with the microscope set to the 5 zoom position. The movable line set in this diagram is colored red for demonstration purposes; normally, it is black. First, set the units of measurement being utilized (inches). Next, set the desired zoom knob position (5), and then focus the microscope until a sharp image of the stage micrometer is obtained. Next, align the movable line set of the Filar micrometer with the first division on the stage micrometer. The meter should now read +000.0. Then, rotate the micrometer's drum knob; this action will cause the movable line set to travel from left to right. Next, stop at the desired stage micrometer division and take a meter reading. In the above example the movable line set traversed twenty stage micrometer divisions, or twenty thousandths of an inch, the exact value covered on the stage micrometer and recorded on the meter.

a micrometer (1 millionth of a meter). Stage micrometers are also used for reference measurements and to calibrate the magnification of toolmakers' microscopes (see Figure 4.14 for an example of a modern toolmaker's microscope).

Finally, all high-end modern stereomicroscope units have digital imaging systems available with software that enables them to be used to make precise measurements at various magnification settings. These systems require calibration with standard references. However, once calibration is achieved, they are capable of making very accurate measurements of minute structural features. Figure 4.15 illustrates the calibration of a Nikon digital image system with a NIST-traceable rule. The calibration and use of these systems varies from manufacturer to manufacturer; thus, calibration will only be discussed in a general manner, while interested readers are referred to the manual supplied with their system.

Before calibration is attempted the imaging system is made ready. In Figure 4.15 the 1× plan Apo objective lens was removed and replaced with a 0.5× plan achromatic objective lens. This will increase the allowable working distance that is needed because the specimens to be examined are a large piece of pipe and large wrenches. Next, the reference rule is placed on the stage, and a sharp image of the rule is obtained at low magnification.

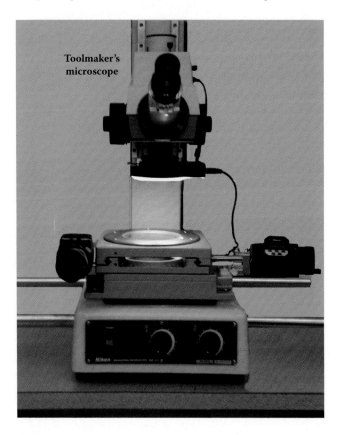

Figure 4.14 A toolmaker's microscope with its x-y stage micrometers.

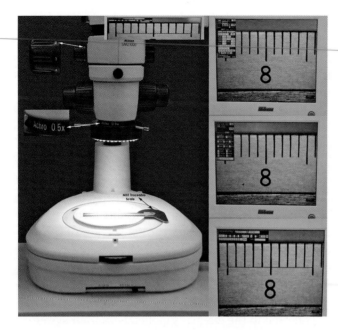

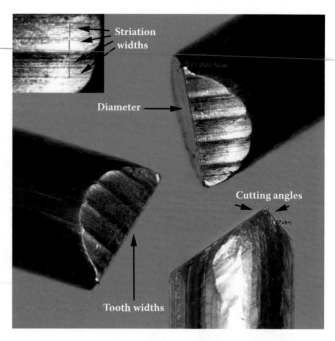

Figure 4.15 In order to calibrate the system, a reference rule is placed on the stage (left), and a sharp image of the rule is obtained at low magnification (top right). Next, the microscope is positioned to the desired setting (position 2), and the image of the rule is adjusted. Then the calibration menu is accessed and a line is drawn from one division on the rule to the desired division (middle right). The numerical value and the units of measurement for the traversed distance (1,000 μm) are inputted into the computer and saved bottom right and top middle.

Then, the microscope's zoom knob is positioned at the desired setting (position 2), and the image of the rule is sharply focused. Next, the calibration menu is accessed and a line is drawn from one division on the reference rule to the desired division. The numerical value and the units of measurement for the traversed distance are then inputted into the computer and saved.

Figure 4.16 Some of the measurements that can be easily made with a modern stereomicroscope and a state-of-the-art digital imaging system.

Next, a reference rule is utilized to check the accuracy of the system. Once the system's accuracy has been checked, the unit is ready to make measurements at the calibrated settings. It is important to remember that the system must be calibrated for each group of magnification settings. Most systems are capable of storing five to ten magnification combinations. Figure 4.16 depicts some of the various kinds of measurements that can be achieved with these systems, a useful tool to have available when conducting toolmark investigation. This type of system will be demonstrated throughout this text.

Collection and Documentation of Toolmarks

5

Toolmarks are a valuable form of physical evidence. The discovery of toolmarks during the investigation of property crimes such as burglary and violent crimes such as robbery, assault, and homicide is often germane to their successful resolution. The classification of a tool used in the incident can frequently be surmised by the thorough documentation, collection, examination, and study of the toolmarks left behind. When questioned toolmarks are found during a search of a crime scene, they should be photographed without delay. Several photographs of each set of toolmarks should be taken. The first photograph should show the overall location and setting of the toolmarks in question. The next exposures should be of an intermediate location depicting the toolmarks in the area where they were discovered. Finally, close-up photographs should be made of the questioned toolmarks. The intermediate and close-up photographs should be taken with and without a ruler (see Figures 5.1 to 5.4). When taking close-up photographs of toolmarks, the camera should be mounted on a tripod, leveled, and held parallel to the plane of the surface being photographed.

Today, digital photography is replacing conventional photography in the majority of disciplines, forensic science included. Since photography is of paramount importance in the documentation of toolmark evidence, key aspects of photography relevant to both conventional (film) and digital photography will be discussed in some detail below.

The 35 mm single-lens reflex (SLR) camera is the primary class of camera currently used at crime scenes and in the forensic laboratory. The SLR camera enables one to view the subject directly through the lens. This feature allows you to preview exactly what will be recorded

Figure 5.1 Overall photograph of door with questioned toolmarks.

Figure 5.2 Intermediate photograph of door jamb with questioned toolmarks.

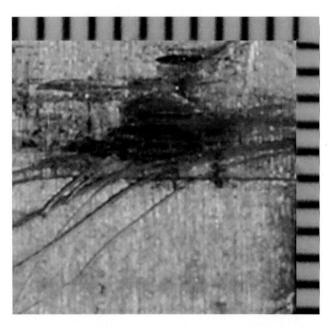

Figure 5.3 Close-up photograph of subject toolmark present on the door jamb.

on the film or digital sensor. Most, if not all, modern SLR cameras have automatic exposure features. These cameras have internal metering systems that measure the intensity of the light on the subject and automatically set the shutter speed and lens aperture opening (*f*-stop) for a given film speed (ISO) setting (typically 200). In addition to several different automatic modes, modern SLR cameras typically have a manual exposure mode that allows one to set the film speed or ISO, the *f*-stop, and shutter speed, thus giving total control to the user. Figure 5.5a depicts a modern professional digital camera. Figure 5.5b illustrates some of the important features of a modern, professional, digital SLR (DSLR) camera. The control panel (frame 1) displays the battery level, shutter speed, aperture stop value, number of available exposures, white balance setting control, shooting mode, and many other important aspects involved in taking quality photographs. The shooting mode dial (frame 2) allows the user to choose between full automatic operation and other modes, such as full manual (M) operation or shutter priority (S) mode, in which the user chooses the shutter speed while the camera selects the aperture that will attain the best exposure. The shooting mode dial also allows for user control over film speed (ISO), white balance (WB), and several other important exposure controls. Frame 3 shows where the available lens' apertures are displayed on the lens, while frame 4 depicts focus distance readings. Finally, frames 5 and 6 show the shutter release button (5) and the autofocus assist illuminator (6).

The use and application of SLR camera lenses for obtaining various images of the same subject are normally explained in regards to their focal lengths. A lens with a focal length of 50 mm is typically referred to as

(a)

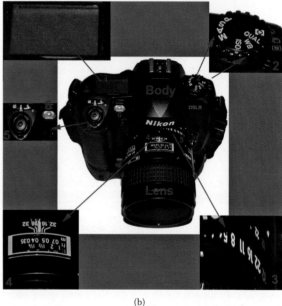

(b)

Figure 5.5 (a) A modern digital SLR (DSLR) camera. (b) A modern DSLR camera with some of its important features. The control panel (frame 1) displays the battery level, shutter speed, aperture stop value, number of available exposures, white balance setting control, shooting mode, and other important aspects involved in taking quality photographs. The shooting mode dial (frame 2) allows the user to choose between full automatic operation and other modes, such as full manual (M) operation or shutter priority (S) mode, in which the user chooses the shutter speed while the camera selects the aperture that will attain the best exposure. The shooting mode dial also allows for user control over film speed (ISO), white balance (WB), and several other important exposure controls. Frame 3 shows where the available lens' apertures are located on the lens ring, while frame 4 depicts focus distance readings. Finally, frames 5 and 6 show the shutter release button (5) and the autofocus assist illuminator (6).

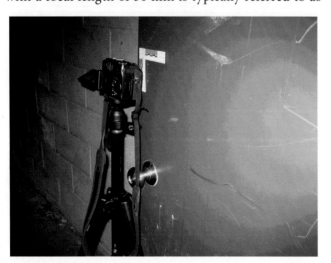

Figure 5.4 When taking close-up photographs, the camera should be mounted on a tripod, level, and held parallel to the plane of the surface bearing the toolmarks. Photographs should be taken with and without a scale.

a normal focal length lens because it produces an image that mimics human vision. In other words, a 50 mm focal length lens produces an image of a subject that appears the same as the image a person would perceive when looking directly at the same subject. Lenses with short focal lengths (e.g., 18 to 35 mm) are normally used to take wide-angle views of a subject, while lenses with focal lengths between 35 and 50 mm are employed to take so-called normal views. Lenses that have longer focal lengths (e.g., 100 to 135 mm) are employed to produce larger images of the same subject, and lenses with focal lengths greater than 135 mm are employed to take close-up views of the subject. When using a given format size as the focal length of the lens used increases, the viewing angle decreases, thereby resulting in an increase in image size. Figures 5.6a–c shows a series of photographs taken at the scene of a burglary. Note as the focal length increases, the viewing angle decreases and the subject's size increases. This series of photographs was taken with a 28 to 300 mm zoom lens. The author believes that a telephoto lens with a range from 18 to 300 mm is ideal for crime scene work, especially that involving toolmark evidence. This lens allows for the taking of a wide range of high-quality photographs, from wide angle to close-ups from the same location, with no changing of lenses, a minimum of photographic equipment, and most importantly, documentation of the untouched pristine crime scene. Only when high-resolution photographs need to be taken of small objects is it necessary to change this lens. In these instances, a fixed-focal-length, macro lens, capable of 1:1 photographs, should be used (e.g., 60 mm). Examples of photographs taken with a 60 mm macro lens are displayed in Figures 5.7a–c.

The shutter speed and the aperture or lens' opening are the two camera controls that allow the user to regulate the quantity of light that reaches the film plane. When the user rotates the aperture control ring on the outside of a lens, the size of the lens opening formed by the sliding metallic leaves composing the internal diaphragm mechanism changes. The opening in the diaphragm can become larger, and allow more light to reach the film plane, or smaller, and result in less light reaching the film plane. Lens openings, or aperture settings, are designated as f-stops. F-stops range in size from larger lens opening to smaller lens opening, typically starting at $f/2.8$, and then decreasing by one full stop increments to $f/5.6$, $f/8$, $f/11$, $f/16$, $f/22$, and $f/32$. The size of the aperture or f-stop also determines how much of the image will be in sharp focus—an effect known as depth of field. As the lens opening or f-stop gets smaller, the depth of field increases, resulting in more of the subject from front to back being in sharp focus. One drawback to decreasing the lens opening in order to increase depth

of field is that each incremental decrease in f-stop from larger to smaller opening results in halving the amount of light that reaches the film plane. Thus, in order to maintain the same exposure level, the shutter speed must be increased by one increment. Figure 5.7a–c illustrates the process of increasing the lens' f-stop in order to increase the image's depth of field while increasing the shutter speed in order to maintain the same degree of exposure.

Light and lighting are an integral part of taking high-quality crime scene and toolmark photographs. The color quality and directionality of the light affect many aspects of the resulting images taken of a subject. The color temperature of the light affects the color reproduction of a subject's color by both color film and digital sensors. Therefore, for either film or digital photography, the system must be balanced for daylight. When color film is employed, this can be achieved by taking the photographs in sunlight, indoors with a flash, with special color-balanced film, or by using color balance or color-compensating filters. In digital photography, this is achieved with the camera's software program. The direction of light and the ability to control light's direction are vital skills for a forensic photographer to possess. The ability to control the directionality of light enables one to show parts of crime scenes that are hidden by heavy shadows, reduce or soften shadows when photographing objects, and enhance the textural appearance of an impression or set of striations. Figure 5.8a and b illustrates the effects overhead lighting and lighting too close to the camera can cause. When lights are placed too close to the camera or directly above the subject, often harsh reflections, hot spots, and glare can obscure the fine details within the subject. These effects can often be corrected by using a diffusing filter to soften the light, using a polarized light filter to reduce glare, and changing the angle or position of the light source.

Moving and lowering the light source away from the camera while changing the angle of the illumination to 45 degrees will often reduce or eliminate problem reflections and glare (see Figure 5.9a and b). In addition, oblique angular lighting is used to enhance the surface details of objects or toolmarks, as shown in Figure 5.10.

The use of tent lighting and the demonstrated lighting techniques to eliminate reflections and shadows when photographing reflective surfaces with toolmarks or small objects is highly recommended by the author. These techniques are useful, relatively easy to utilize, and cost-effective methods to achieve sharp, high-quality, high-resolution, shadow-free images. Several techniques for tent lighting, in combination with varying

52 Color Atlas of Forensic Toolmark Identification

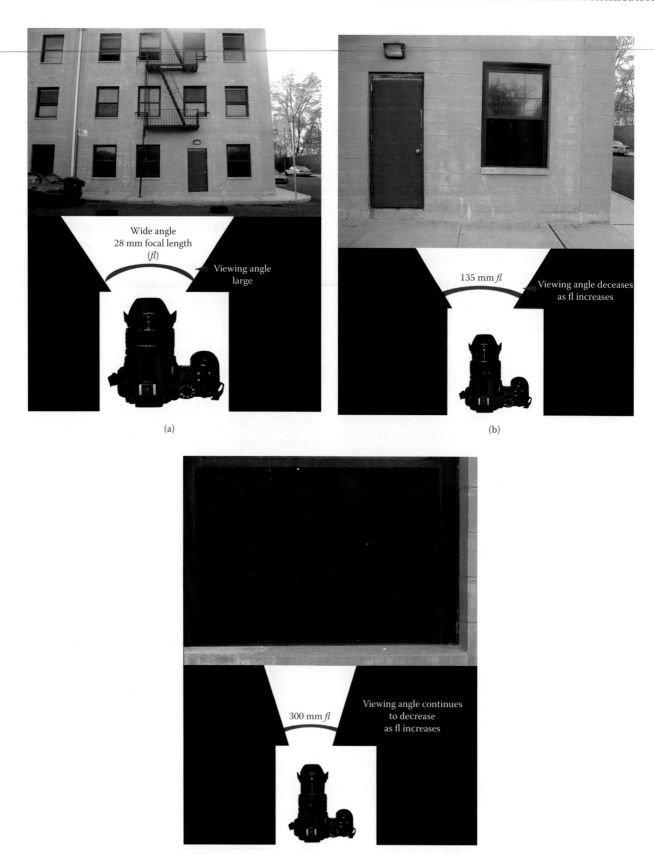

Figure 5.6 (a) An overall photograph of a burglary crime scene taken with a 28 mm *fl* lens. (b) An intermediate photograph of a burglary crime scene taken with a 135 mm *fl* lens. (c) A close-up photograph of a burglary crime scene taken with a 300 mm *fl* lens.

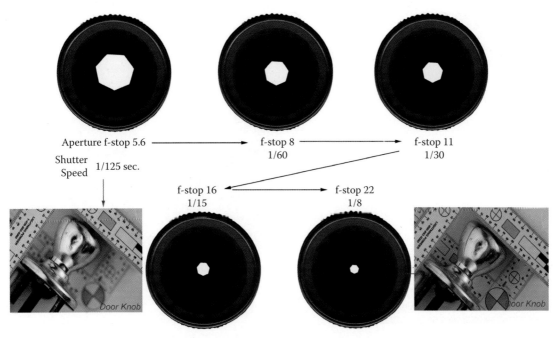

Aperture f-stop 5.6 ⟶ f-stop 8 ⟶ f-stop 11
1/60 1/30

Shutter
Speed 1/125 sec.

f-stop 16 ⟵ f-stop 22
1/15 1/8

As the lens aperture decreases by one f-stop:

(1) its numerical designation increases
(2) the amount of light that reaches the film plane halves
(3) the shutter speed doubles for the same resulting exposure
(4) the depth of field increases and more of the subject is in sharp focus

(a)

(b)

(c)

Figure 5.7 (a) Increasing the lens' f-stop in order to increase the image's depth of field will increase shutter speed in order to maintain the same degree of exposure. Note in the image on the left, taken with f-stop 5.6, only the top ruler is in sharp focus, while in the image on the right, taken with f-stop 22, both rulers are in sharp focus. The distance between both rulers is 60 mm. (b) This photo illustrates the effect of increasing the lens' f-stop in order to increase the image's depth of field while increasing the shutter speed in order to maintain the same degree of exposure. Note in the image on the left, taken with f-stop 2.8 at 1/250 s, the hammer's face is in sharp focus and the ruler is blurry, while in the image on the right, taken with f-stop 32 at ½ s, both the hammer's face and ruler are in sharp focus. The distance between the ruler and hammer's face is 70 mm. (c) The effect of increasing the lens' f-stop in order to increase the image's depth of field while increasing the shutter speed in order to maintain the same degree of exposure. Note in the image on the left, taken with f-stop 4 at 1/500 s, only the top ruler is in sharp focus, while in the image on the right, shot with f-stop 22 at 1/30 s, both rulers are in sharp focus. The distance between both rulers is 18 mm.

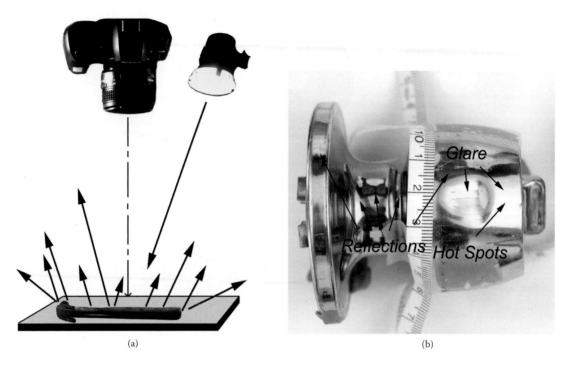

(a)   (b)

Figure 5.8 (a) When lights are too close to the camera or directly overhead, harsh reflections, hot spots, and glare can obscure fine details in the final image. These effects can often be corrected by using a diffusing filter, using a polarized light filter to reduce glare, changing the angle, or changing the position of the light source. (b) A door knob photographed with overhead lighting. Note the severe effects of the resulting glare, hot spots, and reflections.

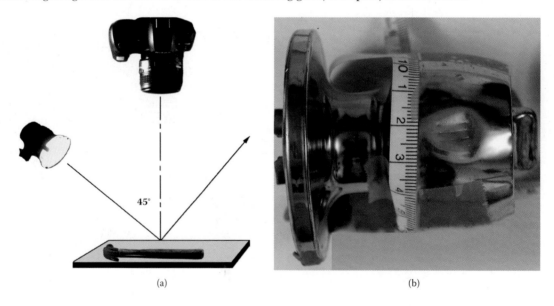

(a)   (b)

Figure 5.9 (a) Moving and lowering the light source away from the camera while changing the angle of the illumination to 45 degrees will often reduce or eliminate problems with reflections and glare. (b) The reduction in glare and reflection achieved by changing the angle of the illumination to 45 degrees.

lighting techniques, can enable the examiner to achieve the best image, as seen in Figure 5.11.

When acquiring digital photographs of toolmark evidence, the following procedure is recommended by the author for general crime scene photographs: (1) a 35 mm SLR digital camera with a complementary metal oxide semiconductor (CMOS) chip, (2) a zoom lens with a focal length range from 18 to 300 mm, (3) a film speed

of ISO 200, (4) a 10–12 megapixel file size, and (5) raw or tiff file formats. When taking close-up or macro photographs of toolmarks, use a macro lens (e.g., Nikon 60 mm *f*/2.8D Micro-Nikkor™ lens). Finally, forensic photography is a very complex subject; the interested reader is referred to the literature.[1–5]

Casting is an important collection procedure often used to collect toolmarks *in situ* at crime scenes. Over the years, the author has researched dozens of media for casting toolmarks. Mikrosil', a two-part epoxy resin, has been found to be the most versatile commercially available preparation for this purpose. Mikrosil comes in several colors: white, black, gray, and brown. The author

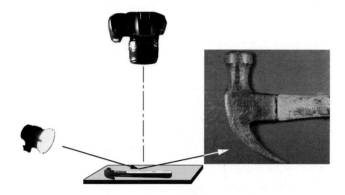

prefers the brown color of Mikrosil because of the superior contrast obtained during stereomicroscopic study. Mikrosil is easy to use both at the crime scene and in the laboratory setting. When it is time to cast the questioned toolmark, the amount of Mikrosil resin needed to cover the area to be cast can be easily estimated, as depicted in Figure 5.12. A piece of wax paper, which is provided in the kit, is placed on top of a clean paper towel. The required amount of resin is dispensed from the squeeze tube, and an equal length of hardener is applied adjacent to the resin, as shown in Figure 5.13. Figure 5.14 illustrates the mixing and application with a spatula. Test to see if the resin is ready to peel off the test surface by removing the excess resin from the spatula (as seen

Figure 5.10 Oblique angle lighting is useful for bringing out the texture present in an object or toolmark.

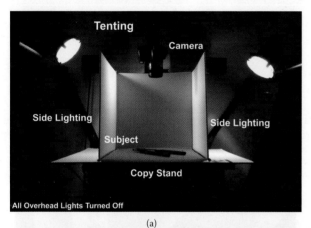

(a)

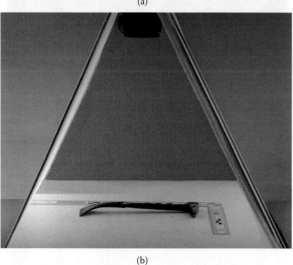

(b)

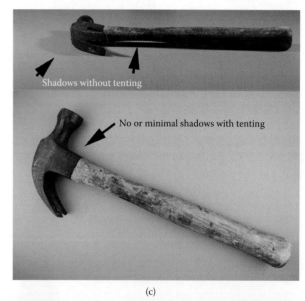

(c)

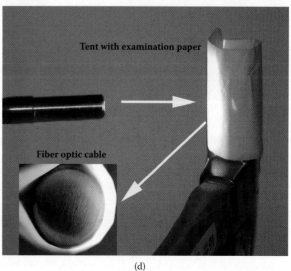

(d)

Figure 5.11 (a) An inexpensive, commercially available, and easy-to-use tenting device set up on a standard MP5 copy stand. (b) A makeshift tent made from poster board, Velcro®, and white deli paper. (c) Tenting reduces shadows, glare, hot spots, and reflections when photographing metallic, shiny surfaces. (d) An improvised tent made from deli paper and wrapped around a hammer head's face to reduce reflection and bring out surface striations.

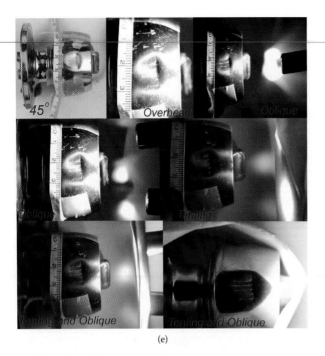

(e)

Figure 5.11 (e) One should experiment with lighting and tenting techniques to achieve the best image.

Figure 5.12 The author's quick and simple method to estimate the quantity of resin needed to cast the entire area of interest.

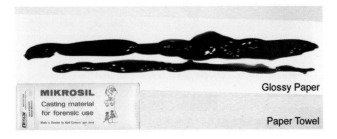

Figure 5.13 Dispensing Mikrosil resin (top) and hardener (bottom).

in Figure 5.15), and then remove the casting material from the test area and photograph as demonstrated in Figure 5.16. The completed cast (Figure 5.17) is ready to be packed for removal to the laboratory.

Mikrosil can also be used to cast screw holes and drill holes. The mixed resin is placed into an appropriate size syringe with a spatula and then slowly pumped into the subject hole. The resin is allowed to set and the cast is carefully removed. The process is demonstrated in Figures 5.18 and 5.19.

Finally, when all documentation of the crime scene is completed, and packaging of the toolmark evidence removed from the crime scene is to begin, consider the following constructs:

Figure 5.14 (1) Thoroughly mix the resin and hardener with a spatula. (2) Apply the resin mixture to the area with a spatula. (3) Cover the entire area of interest. With practice, the whole process should take approximately 5 to 10 min.

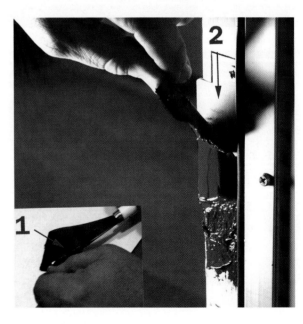

Figure 5.15 (1) Test to see if the resin is ready to be peeled off the test surface by removing the excess resin from the spatula. (2) If ready, proceed to gently remove the resin from the test area.

1. Air dry all biological evidence, such as blood stains on tools or other objects, prior to packaging in a paper-based container.
2. Remove any loose trace evidence from the tool or object and package in a separate container (e.g., a druggist fold).
3. If possible, send the object with the toolmarks to the laboratory for examination.
4. Never package suspect tools with objects containing questioned toolmarks; always package in separate paper-based containers.
5. Package each tool in a cardboard box and secure with plastic ties to limit movement.
6. Seal each cardboard box with evidence tape and mark for identification.
7. Mark each item for identification with complete information of the item's recovery on the outer packaging (who, what, when, where, and why).

Figure 5.16 (3) Remove the entire cast from the subject area and photograph the removed cast.

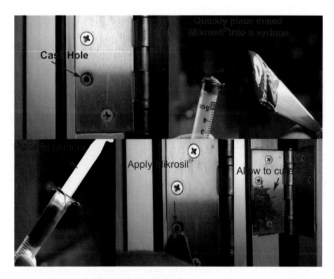

Figure 5.18 The mixed Mikrosil resin is placed into an appropriate size syringe with a spatula and then slowly pumped into the subject hole. The resin is allowed to cure.

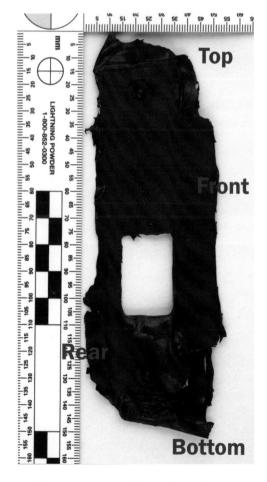

Figure 5.17 A cast removed from the subject area.

Figure 5.19 The cured Mikrosil is then carefully removed from the subject hole. A comparison of the Mikrosil cast of the hole and the questioned screw is shown on the right.

References

1. Scott, C. C. 1969. *Photographic evidence*. 2nd ed., 3 vols. St. Paul, MN: West Publishing Co.
2. Meritt, R. L., and Dey, L. M., Eds. 1976. *Using photography to preserve evidence*. Rochester, NY: Eastman Kodak Co.
3. Sansone, S. J. 1977. *Police photography*. Cincinnati, OH: Anderson, Inc.
4. Blitzer, H. L., and Jacobia, J. 2002. *Forensic digital imaging and photography*. New York: AP.
5. Petraco, N., and Sherman, H. 2006. *Illustrated guide to crime scene investigation*. Boca Raton, FL: Taylor & Francis.

Preparation of Toolmark Standards

6

During the commission of crimes, tools may be employed for a range of purposes. Tools are used in burglaries to force entry into premises, in arson and explosion cases to make bombs and incendiary devices, in robberies to alter weapons and remove serial numbers, and in kidnappings and smuggling to construct containers to imprison people or conceal contraband. Tools are used in sex crimes and homicides to cut off clothing; cut wire, phone cords, textiles, and rope to use as ligatures or restraints; beat, stab, or otherwise assault victims; cut throats, chop off heads, and dismember bodies. As the forensic literature demonstrates, the examination and comparison of the marks left by tools to aid in the solving of crimes in which tools were used have a long history.[1–25]

Although there is an endless diversity of tools and their marks, there are only three primary ways toolmarks are formed by tools: (1) impressing (leaving a mark or imprint on a softer surface by applying pressure), (2) puncturing (piercing an object, leaving a hole or the outlined trace of a hole or opening), and (3) scratching (marring the surface of an object by rubbing or sliding an instrument laterally or up and down in an even or erratic manner upon an object's surface). In real life, toolmarks are typically formed by a combination of any two or all three of these processes.

Impression marks are produced when a tool's working surface is pressed into the surface of a softer material in such a manner as to leave a negative impression of the tool's working surface class characteristics and wear or damage features. Examples of tools that commonly leave impression marks are wrenches, stamps, and seals (see Figure 6.1a and b). Puncture marks or outline marks are created when something or someone is pierced or perforated with an implement (e.g., a bullet hole, as seen in Figure 6.2). Scratch marks are produced when a tool's working surface is caused to slide laterally along the surface of a softer material, in the shape of narrow grooves or channels in the form of a random pattern of striations (see Figure 6.3). Combination toolmarks are a merger of two or more of the toolmark producing processes (see Figure 6.4).

In cases involving toolmark examination and comparison, it is always important to record and document a toolmark's morphology, as well as its exact location and position, relative to other toolmarks and the overall

crime scene. After documentation is completed, it is always preferable to remove the object(s) containing the toolmarks for laboratory study, examination, and comparison with standards made from the suspected tool (see Chapter 6.5 of De Forest et al.[24]).

Scientific investigations involving the use of tools; the presence, classification, and interpretation of toolmarks; the authentication of artifacts from toolmarks; and the

(a)

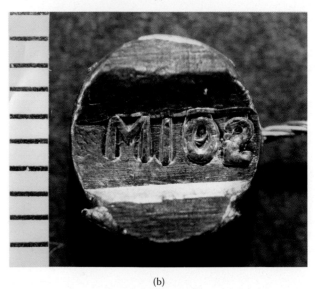

(b)

Figure 6.1 (a) A casework example of impressions made on a pipe bomb by a plumber's wrench. (b) A casework example of impressions made on a lead seal.

association of a particular tool with a group of questioned toolmarks are often quite difficult and challenging. Prior to any conclusion regarding how the questioned toolmarks were made, and well before any comparison standards are prepared, a complete and thorough study of the suspect tool and toolmarks should be conducted. The methods of study are discussed in chapters throughout this text. The data collected during the preliminary examination should be recorded on a data sheet (see Figure 6.5). Any trace evidence on the questioned tool should be documented, collected, if loose; or safeguarded and secured (see Figure 6.6).

The primary objectives of the preliminary study are to collect data in order to determine: (1) the kind of material or substrate the questioned (Q) marks were made on; (2) the physical dimensions and properties of the substrate material; (3) the size, shape, style, and classification of the

Figure 6.4 Casework example of a combination of toolmarks containing two or more elements both impression and scratching or scraping type toolmarks, displaying the class patterns of slotted screwdrivers and a pry bar.

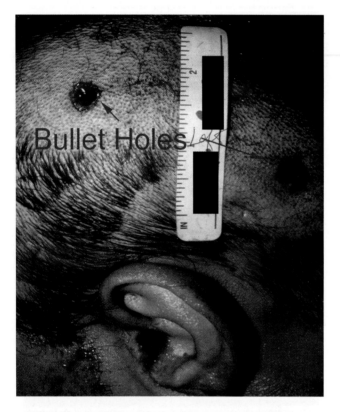

Figure 6.2 Puncture type toolmarks caused by bullets perforating a man's skull.

Figure 6.3 An example of scratches made on a metal seal medallion in order to obliterate or obscure a serial number.

Q Tool Mark Data Sheet

(1) **Substrate Material:**_____

(2) **Dimension:**

    Length _____   Depth _____
    Width _____   Angle _____
    Thickness_____   Diameter_____
    Overall Dimensions _____

(3) **Overall Geometric Shape:**

    Straight Lines _____   Curved Lines_____
    Round _____   Oval _____
    Square _____   Triangular _____
    Other _____

(4) **Describe the Application of Tool:** _____
    _____

(5) **Suspected Tool Available Class:** _____
    Trace Evidence Present Type:_____

(6) **Class Mark:**   Scrape   Impression   Puncture   Combination
    (Circle)

(7) **Tool Type:**
    (Circle)

Figure 6.5 A questioned (Q) toolmark data sheet. The data collected during a preliminary examination should be noted on a data sheet similar to the one shown.

questioned tool that made the Q marks; (4) how the tool's working surface was applied to the surface of the object(s) containing the Q toolmarks; and (5) if the suspect tool (if available) could have been used to make the Q toolmarks. All the information gathered during the preliminary assessments should be utilized in developing a hypothesis concerning how the subject tool was used or misused and how the questioned toolmarks were produced.

Once formed, the hypothesis is tested by direct comparison of replicated toolmarks made with the suspected tool(s) to mimic the questioned toolmarks, prepared in accordance with the hypothesis. The test

toolmarks are made on a substrate material that allows for the complete and accurate 1:1 replication of the test tool's working surface without causing any deleterious change or damage to the working surface of the subject tool. Recent published articles introduced the use of jeweler's modeling waxes for the preparation of toolmark standards.[26,27] The use of modeling wax was introduced, studied, and published by the author in order to broaden the scope and add to the list of tested and approved materials available to the toolmark community for making known test standards.

Treatments of materials such as annealing metal copper sheets to soften the metal before preparing test toolmark standards have also been explored. The copper sheet (18 to 20 gauge) is heated with a propane or methane air torch until it glows a cherry red color. Next, the copper is allowed to slowly air cool. Annealing must be conducted in a fire code resistant ventilated hood apparatus. The resulting annealed copper is many times softer than the original copper sheet. Thus, when a tool (e.g., a pry bar) is scraped across the annealed copper's surface, toolmarks are more likely to form because the softened metal offers less resistance and is easier to work, as seen in Figure 6.7. Annealing can also be performed on aluminum sheets, bars, rods, or wire cable stock. Table 6.1 contains a list of materials that should be or are readily available to the toolmark examiner for the preparation of known test toolmarks. Figures 6.8 through 6.11 depict

Figure 6.6 Four criminal cases in which important trace evidence was found on the tool or substrate involved in the case. The trace materials recovered and used in these cases were (clockwise) smears of green and white paint, red synthetic fibers, lead metal smear, and brown human head hair and human blood.

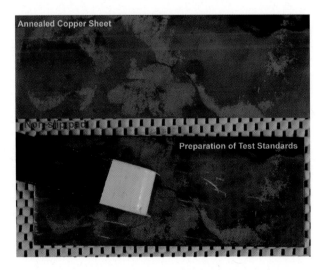

Figure 6.7 Top: An annealed copper sheet is placed on an antislip pad. Bottom: A pry bar is scraped along the metal's surface to produce known test toolmarks.

Figure 6.8 Pliable lead sheets 12 × 12 in. square, and $1/32$ in. thick are available commercially and should be supplied with a materials safety data sheet (MSDS).

some of the materials a forensic laboratory should have on hand for the preparation of known test toolmark standards.

When preparing to make toolmark standards with a suspected tool, an appropriate sized and shaped piece of substrate material possessing the desired properties should be selected. Over the years the author has found that thin metal sheets made of lead yield, without much trouble, reproducible, highly detailed, 1:1 test toolmark standards with compression tools such as vise-grips, pliers, and seals. In Figure 6.12, a ¹⁄₃₂ in. thick lead sheet is wrapped around a 1¼ in. diameter PVC pipe (to simulate a cast iron pipe) then groove-lock pliers' teeth are compressed into the soft lead metal. Figure 6.13 demonstrates the making of vise-grip marks with lead sheeting wrapped around a piece of ½ in. pine. Pine is utilized

for this purpose because it will give a little, yet provide a sturdy support for the lead sheet.

The preparation of test standards for hatchet, axe, drywall hammer, hammers, and other similar tools is usually accomplished as follows: A block of hardwood

Figure 6.10 An assortment of wire for the preparation of test toolmark standards.

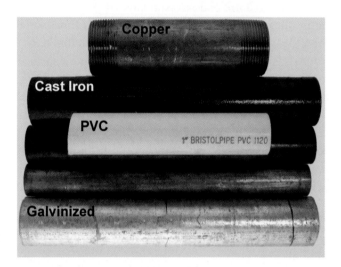

Figure 6.9 An assortment of pipe sections made of PVC, cast iron, galvanized iron, copper, and brass.

Table 6.1   Materials That Should Be on Hand or Readily Available to the Toolmark Examiner for the Preparation of Known Test Toolmarks

Objects	Sizes	Composition
Metal sheets	¹⁄₃₂ in. thick, 12 × 12 in.	Pb, Cu, Al, brass
Pipes	¼ to 3 in. diameter	Al, Cu, Zn, Fe—cast, brass, PVC
Phone wire	1/8 in.	4 strands, Cu, covered
Appliance wire	1/8–¼ in.	Single and multistrand covered
Bone	—	Animal, human
Wood blocks	Various	Soft and hard
Plywood	¼–½ in.	—
Wall board	¼–½ in. thick	Gypsum, concrete
Brake hose	½ in.	Synthetic rubber
Tire	Sections	—
Jewelry modeling wax	Various shapes	Soft, medium, hard
Sculpture wax	2 lb	Soft Red
Sculpture clay	2 lb	Plastilina No. 2

is placed on a piece of ½ in. polypropylene sheeting cushioned with a piece of shock-absorbing membrane and a rubber pad, all positioned on top of a worktable (Figure 6.14). The substrate material is then struck with the subject tool in the hypothesized manner. Depending on the type of tool being studied and the substrate material, the questioned toolmarks are found on, red wax, as well as other substrate materials, can be substituted for the hard wood. In Figure 6.15, a block of soft red sculpture wax was used as the substrate to make hammer face marks without any prior preparation. In some instances, the outer surfaces of the chosen modeling wax may have to be made free of surface marks, scuffs, cuts, scratches, dents, and so on. This can be accomplished in several

ways. The surface of the wax can be gently heated with a heat gun and allowed to air cool, as shown in Figure 6.16, or the surface of the wax can be made smooth by lightly sanding it with a fine-grit sandpaper (200–400 mesh) or by filing it with a fine wax file. After sanding or filing, any wax shavings should be removed with an air gun. Next, any remaining minor abrasions are then removed by swabbing the wax with the organic solvent Wax Brite®. (This process is demonstrated in Figure 6.17.) Application of these treatments will give the treated piece of wax a smooth polished surface. Several of the waxes can be reused over and over again, making their utilization very cost-effective.

In some situations, devices used to hold tools in precise position are useful in the preparation of accurate test standards. In Figures 6.18a and 6.19, a tool holder is utilized to hold each one of the subject tools at precise angles in order to produce the test toolmarks. Each chisel standard is prepared by applying the exemplar tools directly to the working surface of a suitably sized and shaped piece of substrate material in the manner theorized—that both tools were applied to the surface

Figure 6.11 An assortment of materials needed for the replication of toolmarks, including modeling waxes, wood, and sculpting clay.

Figure 6.12 Standard test impressions of the teeth of Irwin™ groove-lock pliers made on a lead sheet wrapped around a section of PVC pipe.

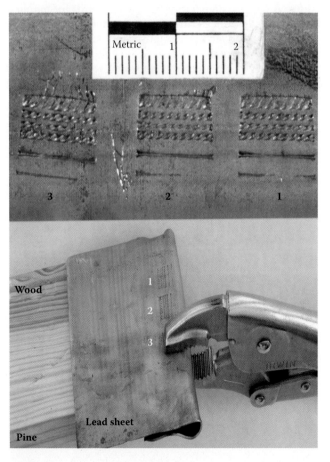

Figure 6.13 Vise-grip teeth marks in lead sheeting wrapped over a piece of ½ in. pine. Pine is utilized for this purpose because it will give a little, yet provide sturdy support for the lead sheet.

containing the questioned toolmarks. In Figure 6.18a a block of green wax is used as the substrate, while in Figure 6.18b a thin sheet of lead is used as the substrate. In Figure 6.18b excess wax is cleared from the toolmarks with a gentle flow of air. In Figure 6.18c the reproducibility of the chisel's striation pattern in the green modeling wax is clearly visible. Figure 6.19 depicts the making of standard screwdriver toolmarks

with an engraver's tool holding device designed to hold the test tool precisely in a compound angular position while the tool is being used to prepare test toolmark standards on a piece of lead. Not using the engraver's holding tool often results in tool chatter, especially when harder metals such as copper or brass are used as the substrate material (Figure 6.20).

Another useful tool for the preparation of toolmark standards is a small miter box, which can be used to facilitate the cutting of precise angles in wood, wax, or metal substrate material (see Figure 6.21).

Yet another device useful for the preparation of test toolmark standards is a small drill guide made by General™. Figures 6.22 and 6.23 illustrate the procedure for preparing a test toolmark hole while using the General drill guide. The drill bit is placed into the chuck, which is then tightened with the chuck key. Next, the desired

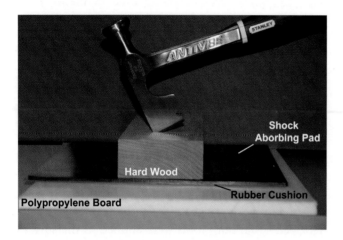

Figure 6.14 The preparation of test standards for hatchet, axe, drywall hammer, hammers, and other similar tools is usually accomplished as demonstrated above. A block of hardwood is placed on a piece of ½ in. polypropylene sheeting cushioned with a piece of shock-absorbing membrane and rubber pad, all positioned on top of a worktable. The wood is then struck with the subject tool.

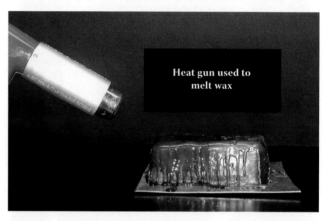

Figure 6.16 To remove heavy scratches or dents, gently heat wax surface with a heat gun and allow to air cool until it returns to its original consistency. Caution: Only melt wax in a fire proof well ventilated hood.

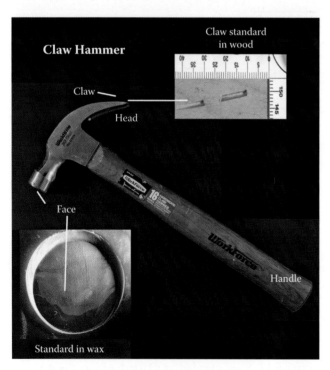

Figure 6.15 Red wax and wood test standards were made with a claw hammer in the same manner as the tested standards were prepared in Figure 6.14.

Figure 6.17 Removal of fine surface marks and scratches from the surface of a piece of modeling wax. The surface of the wax is filed or sanded. Next, any fine abrasions are removed by swabbing the wax with the organic wax solvent Wax Brite.

angle is set on both protractors, which are then locked into place. The depth of the drill bit is set by adjusting the drill's depth control, which is then locked into place. An electric drill is attached to the chuck's rod and the hole is prepared as demonstrated in Figure 6.23.

The illustrations presented in Figure 6.24 clearly demonstrate the ability of jewelry modeling waxes as a substrate for reproducing and retaining class characteristics, wear patterns, and damage features, as well as microscopic size individualizing characteristics.

Standard drill bit holes are prepared in modeling wax with three different types of drill bits: Forstner (F), twist (T), and auger (A). The steps are as follows:

1. Select an appropriate size piece of purple or blue wax.
2. Prepare the toolmarks in the wax as theorized.
3. For drill bits cut wax with band saw to expose toolmarks.
4. Remove excess wax as necessary.

5. Gently remove veil of obscuring wax with solvent as necessary.
6. Mark toolmark standards for identification.

(c)

Figure 6.18 (c) Photomicrographs clearly showing the reproducibility of microscopic striation patterns: both chisel marks were made with the chisel shown in (a) on the piece of green modeling wax shown in (b).

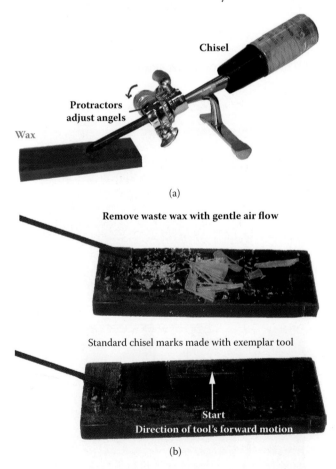

(a)

Remove waste wax with gentle air flow

Standard chisel marks made with exemplar tool

(b)

Figure 6.18 (a) Preparation of toolmark standards being made on a piece of hard green wax. A tool holder with variable vertical and horizontal angle adjustment screws is employed to make the exemplar toolmarks in the manner suggested by Burd and Kirk.[28] (b) An air gun is used to gently remove wax shavings and dust from the surface of the piece of wax.

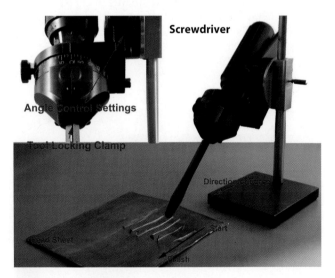

Figure 6.19 Preparation of screwdriver toolmark standards being made on a piece of lead sheet. An engraver's tool-sharpening holder with a variable height adjustment and two angle adjustments holds the test tool to make the exemplar toolmarks in the manner suggested by Burd and Kirk.[28]

Figure 6.25 depicts the replication of the same auger bit's class characteristics and striation patterns in purple modeling wax.

The preparation of ball-peen hammer toolmarks is demonstrated in Figure 6.26a and b. In Figure 6.26a, a ball-peen hammer is caused to strike the surface of a 1 lb block of soft red sculpting wax at an angle of 23 degrees. This process was carried out ten times to determine if the toolmark standards produced were reproducible. All ten toolmarks exhibited the same class characteristics, damage marks, and patterns. In Figure 6.26b, photomicrographs of the ball-peen hammer's face and a toolmark made in red wax are displayed. On the left is the head of a ball-peen hammer with its damaged areas; on the right is an imprint in wax (No. 10 in Figure 6.26a) of the hammer's head. Note the presence of eight damaged

Figure 6.22 A drill guide tool being used to hold a test drill bit at a 15 degree angle. The drill guide can be adjusted from 0 to 45 degrees on either side of the two protractors.

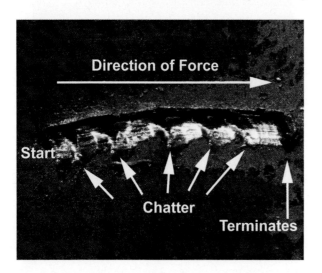

Figure 6.20 Producing chisel toolmarks in copper without using an engraver's holding tool often results in the formation of chatter marks. This is especially common when harder metals, e.g., copper, are used as the substrate material.

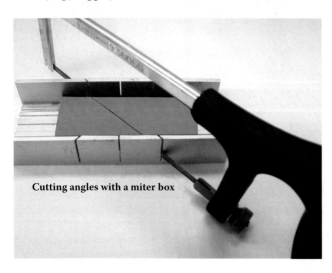

Figure 6.21 A miter box is used to cut a 45 degree angle in a block of substrate material using a hacksaw.

(a)

(b)

Figure 6.23 (a) A drill guide tool being used to hold a test drill bit at a 15 degree angle. (b) A ³⁄₈ in. brad point drill bit is used to prepare a test hole in a block of walnut.

areas within the white circle, and the eight corresponding damaged areas reproduced in the standard wax imprint.

Sculpture clay, or Roma Italian Plastilina made by Sculpture House, is another useful material for reproducing questioned toolmarks with subject tools. This material is available in four different consistencies, from

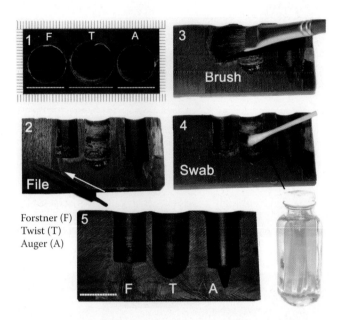

Figure 6.24 A depiction of the entire process used to prepare exemplar standards with purple modeling wax: (1) select an appropriate piece of wax; (2) prepare the toolmarks in the wax as theorized, and cut the wax with a band saw to expose toolmarks; (3) remove excess wax as necessary, (4) gently remove veil of obscuring wax with solvent as necessary, and (5) mark toolmark standards for identification. The scales are in mm.

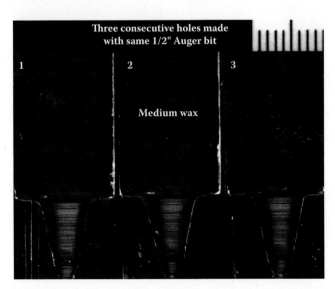

Figure 6.25 Reproduction of three consecutive holes in the same piece of jewelry modeling wax with the same auger drill bit used to prepare the hole marked A shown in Figure 6.24. The scale is in mm.

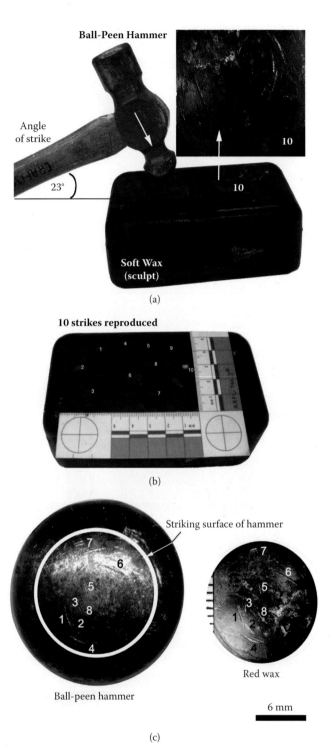

Figure 6.26 (a) A ball-peen hammer striking the surface of a block of soft sculpting wax at an angle of 23 degrees. Ten toolmark standards were produced for comparison purposes. All ten exhibited the same class characteristics, damage marks, and patterns. (b) Photomicrographs of the ball-peen hammer's face and the strike mark depict reproducibility of damage marks and patterns in red modeling wax. (c) The head of a ball-peen hammer with damaged areas; on the right is an imprint in wax (No. 10 in (a)) of the hammer's head. Note the presence of eight damaged areas within the white circle, and the eight corresponding damaged areas reproduced in the standard wax imprint.

Figure 6.27 Medium-consistency No. 2 Roma Italian Plastilina is used in the production of test standards with a subject dagger. Adobe™ PS filter lighting effects option was used to make the interior of the bottom right stab mark visible.

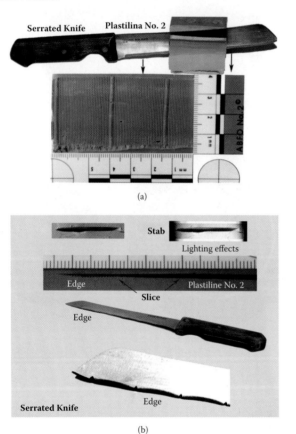

Figure 6.28 (a) Medium-consistency No. 2 Roma Italian Plastilina is used in the production of test standards with a serrated kitchen bread knife. Note the high reproducibility of the knife's serrations. (b) Additional test standards, made in medium-consistency No 2. Roma Italian Plastilina. A slicing motion was used to produce the edge slice depicted in the middle, while a stabbing motion was used to produce the top stab marks. The Adobe PS filter lighting effects option was used to make the interior of the top right stab mark visible.

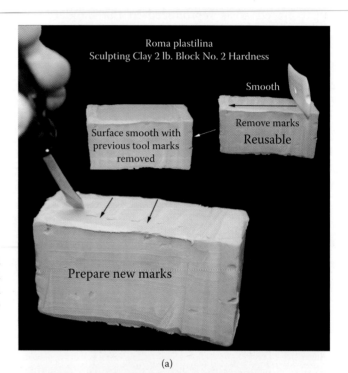

(a)

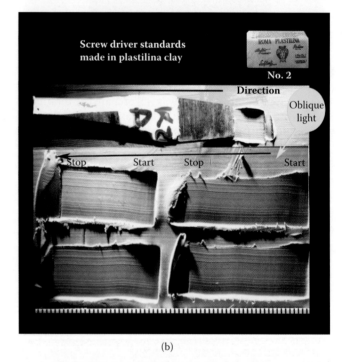

(b)

Figure 6.29 (a) The recycling and reuse of used No. 2 Roma Italian Plastilina to produce screwdriver striation patterns. The old marks are simply removed with a sharp-edged tool and the clay reused as shown. (b) Four screwdriver test striation patterns produced in No. 2 Roma Italian Plastilina. One side of the screwdriver is simply dragged along the surface of the clay while applying enough pressure to break the surface of the material. The tilt angle seems to have little effect on the final pattern produced. All four patterns possess the same striation patterns. Each side of the screwdriver yields different and distinct striation patterns.

No. 1 (soft and extremely pliable) to No. 4 (a hard material). All four consistencies conform to ASTM D-4236 specification and are very safe to use. In addition, this material is very easy to use, inexpensive, and reusable, and its shelf life is over 1 year. The medium No. 2 Roma Plastilina has been found by the author to be a very versatile material for the production of test toolmark standards. The material has been used to produce test standards with knives (see Figures 6.27 and 6.28a

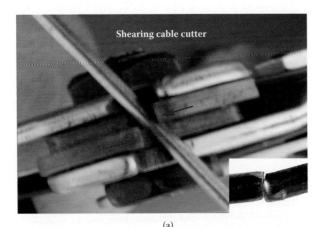

(a)

(b)

Figure 6.30 (a) Production of a test standard with 10 gauge copper cable and a shearing type bolt cutter. Note the side-to-side action of the cutting blades. (b) Production of a test standard with ¼ in. diameter aluminum cable and a point-to-point type bolt cutter. Note the sharp point of each piece of cut aluminum cable. When bolt cutters are used to cut cables, there is normally a residue of the cut material left on the cutting blade's surface.

and b), screwdrivers, and pry bars (Figure 6.29a and b). The test standards produced are 1:1 exact replicas of the tool's features. They will not shrink or change in size or details over time unless the material is reworked.

Finally, copper and aluminum wire strands ranging in gauge size from 24 to 6 have been used successfully by the author in casework for over three decades. In cases that simply involve wire cutters or bolt cutters, these materials are useful in reproducing class patterns and damage features, as well as fine striation patterns. Figure 6.30a and b demonstrates how these materials are used to produce test standards to be used in comparison to questioned toolmarks. In Figure 6.30a, a shearing type bolt cutter is used to cut copper cable, while in Figure 6.30b a point-to-point type bolt cutter is used to cut aluminum cable. When bolt cutters are used to cut cables, there is normally a residue of the cut material left on the cutting blade's surface. The toolmark examiner should always be on the lookout for these traces of metal and other material because they often indicate which portion of the tool's blade was used to make the questioned cut, thereby making it easier for the examiner to produce quality test standards.

After the study of the questioned toolmarks is complete and a hypothesis is formed (Chapter 5), and the test standards are prepared (Chapter 6), the hypothesis is then tested by comparing the questioned and known toolmarks microscopically in order to prove or disprove the hypothesis. Chapter 7 is offered to demonstrate this process.

References

1. May, L. S. 1930. The identification of knives, tools, and instruments a positive science. *Am. J. Police Sci.* 1:246–59.
2. Mezger, O., Hasslacher, F., and Frankle, P. 1930. Identification of marks made on trees. *Am. J. Police Sci.* 1:358-65.
3. Lucas, A. 1935. *Forensic chemistry and scientific criminal investigation.* New York: Longmans, Green.
4. Söderman, H., and O'Connell, J. J. 1936. *Modem criminal investigation.* New York: Funk and Wagnalls.
5. Koehler, A. 1937. Techniques used in tracing the Lindbergh kidnapping ladder. *J. Crim. Law Criminol.* 27:712–24.
6. Wilson, C. M. 1938. The comparison and identification of wire in a coal mine bombing case. *J. Crim. Law Criminol.* 28:873–92.
7. Burd, D. Q., and Kirk, P. L. 1942. Toolmarks: Factors involved and their comparison and use as evidence. *J. Crim. Law Criminol.* 32:679–86.
8. Cowles, D. L., and Dodge, J. K. 1948. A method for comparison of toolmarks. *J. Crim. Law Criminol.* 39:262–64.

9. Burd, D. Q., and Greene R. S. 1948. Toolmark comparisons in criminal investigations. *J. Crim. Law Criminol.* 39:379–91.

10. Greene, Rm. S., and Burd, D. Q. 1950. Special techniques useful in toolmark comparisons. *J. Crim. Law Criminol.* 41:523–27.

11. O'Hara, C. E., and Osterburg, J. W. 1949. *An introduction to criminalistics*, 121–30. New York: MacMillan Co.

12. Kirk, P. 1953. *Crime investigation*, 311–27. New York: John Wiley & Sons.

13. Svensson, A., and Wendel, O. 1971. *Techniques of crime scene investigation*, 98–116. 2nd ed. New York: Elsevier.

14. Hatcher, J., Jury, F. J., and Weller, J. 1957. *Firearms investigation identification and evidence*, 438–41. Harrisburg, PA: The Stackpole Company.

15. Burd, D. Q., and Greene, R. S. 1957. Toolmark examination techniques. *J. Forensic Sci.* 2:297–306.

16. Davis, J. 1958. *Toolmarks, firearms and the striagraph*. Springfield, IL: Charles C. Thomas.

17. Burd, D. Q., and Gilmore, A. E. 1968. Individual and class characteristics of tools. *J. Forensic Sci.* 13:380–96.

18. O'Hara, C. E. 1974. *Fundamentals of criminal investigation*, 705–11. 3rd ed. Springfield, IL: Charles C. Thomas.

19. Good, R. R. 1979. Toolmark identification in a gambling case (identification of illegally manufactured slugs). *AFTE J.* 11:49–50.

20. Harden, L. R. 1979. Toolmarks on a rape case. *AFTE J.* 11:25.

21. Cassidy, F. H. 1980. Examination of toolmarks from sequentially manufactured tongue-and-groove pliers. *J. Forensic Sci.* 25:796–809.

22. Moenssens, A. A., Inbau, F. E., and Starrs, J. E. 1986. *Scientific evidence in criminal cases*, 236–40. 3rd ed. Mineola, NY: Foundation Press.

23. Cassidy, F. H. 1997. Bolt cutter toolmarks. *AFTE J.* 29:484–86.

24. De Forest, P. R., Gaensslen, R. E., and Lee, H. C. 1983. *Forensic science: An introduction to criminalistics*, 383–88. New York: McGraw-Hill.

25. Petraco, N., and Sherman, H. 2006. *Illustrated guide to crime scene investigation*. Boca Raton, FL: Taylor & Francis.

26. Petraco, N., Petraco, N. D. K., and Pizzola, P. 2005. An ideal material for the preparation of known toolmark test impressions. Part 1. *J. Forensic Sci.* 50:1198–201.

27. Petraco, N., Petraco, N. D. K., Faber, L., and Pizzola, P. A. 2009. Preparation of toolmark standards with jewelry modeling waxes. *J. Forensic Sci.* 54:353–58.

28. Burd, D. Q., and Kirk, P. L. 1942. Toolmarks—Factors involved in their comparison and use as evidence. *J. Crim. Law Criminol.* 32:681.

Doing Toolmark Cases

7

An important class of physical evidence that is often detected during the investigation of crimes is impression evidence. One basic variety of this genre of physical evidence is toolmarks. Toolmarks are marks or patterns of marks that are produced by a tool or object while being used. These marks or patterns can be used to identify the tool or objected used in a given event. The tool may be the object used during the commission of a burglary or robbery to gain access into a premises, or it may be the weapon used in an assault or homicide. The type of tool and the manner of use can often be determined by a methodical and systematic examination of the questioned toolmarks. If a subject tool is acquired, known toolmark standards must be made on a substrate similar to the one on which the questioned marks were found. In addition, the test toolmarks must be made in a manner that simulates the production of the questioned toolmarks so a meaningful comparison of the questioned and known toolmarks can be conducted. In many cases, tiny traces of metal, paint, wood, plaster, fibers, polymers, and so on are found on the tool's working surface in the area where the tool was applied to the object. These trace materials should be collected for study before any test toolmarks are made with the subject tool. The examination and comparison of these collected **trace materials** with the questioned substrates can often yield conclusive proof to further bolster the findings.

The fundamental purpose of a comparison of the subject tool with the questioned toolmarks is to demonstrate that the questioned toolmarks were made by a particular tool. Even though this end is rarely achieved, the final goal should be the identification of the individual tool. However, ordinarily the examiner must be content with proving that the questioned impression was made by a tool of the same class or type (e.g., a type of saw).

The means of proof in this type of examination is by comparing patterns of striations produced by independently formed minute ridges and furrows acquired on the tool's working surface or edge during final production or subsequent sharpening and use. The ridges and furrows in turn produce patterns of striations when the tool's working surfaces are scraped or otherwise worked upon the surface of an object composed of a softer material. In casework, the questioned toolmarks are first studied in detail. Test toolmark impressions are then made in the manner it is believed that the subject tool was used to produce the questioned toolmarks. The test impressions are examined; if the class mark is consistent with the questioned class mark, their striation patterns are compared and correlated with those observed composing the questioned toolmark impressions. In theory, the greater the percentage of independent striation marks that are common to both the questioned and known impressions, the stronger is the proof that they were made by the same instrument, since the probability is believed to increase exponentially with the quantity of the number of characteristics. The following will illustrate the various types of toolmark cases encountered in the forensic laboratory and the spectrum of conclusions that can be reached.

Case 1: Pipe and Vise-Grip Arson Investigation

Evidence submitted: One vise-grip (Figure 7.1) and two pieces of gas pipe (Figures 7.2 and 7.3).

Request: Could the vise-grip obtained from the suspect's auto have been recently used to loosen the two sections of gas pipe found at the scene of a suspected arson?

Collected data: Undisturbed old pieces of plumber's string are present on the vise-grip's lower jaw teeth, as seen in Figure 7.4, and both the upper and lower jaws of the vise-grip have deposits of undisturbed rust present on all the serrated teeth, as shown in Figures 7.4 and 7.5.

Figure 7.1 Vise-grip.

Figure 7.2 Pipe with toolmarks. The spacing between toolmarks on the pipe is 4 mm.

Figure 7.3 Pipe with toolmarks.

Figure 7.4 Vise-grip with undisturbed traces of old twine and undisturbed deposits of rust on the serrated teeth of the lower jaw.

In addition, the vise-grip's teeth are 2.8 mm apart on both the upper and lower jaws. Both sections of gas pipe have teeth toolmarks that are 4 mm apart (see Figures 7.2 and 7.6).

Conclusions: The submitted vise-grip was not recently used and did not make the questioned toolmarks present on the two sections of pipe.

Case 2: Gas Explosion Homicide Investigation

Evidence submitted: Two gas pipes (shown in Figure 7.7), one (K2a) from the landlord's basement with toolmarks made with a wrench and one (Q1a) from the scene of a gas explosion in a

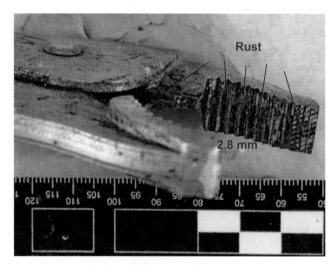

Figure 7.5 Vise-grip with undisturbed deposits of rust on upper jaw.

Figure 7.6 Opposite side of pipe in Figure 7.3. Spacing between teeth toolmarks on the pipe is 4 mm.

building owned by the landlord where a tenant was found dead.

Request: Determine if the toolmarks on the known gas pipe (K2a) are consistent with the toolmarks present on the questioned gas pipe (Q1a).

Collected data: All of the toolmark impressions present on the Q1a pipe were carefully examined with a stereomicroscope under 4× to 20× magnification. The class patterns present on the Q1a pipe were consistent with marks left by a pipe wrench (see Figure 7.7). Linear and angular dimensions of the circled (red) pipe tooth impression on the Q1a section of pipe were measured with a calibrated ocular micrometer and a protractor ocular micrometer. The dimensions were noted (see Figure 7.8).

Next, all of the toolmark impressions present on the K2a pipe were carefully examined with a stereomicroscope under 4× to 20× magnification. The class patterns present on the K2a pipe were consistent with marks left by a pipe wrench (see Figure 7.7). Linear and angular dimensions of the circled (red) pipe tooth impression on the K2a section of pipe were measured with a calibrated ocular micrometer and a protractor ocular micrometer; the dimensions were noted (see Figure 7.8). Both the questioned and known circled tooth impressions were found to have the same class features and dimensions. Both singled out tooth impressions in Q1a and K2a had the shape of a parallelogram, having two sets of equal length, parallel, opposite sides. The questioned (Q1a)

and known (K2a) tooth mark impressions were compared on a comparison microscope. Both tooth impressions were found to possess the same patterns of accidental striation features, as seen in the superimposed images of the Q1a and K2a pipe wrench tooth impressions shown in Figure 7.9.

Conclusions: Both gas pipes possessed toolmarks made with the same pipe wrench.

Case 3: Bank Robbery Investigation

Evidence submitted: One shortened section of rifle and one piece of wooden gun stock (see Figure 7.10).

Request: Could the two sections of rifle ever have been one whole continuous rifle?

Collected data: The wood species composing both pieces of gun stock were studied and identified as black walnut. Next, the cutoff ends of both

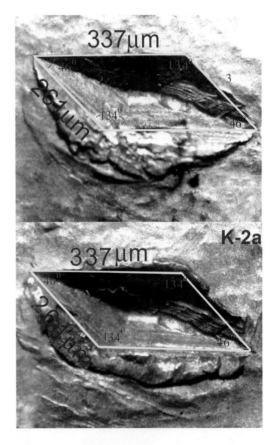

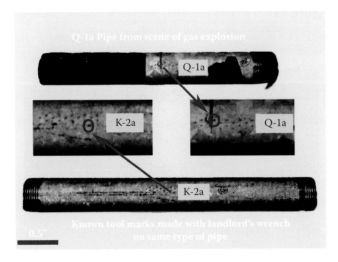

Figure 7.7 Two gas pipes, one (Q1a) from the scene of a homicide and gas explosion investigation, and one with known toolmarks from the landlord's basement (pipe marked K2a).

Figure 7.8 A comparison of the linear and angular dimensions of the Q1a tooth impression (top) and the K2a tooth impression (bottom). Two sets of parallel sides were found to be present. One set of sides was 337 μm in length, and the second set of parallel sides was 261 μm in length. The opposite angles were also equal. The smaller set of angles was 46 degrees and the second set was 134 degrees.

pieces of wooden gun stock were examined and measurements were made with a stereomicroscope equipped with a calibrated ocular micrometer. The cut ends of both pieces of wood stock were placed end to end and aligned. The space between the pieces was measured and determined to be caused by a ⅜ in. width. The size and shape of the cut marks found on and between the two pieces of wood stock indicated that an electric drill (note the chatter marks present on the right, top portion of the gun stock in Figure 7.12) fitted with a ⅜ in. bit was used to cut the wood stock, as indicated in Figure 7.11. The two pieces of aligned gun stock also exhibited a jigsaw match between the rifle's wooden end and the gun stock's end piece, as seen in Figure 7.12.

Conclusions: As depicted in Figure 7.13, the two pieces of gun stock were once one continuous piece of wood constructing the subject rifle.

Case 4: Criminal Possession of Stolen Property

Evidence submitted: One brass gas tank regulator (Q1), recovered in a thrift shop, and one brass gas tank nut (K1), from the complainant's basement (see Figure 7.14). A local man entered a thrift shop and noticed what he identified as his

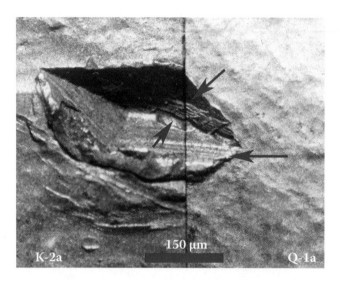

Figure 7.9 Comparison microscope photomicrograph showing one tooth mark on the K2a pipe overlapped with one tooth mark on the Q1a pipe. Note the corresponding accidental striation patterns in both specimens.

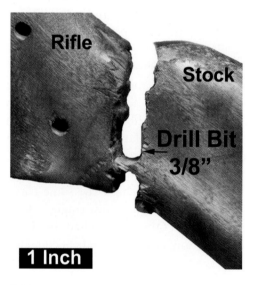

Figure 7.11 The two pieces of gun stock aligned, showing the space caused by a ⅜ in. drill bit.

Figure 7.10 Two sections of rifle-top section were recovered outside the scene of a bank robbery, while the bottom portion was recovered in the suspect's motel room.

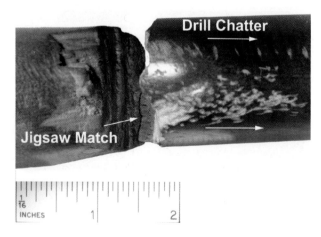

Figure 7.12 The two pieces of gun stock aligned, showing a jigsaw match between the rifle and stock. Note the chatter marks present on the right, top portion of the gun stock.

gas tank regulator valve hanging on the wall for sale. He summoned the police and stated that the valve was stolen from his basement during a burglary committed some weeks earlier. When asked what proof he had of this, he stated he had the gas tank nut that had been cut off of the tank still in his basement. Both items were forwarded to the laboratory for examination.

Request: Could the gas tank nut (K1) and the brass gas tank regulator fitting be associated?

Collected data: The damaged ends of the questioned and known objects were examined closely with a stereomicroscope under magnification ranging from 4× to 30×. Each was determined to have been cut with a hacksaw. Next, both pieces were aligned by inserting the nozzle end of the Q1 gas tank regulator valve into the cut end of the gas tank regulator nut. The saw cut marks were aligned and studied. The alignment of the gas regulator valve nozzle (center) with

Figure 7.13 The alignment of the drilled-off rifle. Note the overall portion of the rifle.

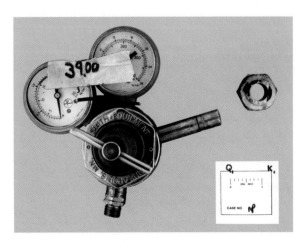

Figure 7.14 One brass gas valve (Q1), left, recovered in a thrift shop, and one brass gas tank nut (K1), right, from the complainant's basement.

the gas tank regulator nut (outside) is shown in Figure 7.15. Note the exact alignment of the numerous cut lines made by the saw's teeth and the many changes in angular direction made during the cutting process. It was determined from the examination of the toolmarks present on the end of the gas tank regulator (Q1) and the gas tank regulator nut (K1) that both pieces of brass were cut simultaneously by the action of a hacksaw, as evidenced in Figure 7.15.

Conclusions: The gas tank regulator was returned to its rightful owner.

Case 5: Homicide by Hanging

Evidence submitted: One noose fashioned from telephone wire (Q1) removed from the body of a nine-year-old boy by the medical examiner during autopsy, killed during a Voodoo rite carried out by a Voodoo priest. In addition, a goat's stomach was found at the crime scene with the boy's body. One length of telephone line wire (K1) from the primary suspect's automobile, as seen in Figure 7.16.

Request: Were the noose and the section of telephone wire ever one continuous length of telephone wire?

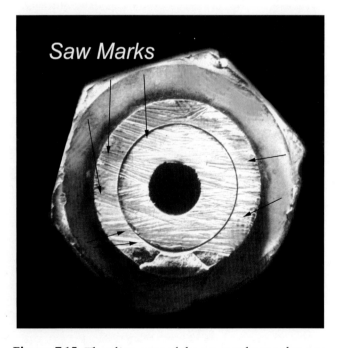

Figure 7.15 The alignment of the gas regulator valve nozzle (center) with the gas tank regulator nut (outside). Note the exact alignment of the numerous cut lines made by the saw's teeth and the many changes in angular direction.

Collected data: Both the questioned (Q1) noose and the known length of telephone line wire (K1) were examined with a stereomicroscope and measured with a calibrated ocular micrometer. Each was found to be composed of the same type of telephone line wire (four different colored 26 gauge pieces of copper wire) encased in white vinyl. Examination of the cut ends disclosed they were cut with a knife. Further examination of two of the cut ends, shown in Figure 7.17, revealed the presence of a jigsaw match. In addition, continuous lines of black soot were found running along both lengths of telephone line wire, further demonstrating that these two pieces of wire were once one continuous length of telephone line wire.

Conclusions: Both pieces of telephone line, Q1 and K1, were once one continuous length of telephone line wire.

Case 6: Narcotics Investigation

Evidence submitted: One piece of sofa upholstery fabric (K1) from the suspect's residence with an impression, and one Davis Industries P-32 pistol (Q1) found five floors below suspect's living room window in grass (see Figure 7.18).

Request: Could the questioned pistol (Q1) be the source of the impression (K1) found underneath the top cushion, embossed in the sofa upholstery, collected in the course of a search pursuant to the arrest of a suspected drug dealer during a buy/bust operation?

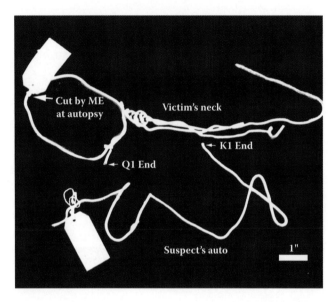

Figure 7.16 Q1 a piece of telephone wire fashioned into a loop removed from victim's neck at autopsy. K1 a piece of telephone wire from the suspect's auto.

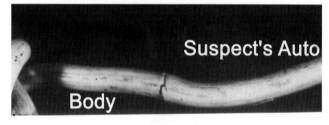

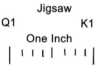

Figure 7.17 The cut ends of the Q1 loop of wire from the body (left), and K1 piece of wire from the suspect's auto demonstrating a jigsaw match.

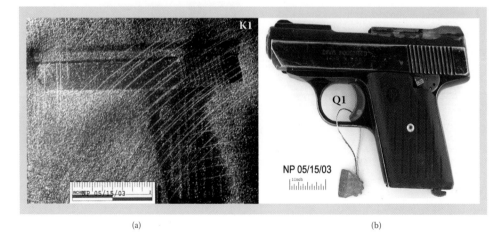

(a)   (b)

Figure 7.18 (a) The piece of upholstery with an impression of a pistol (K1), and (b), the pistol (Q1) obtained during the search of the grass below the suspect's living room window.

Collected data: Both the questioned (Q1) pistol and the known impression (K1) were examined separately. First the pistol was processed for the presence of fibers. One black fiber consistent in all chemical and physical properties with the black-colored fibers composing the sofa's upholstery was found on the pistol. Next, the pistol and impression in the textile were examined for design features. Linear and angular measurements of both were made. Figure 7.19 demonstrates that all the obtained measurements and design features were present in both specimens. Finally, a photographic overlay was made of the pistol and placed directly over the K1 impression on the textile, as shown in Figure 7.20.

Conclusions: It was reported that the K1 impression present on the textile was consistent with having been made by the Q1 P-380p pistol.

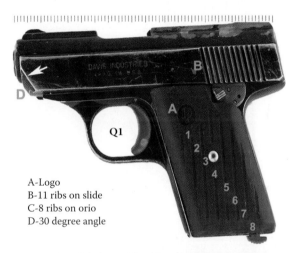

A-Logo
B-11 ribs on slide
C-8 ribs on orio
D-30 degree angle

Davis Industries P-380 Pistol

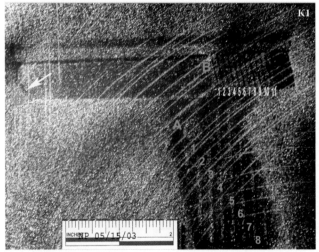

Figure 7.19 The angular and linear measurements and design features observed for the impression and the pistol were found to be consistent in all respects, except for the absence or presence of an impression of a trigger guard and magazine release.

Case 7: Burglary Investigation

Evidence submitted: One padlock with cut shackle as seen in Figure 7.21.

Request: Was the shackle cut off the padlock while the lock was locked or unlocked?

Collected data: The cut end of the shackle, marked B, and the portion of the shackle still protruding

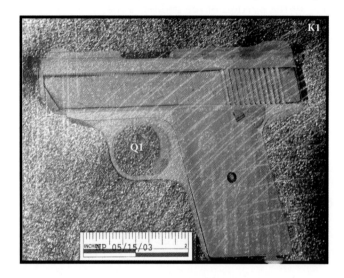

Figure 7.20 The overlay of the Q1 pistol as it appears placed directly over the K1 impression on the upholstery. This type of image processing can easily be done with Adobe Photoshop.

Shackle

Case

Key

Figure 7.21 The questioned padlock showing brass case with key inserted into the cylinder and cut shackle.

from the padlock, marked A, in Figure 7.21 were both examined separately with a stereomicroscope utilizing a range of magnification from 4× to 20×. From the physical appearance of the end of the shackle marked B 1 and 2, and A 3 and 4, on the left side of Figure 7.22, it was evident that a bolt cutter was employed to cut the shackle from the lock. In addition, the position of the portion of the padlock's shackle remaining attached to the lock casing is indicative of the shackle being cut while the padlock was in the unlocked, opened orientation (as seen in Figure 7.22).

Conclusions: The padlock was in the unlocked position when its shackle was cut with a shearing action bolt cutter. Unlocked orientation as shown in Figure 7.21.

Case 8: Homicide Investigation

Evidence submitted: Three pieces of door jamb (Figure 7.23) collected by crime scene analysts

Figure 7.22 Based upon the physical appearance of the ends of the shackle marked B 1 and 2, and A 3 and 4 (on the left), it is evident that a bolt cutter was employed to cut the shackle from the lock. The position of the portion of the padlock's shackle (A) still within the lock casing is indicative of the shackle being cut while the padlock was in the open position.

from the front door of the suspect's residence, the scene of a double homicide, and two screwdrivers (Figure 7.24) collected from the husband's automobile.

Request: Determine if either screwdriver could have been used to simulate a forced entry into the residence.

Collected data: Known K1 and K2 screwdrivers were examined with a stereomicroscope for the presence of trace evidence. Minute smears of blue-green-colored paint were found on the tip end of K2. No trace materials were found on the K1 screwdriver (see Figure 7.25). The specimens of blue-green paint found on K2 were compared

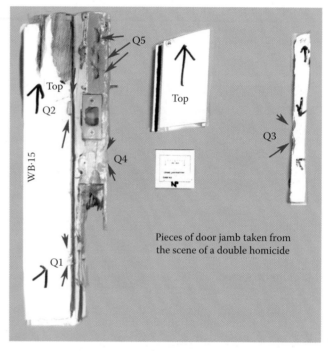

Figure 7.23 Three pieces of door jamb, from suspect's residence, the scene of a double homicide, with questioned toolmarks.

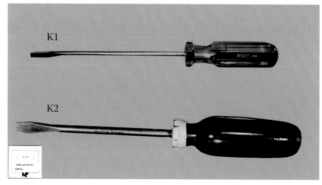

Figure 7.24 Two screwdrivers from suspect's vehicle. K1 has a red handle and a ³⁄₈ in. wide slot tip, while K2 has a ⁵⁄₈ in. wide slot tip.

to the blue-green paint covering areas of the three pieces of questioned door jambs. The blue-green paint found on K2 was consistent in all physical and chemical properties with the questioned specimens from the large section of door jamb. Next, the known toolmark impressions made by the K2 screwdriver in wood (not shown) were consistent in all class characteristics to the Q1, Q2, and Q4 questioned ⅝ in. wide slot screwdriver tip impressions present on the larger section of door jamb (K1). The blade width of the K1 screwdriver was not consistent with any of the questioned impressions.

Conclusions: In the opinion of the author, the questioned impressions, Q1, Q2, and Q4, could have been made by the K2 screwdriver. The K2 screwdriver did not cause the Q3 or Q5 groups of toolmark impressions on the questioned pieces of door jamb. The K1 screwdriver did not cause any of the toolmark impressions on the three pieces of questioned door jamb.

Case 9: Burglary Investigation

Evidence submitted: One lock cylinder from the front door of a burglary scene investigation, seen in Figure 7.26.

Request: Examine lock cylinder to determine if the door lock was picked or otherwise defeated.

Collected data: The lock cylinder was first examined with a stereomicroscope at a range of magnification from 4× to 30× for signs of damage

or tampering. No indications of damage or tampering of the lock cylinder were observed (see Figure 7.27). Next, the cylinder plug was removed and the springs, spacers, and pins (6) were removed.

All six pins were examined for pick marks. Figure 7.28 shows the pick marks on one of the cylinder pins. All six pins had similar-looking pick marks.

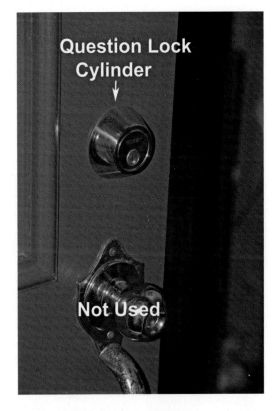

Figure 7.26 Questioned lock cylinder recovered for examination from the front door during a burglary investigation.

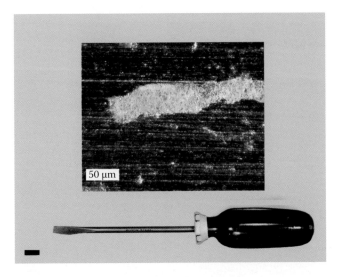

Figure 7.25 The tip of the K2 screwdriver contained green-blue-colored paint. The smaller K1 screwdriver contained no paint on its tip.

Figure 7.27 Questioned lock cylinder received for examination showing no signs of tampering or damage.

Conclusions: From the pick marks detected on the cylinder pins obtained from the lock cylinder it was determined that the questioned lock was picked.

Case 10: Burglary Investigation

Evidence submitted: Photographs of the door and damage to the door and jamb (see Figures 7.29 and 7.30).

Request: Determine if the premises was broken into through the rear basement door.

Collected data: Examination of the inside and outside portions of the basement's rear door

divulged the presence of several toolmarks near the door's lock cylinder and on the door jamb moldings. Close examination of the outside portion of the door and jamb revealed the presence of ¾ in. wide impressions consistent with the tip of a crow bar on the side of the door and on the door jamb, as seen in Figure 7.31. Close scrutiny of the inside portion of the door and jamb revealed toolmarks and signs of the levering action of the tip of a crow bar being forced into the space between the door and the door

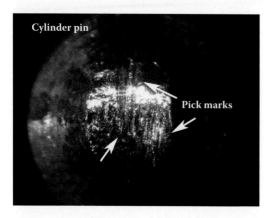

Figure 7.28 Pick marks on one of the pins from questioned lock cylinder. All six pins exhibited similar pick marks.

Figure 7.30 Inside of the basement's rear door showing damage on door and door jamb next to lock cylinder.

Figure 7.29 Outside of rear door of a premises leading into its basement.

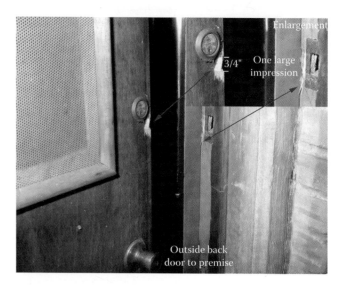

Figure 7.31 Outside of rear door leading from basement showing signs of toolmarks near door lock and on door jamb.

jamb, while the shaft portion of the crow bar was being forced against the jamb and its molding, as depicted in Figure 7.32.

Conclusions: From the toolmarks and damage found on the rear basement door, it was theorized that the building was broken out of and not into.

Case 11: Bomb Investigation

Evidence submitted: The components of a dismantled, unexploded pipe bomb, shown in Figure 7.33. The fragments and debris collected at the scene of a pipe bomb explosion, as seen in Figure 7.34.

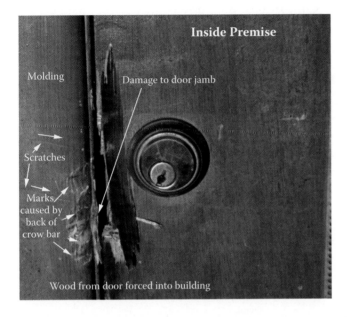

Figure 7.32 Inside of rear door of premises showing more damage than is present on the outside damaged portion of the rear basement door. Damage to the inside door jamb's molding and to the door itself is consistent with the action of a lever action tool such as a crow bar.

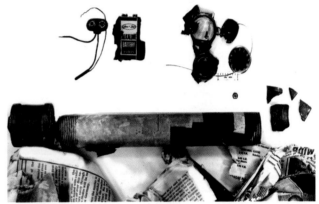

Figure 7.33 A dismantled, unexploded pipe bomb recovered in the alleyway of a high-profile bank's headquarters.

Figure 7.34 Fragments and debris collected at the scene of a pipe bomb explosion.

Request: Determine if the two pipe bombs could have been assembled by the same person.

Collected data: The unexploded pipe bomb was filled with Pyrodex*, a synthetic, low-order explosive substitute for black powder, designed to burn more evenly, and at a higher efficiency than traditional black powder. A few particles and residues consistent with Pyrodex were detected in the debris and fragments collected at the scene of the detonated pipe bomb. The 9-volt battery terminals from the unexploded pipe bomb and from the exploded pipe bomb's debris were wired with 26 gauge, multistrand, black insulated wires in the same manner. In addition, both terminals appeared to have been manufactured out of the same materials. Finally,

the ends of the wires attached to both terminals were cut with the same style of wire cutting pliers (point-to-point). Many of these similarities are demonstrated in Figure 7.35.

Conclusions: Both pipe bomb devices could have been assembled by the same person.

Case 12: Attempted Murder Investigation

Evidence submitted: The victim's outer clothing (Figure 7.36), vest holder (Figure 7.37), and Kevlar* vest insert (Figure 7.38) were submitted for assessment. In addition, a questioned, spent bullet (shown in Figure 7.39), found near the

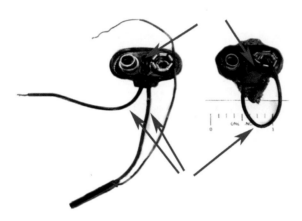

Figure 7.35 Two terminals, on left, from unexploded pipe bomb and, on right, exploded pipe bomb. Note the same manner in which the 26 gauge, multistrand, black insulated wires are attached to the 9-volt battery terminals.

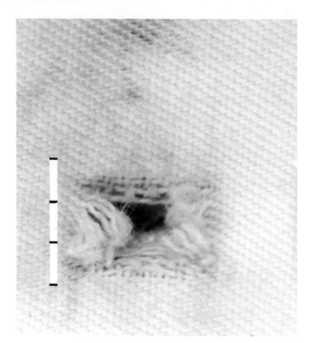

Figure 7.37 Layer 4 Kevlar insert holder.

Figure 7.36 Outer clothing of a shooting victim showing top (1) to bottom (3) layering.

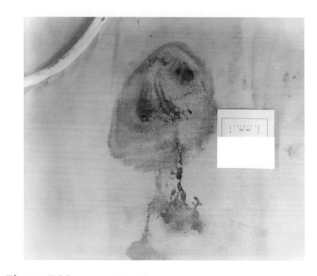

Figure 7.38 Layer 5 Kevlar vest insert.

scene of a shooting, was submitted for comparison with the vest.

Request: Determine if the questioned bullet struck the victim, causing the holes and impact marks present on the victim's clothing and body.

Collected data: The holes and impact marks present on the victim's clothing were carefully examined with a stereomicroscope under a range of magnification from 4× to 40×. Linear and angular measurements were made of the holes and marks. Several of the holes were tested for the presence of gunshot residue. Lead residues in the form of bullet wipes were found on all of the garments. An impact lead pattern (not shown) was also present on the front portion of the Kevlar insert. The impression on the surface of the bullet was carefully studied. A few of the fibers from the questioned bullet were removed and studied with a polarized light microscope. Red-colored polyester and cotton fibers, colorless polyester and cotton fibers, and yellow-appearing Kevlar fibers were found on the bullet. The fibers from the bullet were compared to the fibers composing the victim's garments. All of the questioned fibers from the bullet were consistent in all physical, optical, and chemical properties with the known fibers composing the victim's clothing and body

Figure 7.39 Questioned bullet found near scene of shooting.

armor. The impression found on the bullet's surface was compared to the textile weave pattern used to construct the Kevlar body armor insert and found to be consistent. In Figure 7.40 (left), the bullet's image is laid on top of the vest insert using Photoshop. In Figure 7.40 (right), red-colored polyester and cotton fibers as well as yellow-appearing Kevlar (aramid) fibers are present on the bullet's surface.

Conclusions: From the fibers and textile weave pattern impressions found on the bullet, it was concluded that the questioned bullet was the one that struck the victim, causing his injuries.

After study of the questioned toolmarks is complete, a hypothesis is formed (Chapter 5), the test standards are prepared (Chapter 6), and the hypothesis is tested (Chapter 7), one must statistically assess the conclusions in order to further evolve the discipline of toolmark examination from an art into a science. Chapter 8 is offered to assist toward this end.

Figure 7.40 Questioned bullet found near scene of shooting compared to the textile weave pattern of the Kevlar vest insert. On the left, the bullet's image is laid on top of the vest insert using Photoshop. On the right, red-colored polyester and cotton fibers as well as yellow-appearing Kevlar (aramid) fibers are present on bullet's surface.

How Statistical Pattern Comparison Methods Can Be Applied to Toolmarks

8

Introduction

Over the course of the last two decades, DNA profiling has grown to be one of the most widely known and applied techniques for the identification of biological samples in forensic science. Arguably, the "fame" of DNA profiling is responsible for the courts' current interest in the raising of standards for scientific examination of all forms of physical evidence (e.g., toolmarks, soils, fingerprints, gunshot residue, etc.). It is undoubtedly the clear applicability of simple statistical methods to DNA profiling techniques that lies at the core of its success.

Unfortunately, there are no standard methods or protocols for the application of probability and statistics to the analysis and comparison of toolmarks. In order to begin to address this problem, here we propose and describe several methods for objective, numerical computational pattern matching that can be applied to toolmarks.* Indeed, Moran remarks that "the actual mechanics of the toolmark identification process involves the use of our cognitive ability to first recognize identification through pattern matching."[1] The theory and algorithms of **statistical pattern recognition** give methods for what Moran calls "the quantitative difference between an identification and non-identification."[1] Industries, particularly those that employ some type of sorting into categories, face similar problems as those faced in the examination of physical evidence in forensic science. They have been applying statistical pattern recognition techniques for the automation of assorted classification tasks for approximately the last half century.[2-6]

The examination of similarities and dissimilarities between pieces of physical evidence is based on comparison of the evidence's physical features. The Association of Firearms and Toolmark Examiners (AFTE; www.afte.org) is the *de facto* group that has set the standards for firearms and toolmark examination. The AFTE theory of identification as it relates to toolmarks states (boldface added for emphasis):[1,7]

A. The theory of identification as it pertains to the comparison of toolmarks enables **opinions** of common origin to be made when unique surface contours of two toolmarks are in **sufficient agreement**.
B. This sufficient agreement is related to significant duplication of random toolmarks by correspondence of pattern or combination of patterns of surface contours.
   a. Significance is determined by **comparative examination** of two or more sets of surface contour patterns comprised of individual peaks, ridges and furrows.

Numerical classification methods[3,4,8] are of particular interest because they have the potential of assigning objective quantitative measures to the words *sufficient agreement* and *comparative examination*.

AFTE theory of identification further specifies certain features and their comparison:[1,7]

[B] b. Specifically, the relative height or depth, width, curvature and spatial relationship of individual peaks, ridges and furrows within one set of surface contours are defined and compared to corresponding features in a second set of surface contours.

These features can be subclass or individual characteristics of toolmarks. Specifically the AFTE definitions are:[7,9]

Subclass Characteristics—Discernable surface features of an object which are more restrictive than CLASS CHARACTERISTICS in that they are:
1. Produced incidental to manufacture.
2. Are significant in that they relate to a smaller group source (a subset of the class to which they belong).
3. Can arise from a source which changes over time.

Individual Characteristics—Marks produced by the random imperfections or irregularities of tool surfaces. These random imperfections or irregularities are produced incidental to manufacture and/or caused by use, corrosion, or damage. They are unique to the tool and distinguish it from all other tools.

---

* In this chapter we use the following terms interchangeably: numerical computational pattern matching, toolmark pattern comparisons, and pattern recognition.

As a note of caution, AFTE states:[7]

Caution should be exercised in distinguishing SUB-CLASS CHARACTERISTICS from INDIVIDUAL CHARACTERISTICS.

In keeping with the AFTE theory we will adopt the same definitions; however, we will refer to both subclass characteristics and individual characteristics of the tool's working surface or toolmark simply as **features**.* We have chosen this convention because statistical pattern comparison algorithms would detect both similarities (possible subclass characteristics) and dissimilarities (individual characteristics) between sets of features for many different toolmarks. We agree that caution still needs to be exercised when applying any statistical pattern comparison methods if the working set of toolmarks is small. In such a case, the algorithms may identify subclass characteristics as individualizing a toolmark simply because they do not have enough other toolmarks to make comparisons too. The reverse is also true, however. Similarities or, more importantly, differences between the toolmark features, which may not be apparent or discernible under microscopic examination, may be discovered by computational processing. Essentially, individual characteristics may be discovered within what appears to be subclass characteristics under the microscope. For these reasons alone, statistical pattern recognition should never be ubiquitously and blindly applied to toolmark analysis. Below we will describe ways in which toolmark features can be manually and automatically collected and prepared for statistical comparisons.

With the objective quantification of features in a toolmark's surface, research questions that arise are:

- What features should we use for numerical comparisons?
- Does one need to use all features (which in principle could be infinite), or is it sufficient to choose a finite number of features?

The AFTE theory states that (boldface added for emphasis):[1,7]

 c. Agreement is sufficient when it exceeds the **best agreement** demonstrated by toolmarks **known** to have been produced by different tools and

is consistent with agreement demonstrated by toolmarks **known** to have been produced by the same tool.

In order to quantify "best agreement" and toolmarks of "known" identity, a database can be used to record the features of the tool or toolmark. With a database it becomes relatively easy to apply multiple similarity measures to study their efficacy. Further research questions that arise are:

- How do the identification and comparison accuracy vary with the set of features used?
- What is the likelihood of a false positive "match" given a set of measured features?

Answers to these questions can help to quantify what is stipulated in the AFTE theory below (boldface added for emphasis):[7]

 d. The statement that "sufficient agreement" exists between two toolmarks means that **agreement is of a quality and quantity** that **the likelihood another tool could have made the mark is so remote** as to be **considered a practical impossibility**.

Statistical methods used for justifying DNA profiling have done just that; i.e., they show that the likelihood that two unrelated people have the same DNA profile is "so remote as to be considered a practical impossibility." DNA profiling, however, works because of Mendel's laws of inheritance, specifically the law of independent assortment. Its mathematical generalization for populations, the Hardy-Weinberg and linkage equilibria, allows one to multiply together frequencies of alleles (the "features" of DNA typing) at assorted loci and thus find the probability of particular profiles occurring.[10] Multiplication of allelic frequencies is justified by Mendel's experimental observation of the statistical independence of allele segregation and assortment of chromosomes.[11] In general, the same multiplication of feature frequencies (i.e., probabilities) may not be justified for arbitrary forms of physical evidence. This is true for the specific category of toolmarks because of the following reasons:

- It is difficult to consider measuring the frequencies of even a finite number of features within a large enough sample of the whole "population" of tools to obtain a reasonable level of confidence in their value. Much more research is needed on this issue.
- Statistical independence for the probabilities (i.e., frequencies) of the selected features may be difficult or impossible to prove.

---

* All of the discussions in this chapter apply to the tool's working surface and the toolmarks it is capable of imparting. For brevity, we will only make reference to the toolmark itself. Also for the sake of brevity, we will refer to toolmark striation patterns and toolmark impression patterns in a unified way, simply as **toolmark patterns**. We do recognize, however, that in practice striation and impression patterns are very different.

- Most importantly, the features of tools are mutable over time. Allelic frequencies are assumed not to change.

Thus, important questions for the application of mathematics to the study of toolmarks are:

- What statistical methods should be used for examining features of toolmarks?
- Is there a better numerical comparison method than all others, or are the methods case dependent?
- What is the distribution of percentages for "matching" features from impressions known to have been made by the same tool?[12]
- Can toolmark data be used to generate estimates of a chance match with a high degree of confidence?[12]

In order to begin to answer these questions, below we give an overview of statistical pattern comparison as it can apply to toolmark analysis. The first step in this analysis is the collection of feature data from toolmarks. Next, we will discuss the two general ways to use statistics for the comparison toolmark patterns. The goal of these two general approaches is to construct mathematical discriminant functions or **decision rules**. The two methodologies, however, differ in the way they go about achieving this goal. The **classical methods** of statistical pattern comparison require explicit probability mass functions (histograms), probability densities or their integrals, and probability distributions in order to rigorously find decision rules.[13] **Postclassical methods** of statistical pattern comparison, on the other hand, do not require this much information. Instead, this set of methods seeks to construct decision rules directly from the measured data.[13] Both paradigms have their strengths and weaknesses, and for this reason, a battery of statistical tests should be used on any toolmark comparison task if possible. As we progress through the overview, we will point out pros and cons with both approaches as they apply to toolmark analysis. We further argue that the postclassical methods, which specifically support vector machines, are very suitable for toolmark comparison work because they perform well in a wide variety of applications using less data, and they have nice mathematical properties (e.g., consistency and adjustable generalizability).

The list of statistical pattern comparison methods we describe below is certainly not exhaustive. Over the course of the last 50 years, a smattering of statistical models and statistical studies aimed at toolmark analysis (mostly for firearms) have appeared in the literature.[14–39] Nichols' reviews give excellent background and insightful overviews of most of these studies.[40–42] We chose to focus on methods for the construction of numerical decision rules because we feel they offer the best opportunity to bring more objectivity to the field of toolmark analysis. For those readers who desire readable texts on statistics or a refresher in basic probability and statistics, books by Gonick, Donnelly, Bertsekas, and Rencher are all excellent, contain many examples, and are even enjoyable to read.[43–46] Chapters in Butler and by Morgan and Bartick are also excellent and relevant to forensic science.[10,47] To begin our discussion, we start with a simple example.

A Simple Illustrative Example

Here we consider a common situation met in toolmark analysis: whether or not a striated toolmark found at a crime scene matches the striations made by a suspect tool. As we progress through this section, we hope the reader will see how concepts from statistical pattern recognition can be applied to common tasks of the toolmark examiner, and how these statistical tools can provide a framework for a mathematical foundation of the field. Note that the examples provided below are hypothetical and are meant to show how statistical pattern comparison can be applied to toolmarks.

Say a specific striation pattern, *CS*, is found embedded in a metal windowsill at a crime scene. Next, consider a set of exemplar striation patterns, *EX*, made with known tools, including the tool suspected to have left the impression at the crime scene. Each tool in the exemplar set has the same class characteristics and is used to make several impressions. Using the classical methods of pattern comparison, such as those used for DNA profiling,[10] the set *EX* should contain a very large number (theoretically infinite in size) of striation patterns made by a very large set of tools (theoretically infinite in size as well).[45,46] Next, a **probability mass function** (pmf; i.e., a **histogram**) needs to be constructed for the frequencies of measured **features** produced by each tool in *EX*.[45,46,48] For example, say we have two tools that were used to make all the striation patterns in *EX*. Then a simple feature could be the number of striation lines in each pattern.[49] These measurements could be used to produce the hypothetical histogram shown in Figure 8.1.

Probability density functions (pdfs) can then be found from experimentally determined histograms by extracting parameters for an assumed parametric density (such as the Gaussian density) or fitting the histogram frequencies to a nonparametric density. Figure 8.1 also shows a Gaussian pdf overlaying the histogram that was fit with the average and standard deviation computed from the data. In fact, using various sized runs of

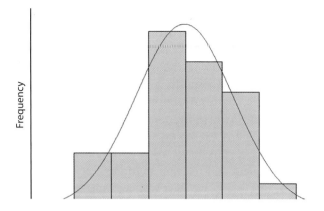

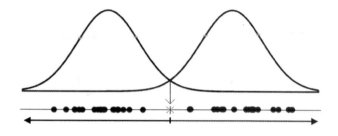

Figure 8.1 A histogram (probability mass function) constructed from the numbers of lines in hypothetical striation patterns made by, say, multiple random jabs of a screwdriver into jeweler's wax. The smooth curve superimposed over the histogram is the Gaussian probability density function fit with the data.

Figure 8.2 Pdfs generated from the number of lines in random striation patterns made by, say, two different hypothetical screwdrivers. Each dot represents the number of lines in a particular striation pattern. The blue dots and pdf are for screwdriver 1, and the red dots and pdf are for screwdriver 2. Note that this situation is a special case of the Bayesian decision rule where the a priori probabilities are equal.

continuous matching striae (CMS) as features, Neel and Wells recently constructed such histograms for large sets of 2D and 3D striation patterns.[19] The frequencies they estimated from their data showed approximate exponential decrease as the size of the CMS runs increased.

Note that the fitting of a pdf to the frequency data is not strictly necessary or even possible. Some of Neel and Wells' fits show significant deviation for exponential decay in some regions (cf. Neel and Wells,[19] Graph 2, for example). The use of pdfs over pmfs in toolmark analysis will be dependent on the chosen features measured in the toolmark pattern. For example, if the features are continuous in nature and there are many to measure, such as the widths of the striation lines in the pattern, then it may makes sense to fit the discrete histogram of feature frequencies to a continuous pdf. On the other hand, if the features are discrete and sparsely occurring, like the number of different subclass characteristics at a particular location on the working surface of the tools, then it may make more sense to simply use a histogram of their frequencies. This is, in fact, the situation that occurs for short tandem repeat (STR)–DNA profiling. STRs at a locus are like subclass characteristics at a particular location of a tool's working surface.[42] It makes no sense to fit continuous pdfs to the frequency data for STRs because there are only a few alleles that can occur at each locus.

While, generally speaking, more "mathematical machinery" is available to be exploited if one uses toolmark features commensurate with continuous pdfs, the use of histograms is not a major hindrance.[3,4,6] This is especially true if the estimated probabilities of occurrence for features (represented by their measured frequencies) are statistically independent. In this case the product rule for probabilities can be used to construct a

very simple and effective discrimination model. In fact, it is the model of statistically independent frequencies of alleles at STR loci that is the foundation of modern DNA profiling, and what makes it such a powerful discrimination technique.

For illustration purposes and to take full advantage of the mathematics of statistical pattern recognition, we will assume throughout this chapter that pdfs can be built from the measured frequencies of arbitrary features in toolmarks. Figure 8.2 displays two pdfs built with the number of lines in striation patterns made by two hypothetical tools.

Note the point marked with an asterisk. This is the number of striation lines where the pdfs cross and is called a decision point.[3] If unknown pattern CS contains a number of striation lines to the left of this decision point, the examiner should assign CS to tool 1. In this region the value of pdf 1 is larger. If instead pattern CS contains a number of striation lines that fall to the right of this decision point, the examiner should choose CS's identity as tool 2 because pdf 2 is larger in this region. Note for one measured feature, the pdfs are two-dimensional, and where they cross produce only decision points. Decision points are the decision rules for a one-dimensional feature space.

This admittedly oversimplified example can be easily generalized to situations where an arbitrary number of features are measured or counted for a particular toolmark. Figure 8.3 shows pdfs fit from histograms for the two measured features: the number of striation lines (feature 1) and average width of striation lines (feature 2) left by random jabbing of a hypothetical screwdriver into a slab of green Ferris™ wax.[50,51]

Note that for two features, the pdfs are three-dimensional. The solid line separating the two data sets is called a decision curve and is a decision rule

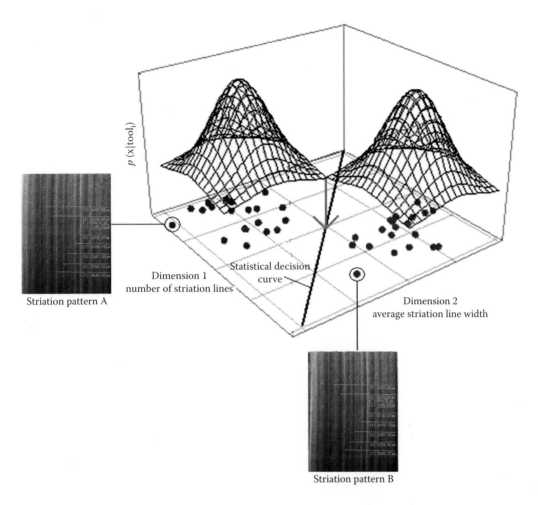

Figure 8.3 Pdfs for the features made by two different hypothetical screwdrivers: dimension 1, number of lines in a random striation pattern; dimension 2, average width of striation line in a random striation pattern. The blue dots are for screwdriver 1 and the red for screwdriver 2. The green arrow points to a decision rule. Equal a priori probabilities are assumed.

for a two-dimensional feature space. If an unknown striation pattern, say CS has 400 striation lines with an average width of 2 μm, the examiner should assign it to tool 1 (pdf 1 is larger in this region). If instead CS has 600 striation lines with an average width of 3.5 μm, the examiner should assign the pattern to tool 2 (pdf 2 is larger in this region).

Generalizing, three measured features (i.e., 3D data) yield decision rules that are surfaces. Higher-dimensional data yield decision rule hypersurfaces. For simplicity, we will refer to any of these geometric discrimination functions (points, curves, surfaces, etc.) simply as decision rules regardless of their dimension. It is these decision rules that are the main object of interest for statistical pattern classification applied to toolmark analysis. They divide up the measured data into decision regions or "classes," thereby allowing an unknown impression pattern to be assigned to a particular tool, depending on which class its measured features fall into.

Falsifiability and Generalizability in Toolmark Pattern Analysis

The process of comparing toolmark impressions is an empirical science. Just as with any empirical science, it is based on inductive reasoning; i.e., given a set of observations, one draws general conclusions.[52] Of course, generalizations based on specific observations are not necessarily valid conclusions. Thus, when building a theory of comparative science based on a finite number of empirical observations (e.g., toolmark analysis), one must be careful to justify the inductive step involved. What this means for the application of statistical pattern recognition to toolmark analysis is that forensic toolmark examiners must be especially careful with the algorithms they choose and how they construct their studies. The "shape" of decision rules (e.g., linear, curved, amorphous, etc.) is in general not unique and depends on the algorithm employed, which may rest on potentially false assumptions. Some decision algorithms are more reliable than others. When they are used to examine evidence, this is an extremely important issue. Not all decision rules are created equal!

The demarcation problem of inductive reasoning is concerned with the formal mechanism to distinguish between a true empirical science and a pseudoscience (i.e., junk science). Since the 1930s the cornerstone of demarcation has been Karl Popper's criteria of falsification.[53] Essentially, if a theory can explain every observation that falls into its purview, then it is **nonfalsifiable** and thus does not have a necessary condition to be a valid science. For an empirical science to be valid, there will inevitably exist some observations that will not fit any possible explanation within its framework but do fall within its domain.[13,53] Any theory of toolmark comparison at a minimum *should not* be nonfalsifiable if it is truly a science and presented as a valid theory in a court of law.

From a somewhat less abstract standpoint, one can think of algorithms that determine decision rules for toolmark patterns as "learning machines." A pattern comparison system (i.e., a learning machine) is nonfalsifiable if it can identify the specific tool that generated any toolmark, no matter how much or how little data are given. Geometrically this means that a nonfalsifiable learning machine can divide any feature data into arbitrary groups in arbitrary ways to produce any "explanation" of the data desired.[13] Needless to say, a nonfalsifiable toolmark pattern comparison algorithm is not reliable, and care must be taken in order to avoid such a thing. An example of a simple nonfalsifiable decision rule is shown in Figure 8.4.

Learning machines can be classified into two broad categories: those that are supervised when learning to classify patterns and those that are unsupervised. It is impossible to assess the reliability of unsupervised learning machines, and thus they are not a good primary pattern recognition tool to use in forensic science (although they would be useful in confirming the results of supervised learning machines). Supervised learning machines, however, produce decision rules by being presented with feature data of known identity. Their performance can then be tested by presenting them with known but unlabeled data from an appropriately sized test set. The best pattern comparison systems have the smallest risk of misclassifying data they have not been trained with; however, they are certainly not nonfalsifiable. A small risk of misclassification on data of unknown identity is called good **generalization**. In order to promote trust and reliability with the courts, statistical pattern comparison algorithms for toolmark analysis need to consistently generalize well yet be falsifiable.

Next we discuss the conditions toolmark pattern comparison methods need to satisfy in order to be

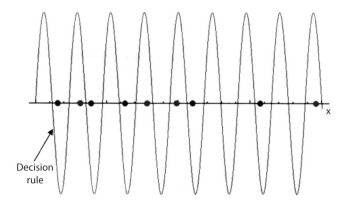

Figure 8.4 A decision rule perfectly separating group 1 blue dots from group 2 red dots. This decision rule is a sine wave where sin(x) is negative for group 1 and positive for group 2. No matter how many new red and blue dots are added to the data set, a sinusoidal decision rule can be found to perfectly separate them. A learning machine that can produce decision rules that can separate data into arbitrary groups is nonfalsifiable. Such a conundrum is also known as overfitting. Nonfalsifiable learning machines generalize very poorly and are a danger that can be encountered when applying statistical pattern comparison to toolmark analysis.

falsifiable but generalize well. The following will necessarily be somewhat abstract but needs to be stated for the record. Below we follow closely the books by Vapnik[13] and Scholkopf and Smola.[54]

Both general methodologies of statistical pattern comparison discussed in this chapter (classical and postclassical) ultimately boil down to what is called **minimization of a risk functional**. A risk functional is a mathematical expression that quantifies the loss encountered when a pattern is misclassified. Its minimization is a natural place to begin the construction of a pattern comparison theory. The form of the "true" risk functional is given as

$$R = \int L[\mathbf{x}, y, g(\mathbf{x})] dP(\mathbf{x}, y),$$

where $L[\mathbf{x},y,g(\mathbf{x})]$ is the loss functional that returns a penalty every time a decision rule, $g(\mathbf{x})$, misclassifies a pattern $\mathbf{x}$, i.e., when $g(\mathbf{x}) \neq y$. $P(\mathbf{x},y)$ is the joint probability distribution over all possible patterns $\mathbf{x}$ with pattern labels y. The risk functional essentially adds up the losses for all the misclassifications made when examining all patterns. An integral of this form is called an expectation value and represents the theoretical average loss for a pattern recognition task. The loss functional is not unique and dependent on the problem at hand, e.g., probability density estimation, pattern comparisons, etc.

Needless to say, calculating the "true" risk functional for a pattern comparison task of one toolmark to any other possible toolmark is impossible. What is used instead for practical applications is the empirical risk functional:

$$R_{\mathrm{emp}} = \frac{1}{n} \sum_{i=1}^{n} L[\mathbf{x}_i, y_i, g(\mathbf{x}_i)].$$

Here empirical risk is calculated based on a sample set of toolmark patterns of size n. Minimization of this functional with respect to a set of decision rules G, $(g \in G)$ is called the **empirical risk minimization** (ERM) principle and leads to various practical pattern recognition algorithms.[3–6,13,54] The ERM, however, needs to be consistent or the decision rules derived from it may be nonfalsifiable. **Consistency** of ERM is heuristically defined as follows:

> As the number of samples in the data set grows (to infinity) the decision rule that minimizes R_{emp} also yields the lowest possible value for test error achievable by minimizing the true risk functional itself.[54]

Consistency of the ERM principle ensures falsifiability and circumvents having to construct and minimize R explicitly since the decision rule derived from the data set should asymptotically yield the same results in terms of test error.[52,54] In general, G is an infinite set of decision rules, and the decision rule that yields the absolute minimum R_{emp} may (and probably will) be nonfalsifiable. Thus, it turns out that consistency of ERM depends critically on the choice of decision rules used in the minimization. The mathematics that give the necessary and sufficient conditions for the consistency of ERM also induce parameters from which restrictions on the decision rules can be inferred. Full details of the necessary proofs are given in Vapnik's book.[52]

Ensuring the consistency of ERM is an abstract idea but has two very practical consequences for toolmark analysis. First, it guarantees falsifiability, which is important because it mathematically establishes to the courts that statistical pattern comparisons of toolmarks satisfy the necessary and sufficient tenants to be called a science. Second, the restrictions that need to be placed on decision rules, g (drawn from G), give us "adjustment knobs" to control the generalizability of the pattern comparison algorithm.

Toolmark Data Collection

The starting point for the statistical analysis and comparison of any set of patterns is the collection of features of the toolmark pattern surface. Every measurement of a feature is a random variable X_i.[55] Collection of various impression features into a list constitutes the feature vector, **x**, for that impression.[5,56] A vector is just a list of numbers. So, for example, if we count the striation lines and determine the average striation line width for a set of one hundred screwdriver striation patterns made in wax, then we could assemble one hundred "lists" of two values:

$$\mathbf{x}_i = \begin{pmatrix} \text{number of striation lines} \\ \text{average width of a striation line} \end{pmatrix} \quad i = \{1,2,3,\ldots,100\}.$$

Each feature vector, **x**, would thus be two numbers representing some information on the toolmark pattern's surface. The number of characterizing values recorded in a feature vector is called the vector's dimension and is not restricted. Thus, feature vectors are just "containers" for toolmark information (i.e., subclass and individual characteristics).

Feature data can be collected in the traditional way (i.e., by hand) or in a more automated fashion. Hand collection can be done by the expert's identification of specific sites on a toolmark surface using stereomicroscopy.[49,57] A standardized reference frame for measurements and counting can be established using various Whipple and Howard micrometer disks in conjunction with the Abbott grid methodology.[58,59] Digital photography combined with specialized computer-aided design software can also be used to help automate the feature data collection process.[60,61]

Fully automated collection of toolmark data can be accomplished with high-resolution 3D laser scanning. This method would capture essentially all the information that can be known by mapping the coordinates of the toolmark's surface. Caution must be exercised with such automated data collection because the surfaces of the different objects must be carefully aligned. This is necessary because the same coordinate system must be used across all the toolmarks in a working set. Computationally this alignment issue is called the registration problem and has been attacked by several authors.[62–65]

Recently, National Institute of Justice funding has been used to develop a commercial 3D bullet comparison system based on confocal microscopy.[30,31] The system, now incorporated into Forensic Technology, Inc.; IBIS BulletTRAX-3D®, partially circumvents the registration problem by computing a similarity score between all possible orientations (with respect to land-engraved areas) of pairs of bullets. Unfortunately, due to the commercial nature of the product, all of the details of how the system functions are not available as the technology is proprietary, and furthermore, little has been published.

Once tool and toolmark data have been collected, they can be perpetually stored in a standard database such as Oracle or mySQL. Issues certainly would arise as to the organization and categories required for the data to be stored. While significant attempts have been made at the construction and maintenance of such a database, much more research is needed in this direction.[32,66,67] The issue of categories to include in the database becomes moot if the entire 3D scanned surface is stored (if disk space is no object, of course!). The entire surface or any feature from that surface can be included in the statistical pattern comparison procedure. We conclude this section by noting that once toolmark data have been recorded, the construction of feature vectors trivially follows by just assembling the desired features into a list.

Some Common Data Preprocessing Methods

For the sake of more completeness we now briefly mention some data preprocessing techniques. Note that many authors describe these methods not simply as preprocessing techniques, but as full-fledged statistical modeling and discrimination techniques of complicated data. We use the adjective *preprocessing* not to diminish their value, but rather because, in and of themselves, they do not produce decision rules as we have defined them in this chapter. The results of the methods discussed in this section can be used with any of the statistical pattern comparison schemes we mention below.

Principal component analysis (PCA) is a multivariate procedure that is used to reduce the dimensionality of a data set ($\mathbf{X}$) to a new data set ($\mathbf{Z}_{pc}$) of derived variables.[46,68] The derived variables are linear combinations of the original variables

$$Z_{ij} = \sum_{l=1}^{p} a_{il} X_{il}$$

or in matrix form

$$\mathbf{Z}_{pc} = \mathbf{X}\mathbf{A}_{pc}^{T}$$

where the superscript T is the transpose of $\mathbf{A}_{pc}$. In the context of toolmark analysis, $\mathbf{X}$ is a collection of toolmark pattern feature vectors, $\mathbf{x}_i$. These feature vectors are stacked on top of each other as rows. If each toolmark pattern contains p empirical measurements (i.e., $\dim(\mathbf{x}_i) = p$) and there are n total toolmark patterns, then $\mathbf{X}$ is an $n \times p$ matrix.

Principal component analysis on a data matrix $\mathbf{X}$ simply rotates the coordinate axes of the data in feature space. Thus, the above equation is a transformation of the data ($\mathbf{X}$) into the basis of principal components. The entire set of derived variables is equivalent to the original data ($\mathbf{X}$). The new data set ($\mathbf{Z}_{pc}$), however, orders the variables (columns) according to the amount of variance of the data set they contain, from highest to lowest. If the first few variables in $\mathbf{Z}_{pc}$ contain a majority of the variance, then the remaining variables can be deleted with a minimum loss of information contained in the data. The dimensionality of the data set is then effectively reduced to include only those variables that adequately represent the data. As a note of caution, while the information contained in the low variance variables of $\mathbf{Z}_{pc}$ that are removed may not be important to the overall structure of the data, they may contain the derived features needed to discriminate between different samples.[68]

The matrix $\mathbf{A}_{pc}$ contains the p principal components as rows and is computed by diagonalizing the $p \times p$ covariance matrix ($\mathbf{S}$) of $\mathbf{X}$:

$$\mathbf{S}\mathbf{A}_{pc}^{T} = \mathbf{A}_{pc}^{T}\Lambda.$$

Standard eigenvector and eigenvalue routines can be used to determine the PCs $\mathbf{A}$ (the eigenvectors of $\mathbf{S}$) and their variances Λ (the eigenvalues of $\mathbf{S}$). The ratio of eigenvalues

$$\lambda_i \bigg/ \sum_{j=1}^{p} \lambda_j \quad \Lambda = diag(\lambda_1, \lambda_1, \ldots \lambda_p)$$

gives the proportion of variance explained by the ith principal component and is useful in selecting the number of principal components required to adequately represent the data. Note that PCA does not assume any prior grouping of the toolmark patterns into known groups.

Canonical variate analysis (CVA; also called Fisher discriminant analysis, linear Fisher discriminant analysis, and linear discriminant analysis) seeks to characterize the ratio of between-group variance ($\mathbf{B}$) to within-group variance ($\mathbf{W}$).[46,56,69] Unlike PCA, canonical variate analysis requires that different samples of toolmark patterns are labeled with their identity and fed into the algorithm as groups. These a priori labeled toolmark pattern samples serve as a training set in order to compute the canonical variates (CVs). Geometrically, the CVs define axes onto which the data are projected that best separate the samples into discrete clusters.[46,69] In p-dimensional space, K-1 canonical variates can be computed. However, CVA can also be used to reduce the dimensionality of the data by retaining only the first few CVs. Additionally, like PCA, CVA can be formulated as an eigenvector-eigenvalue problem, with the magnitude of the eigenvalues providing a guide as to the number of CVs to be retained. The CVs, $\mathbf{A}_{cv}$, and their eigenvalues Λ_{cv} are computed by diagonalizing the matrix $\mathbf{W}^{-1}\mathbf{B}$ with

$$\mathbf{B} = \sum_{i=1}^{k} n_i (\overline{\mathbf{X}}_i - \overline{\mathbf{X}}) \otimes (\overline{\mathbf{X}}_i - \overline{\mathbf{X}})^{\mathrm{T}}$$

and

$$\mathbf{W} = \sum_{i=1}^{k} \sum_{j=1}^{n_i} (\mathbf{X}_{ij} - \overline{\mathbf{X}}_i) \otimes (\mathbf{X}_{ij} - \overline{\mathbf{X}}_i)^{\mathrm{T}}.$$

A standard inversion method is used to invert nonsingular $\mathbf{W}$. $\mathbf{X}_{ij}$ represents the jth toolmark pattern in the ith sample, and $\overline{\mathbf{X}}_i$ is the average of all the toolmark patterns in the ith sample. Note that there are n_i toolmark patterns in sample i. Because the eigenproblem for CVA

$$\mathbf{W}^{-1}\mathbf{B}\mathbf{A}_{cv}^{\mathrm{T}} = \mathbf{A}_{cv}^{\mathrm{T}}\Lambda_{cv}$$

is not symmetric, its eigenvectors are not guaranteed to be orthogonal. Thus, unlike in PCA, the CVs are not necessarily at right angles to each other.[46] The data are then transformed to the basis of (retained) CVs as

$$\mathbf{Z} = \mathbf{X}\mathbf{A}^{\mathrm{T}}.$$

Orthogonal canonical variate analysis (OCVA) seeks to find axes in p-dimensional feature space (defined by the data set) that maximize the ratio of between-group to within-group variance as in CVA.[70] OCVA, however, has the additional restriction that the axes it finds are orthogonal to each other as in PCA. Because of the added constraint, the OCVA procedure cannot be formulated as an eigenproblem. As prescribed by Krzanowski,[70] one must first form the equation of weighted variables, V, for the ith OCV:

$$V = \mathbf{e}_i^{\mathrm{T}}\mathbf{B}\mathbf{e}_i / \mathbf{e}_i^{\mathrm{T}}\mathbf{W}\mathbf{e}_i$$

where $\mathbf{e}_i$,

$$\mathbf{e}_i^{\mathrm{T}} = (y_1, y_2, \ldots y_p)_i$$

is a vector of variables to be determined. Next, the Lagrangian

$$L(\mathbf{e}_i, \lambda) = V - \sum_{j=1}^{i} \lambda_j (\mathbf{e}_j^{T}\mathbf{e}_j - 1)$$

is formed and maximized to determine the values of the variables in $\mathbf{e}_i$ and Lagrange multipliers λ_i. A standard maximization routine can be used to perform this optimization task. The resulting OCVs, $\mathbf{e}_i$, are collected (as rows) into the matrix $\mathbf{A}_{ocv}$. The above procedure is repeated for the desired number of OCVs. A total of K-1 OCVs can be computed; however, like the multivariate methods described above, the goal is to reduce the dimensionality of the data. Like PCA and CVA, the OCVs can be ordered in increasing importance. The Lagrange multipliers serve this task in OCVA; however, they no longer represent variances as in PCA.[70] The data in $\mathbf{X}$ can then be transformed to the basis of (retained) OCVs as

$$\mathbf{Z} = \mathbf{X}\mathbf{A}_{ocv}^{\mathrm{T}}.$$

Classical Methods to Determine Statistical Decision Rules for Toolmark Analysis

The classical methods of statistical pattern comparison determine decision rules using knowledge of the probability mass functions, probability density functions, or probability distributions (all will be called probability functions for brevity).[3] The probability functions can have an assumed form that is dependent only on parameters derived from the measured data. One of the most widely used parametric probability densities is the so-called bell curve (Figure 8.5):

$$p(x) = \frac{1}{\sqrt{2\pi}s} e^{-\frac{1}{2}\left(\frac{x-\bar{x}}{s}\right)^2}.$$

Toolmark features, however, may not be distributed according to any known parametric probability density or mass function. In this case, one can try to fit the toolmark feature data to a nonparametric probability density, or simply use the probability mass function derived from frequencies of features. A popular scheme to fit nonparametric densities is the method of Prazen windows. The details of this method are straightforward but lengthy and will not be presented here. See Duda et al. or Theodoridis and Koutroumbas for more information.[3,4]

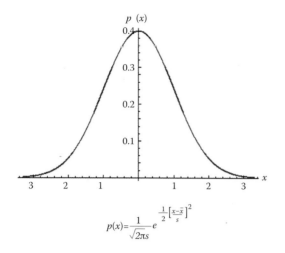

$$p(x) = \frac{1}{\sqrt{2\pi}s} e^{\frac{1}{2}\left[\frac{x-\bar{x}}{s}\right]^2}$$

Figure 8.5 Graphical depiction of the bell curve or Gaussian density. The parameters of the Gaussian density are the data's average, $\bar{x}$, and standard deviation, s. For the above graph, $\bar{x} = 0$ and $s = 1$.

As a note of caution, when using nonparametric densities one must be aware that they suffer from the **curse of dimensionality**. This means that the amount of data required for an accurate nonparametric density increases exponentially with the dimension of the feature vectors used. This can be a severe drawback for their application to toolmark analysis if research ultimately shows that many features (i.e., dimensions) are required to characterize many or all types of toolmarks.

A naïve assumption for high-dimensional-pattern classification tasks that often works well in practice is that all components of the feature vector are statistically independent. This allows one to write a high-dimensional probability function simply as a product, e.g.,

$$p(\mathbf{x}\,|\,\text{tool}_i) = \prod_{i=1}^{\dim(\mathbf{x})} p(x_j\,|\,\text{tool}_i).$$

To our knowledge such an assumption or deviations from it have never been tested for toolmarks. This can be a very fruitful area of research. If it turns out that the assumption of feature vector component independence is bad, then the amount of data required for a robust pattern comparison study based on nonparametric method may be too prohibitive. Vast databases of tool surfaces may aid in the construction of high-dimensional nonparametric densities, and more research is needed in this direction.

In an effort to circumvent the curse of dimensionality, Bachrach has developed a "similarity score"-based approach for the intercomparison of land-engraved areas found on fired bullets.[30,31] This system computes a numerical similarity between vector profiles of bullets obtained from 3D digital photography. The similarity score is a complicated function of the profiles

but essentially relies on the angle between the profile vectors.[30] Bachrach's procedure produces one-dimensional data of similarity scores between pairs of bullets that can be used to plot histograms, which are then employed in various forms of classical hypothesis testing.[31] Evidently this scheme has been incorporated into Forensic Technology's IBIS system.

Once probability functions of the toolmark features have been determined, statistical pattern comparisons can then be carried out. Say we have a set of k tools capable of leaving impression or striation patterns, and we have constructed several probability densities for features vectors of different tools, $p(\mathbf{x}|\text{tool}_i)$. Decision rules enabling a tool's identification are explicitly given by the values of feature vectors $\mathbf{x}$ for which $p(\mathbf{x}|\text{tool}_i) = p(\mathbf{x}|\text{tool}_j)$ for all $i,j = \{1,\ldots,k\}$. These implicit functions of $\mathbf{x}$ are obviously difficult to determine for all but the simplest probability densities. Instead, what is typically done in practice is to plug the feature vector from a toolmark into each $p(\mathbf{x}|\text{tool}_i)$ and choose a tool identity that yields the largest value. This procedure is symbolically given as

Choose tool_i for:

$$\arg \max_{i=\{1,\ldots,k\}} \left[p(\mathbf{x}|\text{tool}_i) \right]$$

Often the above equation is referred to as a decision rule. Even though it does not explicitly designate the intersections between pdfs or probability distributions as a decision rule does (the way we have defined it), it accomplishes the same task. Pictorially this equation looks like Figure 8.6.

The scheme Bachrach developed for the latest IBIS system evidently can work on this principle.[31] Empirical

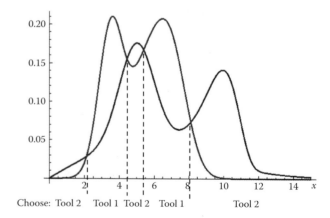

Figure 8.6 Pictorial display of the equation

$$\arg \max_{i=\{1,2\}} \left[p(x|\text{tool}_i) \right]$$

for some measured feature of a toolmark. The red pdf is for the data generated by tool 1 and the blue curve for tool 2.

pdfs of a specific similarity metric are built using the best (matching) and second best (nonmatching) scores between bullets of various manufactures fired through various make and model barrels. This should allow the system to determine decision rules (Bachrach refers to them as "optimal thresholds") as to whether or not a bullet is likely to have been fired through a particular barrel.[31] Using this procedure, the system should also be capable of computing estimates of type I and type II errors familiar from classical hypothesis testing (cf. ref. Bachrach,[31] Figure 8).[71,72]

Since classical methods assume or construct a known conditional probability density $p(\mathbf{x}|\text{tool}_i)$, discrimination of toolmarks can in principle exploit Bayes' theorem:

$$P(\text{tool}_i\,|\,\mathbf{x}) = \frac{p(\mathbf{x}\,|\,\text{tool}_i)P(\text{tool}_i)}{p(\mathbf{x})}.$$

This formulation of Bayes' theorem determines the **a posteriori** (subsequent) probability, $P(\text{tool}_i|\mathbf{x})$, that tool_i is responsible for the toolmark encoded by the feature vector $\mathbf{x}$. The term $p(\mathbf{x})$,

$$p(\mathbf{x}) = \sum_{i=1}^{k} p(\mathbf{x}\,|\,\text{tool}_i)P(\text{tool}_i),$$

is usually referred to as the "evidence"[3] and is essentially a scale factor that guarantees that the sum of all k a posteriori probabilities is unity. $P(\text{tool}_i)$ is the **a priori** (prior) probability and represents the known information that out of all other tools in some predetermined population, tool_i is responsible for the toolmark.[73] Decision rules can reflect this prior knowledge (if available) via the Bayesian decision rule:

$$\arg \max_{i=\{1,\dots,k\}} \left[P(\text{tool}_i\,|\,\mathbf{x}) \right].$$

In words, this equation means: choose the identity of an unknown toolmark (encoded by the feature vector $\mathbf{x}$) as having been produced by tool_i that yields the largest a posteriori probability. Using the same probability densities shown in Figure 8.6, we can visualize the Bayesian decision rule for two tools with, say, $P(\text{tool}_1) = 0.3$ and $P(\text{tool}_2) = 0.7$ (i.e., tool 1 has a known 70% chance of having made the mark and tool 2 a 30% chance; cf. Figure 8.7).

Notice how the decision regions have changed between Figures 8.6 and 8.7. Figure 8.7 implicitly assumes both a priori probabilities are 50%. As the a priori probabilities change with either the addition of new knowledge or better estimates, the decision regions

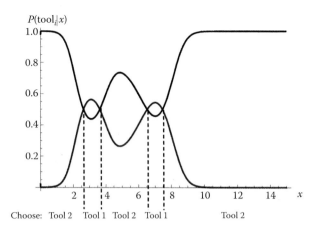

Figure 8.7 Pictorial display of the Bayesian decision rule

$$\arg \max_{i=\{1,2\}} \left[P(\text{tool}_i\,|\,x) \right]$$

for some measured feature of a toolmark. The red curve is for tool 1 and the blue curve for tool 2.

will change as well. For this reason it is crucial to have accurate and objective a priori probabilities when using Bayes' theorem. This is also true of the probability densities $p(x|\text{tool}_i)$.

Bayesian decision rules are very powerful because they can be shown to yield the lowest probability of making an error of any decision rule.[3] Unfortunately, a way in which to accurately and objectively determine the values of a priori probabilities, $P(\text{tool}_i)$, is not uniquely defined. Some applications of Bayes' theorem in toolmark analysis have already been carried out.[14–18] So far, these Bayesian statistics-based toolmark studies all involve one or more subjective estimates of terms used in Bayes' theorem. We believe that since toolmark analysis has so often been criticized as overly subjective, our description of classical methods of statistical discrimination applied to toolmarks needs to remain objective; i.e., measured frequencies need to be used in the ultimate determination of probabilities. In the interests of minimizing bias and maximizing objectivity, a very large sample of tools and toolmarks should be employed for comparison studies using Bayes' theorem and probability functions in general, if the conclusions are ultimately to be judged reliable by the courts.[13,52]

In order to facilitate pattern recognition tasks in practice, often common parametric probability densities are assumed.[2–5] As already mentioned, a popular parametric probability density to assume is the Gaussian density.[46] In multivariate form it is given as

$$p(\mathbf{x}) = \frac{1}{\left(\sqrt{2\pi}\right)^{\dim(\mathbf{x})} \sqrt{\det(\mathbf{S})}} \exp\left(-\frac{(\mathbf{x}-\bar{\mathbf{x}})^{\mathrm{T}}\mathbf{S}^{-1}(\mathbf{x}-\bar{\mathbf{x}})^{\mathrm{T}}}{2} \right),$$

where $\mathbf{S}$ is the covariance matrix and $\det(\mathbf{S})$ its determinant.[46] The assumption of normally distributed toolmark data leads to the equations of linear classification analysis,[46] also often called linear discriminant analysis (LDA).[56] The decision rule of LDA for k different tools is given as

Choose tool$_i$ as the identity of toolmark $\mathbf{x}$ for:

$$\arg \max_{i=\{1,\dots,k\}} \bar{\mathbf{x}}_i^{\mathsf{T}} \mathbf{S}_{pl}^{-1}\mathbf{x} - \frac{1}{2}\left(\bar{\mathbf{x}}_i^{\mathsf{T}} \mathbf{S}_{pl}^{-1} \bar{\mathbf{x}}_i \right) + P(\text{tool}_i | \mathbf{x})$$

Here $\mathbf{S}_{pl}$ is a pooled covariance matrix of all the toolmarks of all the tools used for a particular study or in a database.[46] Note that including quadratic terms in the above decision rule, parabolic (as opposed to linear) decision rules may be computed.[46] Such a quadratic classification scheme also assumes the multivariate normal distribution of data and is often referred to as quadratic discriminant analysis (QDA).[56] These approaches to classification are relatively robust for data deviations from normality and have found wide applications outside the field of toolmark analysis.[3,56,74–80] Whether or not these classifications methods will work well for real-life toolmark examination casework remains to be seen.

Postclassical Methods of Statistical Pattern Classification Toolmark Analysis

Postclassical methods for statistical pattern comparisons do not use explicit knowledge of the underlying pdfs in order to determine decision rules. Instead, toolmark pattern data of known identity are used to compute decision rules that map each toolmark to its assigned identity label. Thus, postclassical methods directly train decision rules to recognize the identity of a toolmark based on its features. The general functional form of decision rules can be linear or nonlinear, both having advantages and disadvantages.[3,4,6] Nonlinear rules can be trained to recognize very complicated toolmarks; however, they are difficult to compute and have little control over the possibility of overfitting.[3,13,52] Linear decision rules tend to be much easier to compute but can be much less flexible than their nonlinear relatives.[3,6]

Neural networks (NNs) are the dominant technique used to compute nonlinear decision rules.[2,6] They experienced a period of rapid development during the late 1980s and early 1990s due to widespread interest in artificial intelligence and led to a plethora of available software. These methods have their roots in modeling of neural processes for biological systems. Our description of neural networks closely follows that of Bishop.[6]

A (supervised) NN identifies patterns via training. The toolmark examiner presents the NN feature vectors of various toolmark patterns as well as labels for their identity. The NN then learns decision rules to identify each pattern with an acceptable level of empirical risk (i.e., apparent error rate). The most common kind of NN, called a **multilayer feed forward network**, constructs nonlinear decision rules in the following way. First, K linear combinations of measured features, x_i, from toolmark patterns $\mathbf{x}$ are constructed by guessing an initial set of **weight coefficients** $w_{j,i}^{[1]}$:

$$c_j^{[1]} = \sum_{i=1}^{p} w_{j,i}^{[1]} x_i + w_{j,0}^{[1]},$$

where $j = \{1, \dots, K\}$ and $p = \dim(\mathbf{x})$. The $c_j^{[1]}$ are the first set of **activation coefficients** and $w_{j,0}^{[1]}$ are a set of first-layer **offset coefficients**. K is the number of **neurons** or **nodes** (linear combinations) in the first layer of the network. The first-layer activation coefficients are then transformed to a first set of output values, $o_j^{[1]}$, using a differentiable activation function, $a^{[1]}$,

$$o_j^{[1]} = a^{[1]}(c_j^{[1]})$$

that typically looks like a stretched-out letter s (e.g., sigmoid functions, hyperbolic tangent functions, etc.; cf. Figure 8.8).

The reason activation functions are used to transform the activation coefficients is that they give approximate 0, 1 responses, like a yes/no answer. These output

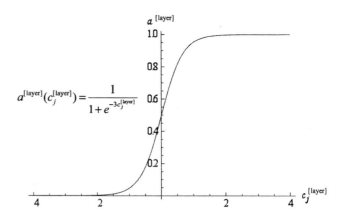

Figure 8.8 A sigmoid activation function for an arbitrary layer of neurons in a neural network. Note how the activation function varies continuously from the range 0 to 1. This behavior gives each neuron a continuous "on-off" switching-like ability. The continuity of the activation function is important in obtaining efficient algorithms for determination of the weights at each neuron.

values are themselves linearly transformed as they are passed to the second layer of L neurons:

$$c_j^{[2]} = \sum_{i=1}^{K} w_{j,i}^{[2]} o_j^{[1]} + w_{j,0}^{[2]} \quad j = \{1,\ldots,L\}$$

producing the second-layer activation coefficients, $c_j^{[2]}$, which are subsequently transformed by a second set of activation functions, $a^{[2]}$:

$$o_j^{[2]} = a^{[2]}(c_j^{[2]}).$$

The process can continue through any number of layers, each with a variable number of neurons, until desired output values are reached. The output values emerging from the final layer are the identity labels assigned by the neural network to the toolmark patterns.

A neural network with Q layers and k neurons in the final layer constructs k decision rules essentially by building up k composite functions from Q nonlinear transformations of linear functions of the data. For a two-layer neural network constructed to describe k toolmark patterns, the decision rules g are

$$g_k(\mathbf{x}) = a^{[2]}\left(\sum_{j=1}^{K} w_{k,j}^{[2]} a^{[1]}\left(\sum_{i=1}^{p} w_{j,i}^{[1]} x_i + w_{j,0}^{[1]} \right) + w_{k,0}^{[2]} \right).$$

The trick to the functioning of NNs is to devise an efficient algorithm to determine the weight coefficients, $w_{j,i}^{[R]}$, at each level, R, for each neuron. Because the activation functions are differentiable, this can be done in a standard way with the so-called back propagation algorithm.[3,6] Below is shown a plot of 2D features of two hypothetical tools (cf. Figure 8.9). The black line is a plot of the output decision rule from a two-layer neural network employing sigmoid activation functions.

Thus far we know of only one application of neural network application to toolmarks (bullet striations).[28] Clearly more studies are needed in this direction.

A major drawback to the use of NNs is that forensic toolmark examiners may need to have expert knowledge to adjust various NN parameters in order to obtain reliable performance.[3] Also, NNs have little control over the possibility of overfitting the data they are trained with.[13] Overfitting leads to a partially or totally nonfalsifiable set of decision rules, which is a dangerous prospect for forensic science applications. That said, estimated error rates for the identification of toolmarks that a NN has not been trained with can be computed using the error

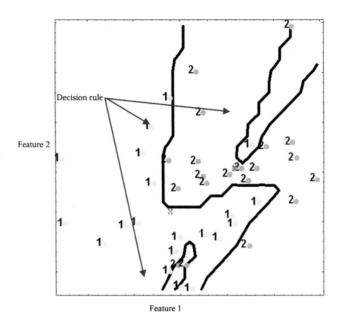

Figure 8.9 Plot of hypothetical two-dimensional features from two toolmark patterns. The yellow dots are the 2D features made by tool 1 and the green dots are the 2D features made by tool 2. A two-layer neural network was used to generate the very nonlinear (and very overfit!) decision rule shown in black.

rate methods detailed below. So far, this has not been done in forensic toolmark analysis.

A state-of-the-art alternative to NNs that also transcends many of their problems is the **support vector machine** (SVM). Small sample sizes are inevitable for many statistical studies of toolmarks. Statistical learning theory and its practical application, the SVM, were developed in response to the need for reliable statistical discriminations within small-sample studies. SVMs like NNs seek to determine decision rules in the absence of any knowledge of probability densities for the data. For pattern classification tasks, statistical learning theory prescribes minimizing the probability of misidentification (risk) by simultaneously minimizing empirical risk (based on the sampled data) and adjusting an appropriately chosen "regularization functional."[13,52] This procedure produces an algorithm that determines linear decision rules with maximum possible margins for error. In practical applications, the problem of determining the maximum margin classifier is formalized in terms of an optimization of a vector of Lagrange multipliers λ:[4,13]

$$\max_{\lambda} \quad \sum_{i=1}^{n} \lambda_i - \frac{1}{2} \sum_{i=1}^{n} \sum_{j=1}^{n} \lambda_i \lambda_j y_i y_j k(\mathbf{x}_i, \mathbf{x}_j)$$

subject to

$$\sum_{i=1}^{n} y_i \lambda_i = 0, \ \sum_{i=1}^{n} \lambda_i = 1 \ \text{and} \ 0 \leq \lambda_i \leq C \ \text{for all} \ i = \{1,\dots,n\}.$$

Given sample patterns of toolmarks made by two different tools, this maximization procedure picks out toolmark patterns x_i that lie on the margin between the two samples. It is these special toolmark patterns that are the **support vectors** (SVs). The decision rule is given as[6,13]

$$g(\mathbf{x}_i) = \text{sign}\left(\sum_{j=1}^{n} \lambda_j y_j k(\mathbf{x}_i, \mathbf{x}_j) + b \right)$$

where the offset b is

$$b = \frac{1}{\#(\text{SVs})} \sum_{i=1}^{\#(\text{SVs})} \left(y_i - \sum_{j=1}^{\#(\text{SVs})} \lambda_j y_j k(\mathbf{x}_i, \mathbf{x}_j) \right)$$

and the sums are taken only over the support vectors. Figure 8.10 shows a plot of 2D features made by two hypothetical tools. The black lines denote the edge of the maximum margin of separation between the two sets of features. The SV toolmark patterns are the fat points lying on the margin lines. These SVs are used to compute the blue decision rule lying directly in the middle of the margin.

There are two drawbacks to the use of SVMs in toolmark analysis, one major and one minor. First is the (major) problem that the SVM methodology does not generalize nicely to the situation when more than two tools are involved. The "band-aid" solution, which

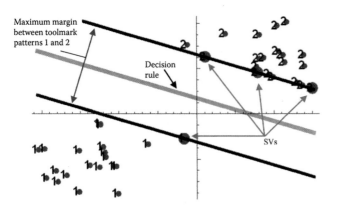

Figure 8.10 Two-dimensional features of toolmark patterns made by two hypothetical tools. The patterns of tool 1 (purple) are separated from those of tool 2 (maroon) by the black lines defining the maximum margin. The fat points are the support vectors defining the maximum margin and the decision rule (the blue line). No other decision rule can be drawn in to separate these toolmark patterns by a wider margin than the one shown.

is also the most popular, because it tends to work well in practice, is to divide the toolmark patterns into two groups. That is, either compute SVs for only pairs of toolmark patterns at a time (**one vs. one method**) or choose one set of toolmark patterns to be tool 1 and the remaining patterns to be tool 2 in a round-robin fashion (**one vs. all method**). Both of these multigrouping methods can lead to unclassifiable regions, and thus a voting procedure must be employed.[3,4,6,81,82] While this is an acceptable situation for most industrial applications, it is a problem for forensic toolmark analysis because it makes methods for error rate estimation difficult to apply. More research is needed in this direction. Note that genuine multigroup SVM algorithms do exist but are not yet in widespread use.[82,83] They may perhaps provide an acceptable solution to this dilemma.

The second problem encountered with SVMs actually turns out to be quite amenable to solution. Note that the output SVM decision rules always have the form of a line. While it is difficult to change this fact, it turns out to be not difficult to bend and twist data space around so that toolmark patterns can (usually) be linearly separated. This is the basis of **kernel** tricks.[8,84] The kernel, $k(\mathbf{x}_i, \mathbf{x}_j)$, is a generalization of the dot product between two vectors and essentially allows the computation of linear decision rules that perform well in highly nonlinear data spaces.

Note that almost all kernels contain parameters that would need to be adjusted by the toolmark examiner for the study at hand.[8] Obviously the more knobs one has to adjust to use a method, the more likely errors will be made. To this end, methods for computing optimal kernels have recently become available with the advent of more efficient **semidefinite programming** (SDP) algorithms.[85] SDP algorithms are generalizations of more common linear programming routines from operations research.[86] Kernels are actually positive semidefinite matrices, and these new SDP algorithms can lead to very powerful yet easy-to-use SVMs. Forensic toolmark examination needs to be at the forefront of application of these new computational tools.

Error Rate Analysis

An **error** is defined as a misclassification of a toolmark by the examiner (human or machine). This occurs when the examiner does not identify the unknown toolmark as having been made by the suspect tool when indeed it had, or the examiner identifies the unknown toolmark as having been made by the suspect tool when indeed it had not. Methods to assess the rate at which a statistical toolmark pattern comparison system makes errors obviously cannot be overemphasized. Error rate analysis for toolmarks, however, is a daunting task for numerous reasons. In general, copious amounts of exemplars need be examined and their feature data recorded. Hatcher et al. notes that no examiner can hope to examine all but a tiny fraction of firearms alone.[87] Also, there is not a general way in which to carry out error rate analysis for pattern comparisons.

In order to begin to address this problem, we will give an overview of a few methods that can be applied to compute approximate error rates. Note, however, that the schemes presented need to be validated with a great deal of research in the future. Because it is familiar to the forensic science community at large, we start with a summary of how error rates are computed for DNA profiling and attempt to make some analogies with toolmark pattern comparisons.

Error rates for DNA profiling are generally referred to as **random match probabilities** (RMPs). These values are actually very simple to calculate with available data. To begin, fifteen loci have been selected by experts as being highly variable areas on DNA for short tandem repeats (STRs) of two to six base pairs that repeat their sequence multiple times.[10] Each STR is an allele. The measured feature data consist of the frequencies at which particular STR alleles occur at these loci. For example, Butler et al. found that allele 8 (i.e., an STR of eight repeats) occurred at the locus TH01 in 8.4% of their U.S. Caucasian sample (cf. Butler et al.,[88] Table 1, column 3, line 4). Two alleles occur at every locus and are assumed to sort independently at meiosis. The logical result of this is the Hardy-Weinberg and linkage equilibria, which imply that the probabilities of occurrence for particular STR alleles at various loci are statistically independent (i.e., like rolling two unconnected, fair dice). Independent probabilities can be multiplied, so considering a large sample of the U.S. Caucasian population, the probability that at locus TH01 allele 8 (8.4%) and allele 9.3 (36.8%) occur together is 3.1% (0.084 × 0.368; cf. Butler et al.,[88] Table 1, column 3, lines 4 and 7). Repeating this process for twelve more loci yields vanishingly small probabilities for particular combinations of STR alleles at those loci; i.e., the probability that any two unrelated people have the same particular DNA profiles is virtually zero. This, of course, is all based on the assumption of statistical independence of the assortment of genes.[10]

Two problems come into play if one attempts to directly extend this DNA profiling philosophy to toolmarks. The first is whether or not arbitrary toolmark features are statistically independent. Statistical independence is a strong mathematical property that stipulates that the features are not only linearly uncorrelated,

but also nonlinearly uncorrelated.[71,89] That is, for two statistically independent features **x** and **y** from the same toolmark,

$$\text{Cov}\big[\phi(\mathbf{x}),\phi(\mathbf{y})\big]=0 \text{ for any function } \phi,$$

and thus

$$p(\mathbf{x},\mathbf{y})=p(\mathbf{x})p(\mathbf{y}).$$

Above, Cov is the covariance that is directly related to correlation.[46,89] It is likely that many, if not most, features present in an arbitrary toolmark are statistically independent, but then again many may not be. To be rigorous, statistical independence of features must be theoretically proven or empirically demonstrated on a large relevant data set. In DNA profiling, independence is tested for by computing frequencies of genotypes at loci using observed allelic frequencies at those loci and comparing this list to a list of frequencies of the same genotypes drawn from a database.[10] The χ^2-test is used to make the comparison, and if no statistically significant difference is computed, the alleles are certified as being statistically independent.

Note that if toolmark features are normally distributed and their covariance is zero, then they are statistically independent.[89] Proving normality of features is not so easy, however, because one needs a great deal of data to construct the density function empirically at a high level of reliability.[3,4] If normality can be established, then vanishing covariance (i.e., the features are uncorrelated) is easy to take care of with a method like principal component analysis.[68,89] This is, in fact, the approach Kennedy et al. took in establishing that bare footprints are essentially unique.[90,91] In a very well-constructed and rigorous study, this group of researchers digitized over nine hundred bare footprints and extracted various one-dimensional features (distances, angles, etc., between landmarks on the foot). They then used these data to show that each feature followed the normal distribution, and thus could be transformed to an uncorrelated and therefore statistically independent set of new variables. They then used the sample variance (i.e., estimated population variance) and intrapersonal variance of each new variable as parameters to compute a random match probability for that variable. Since each new variable is statistically independent of all others, they were able to multiply their random match probabilities together and found (not surprisingly) a vanishingly small joint random match probability for multiple features.

The methods of Kennedy et al. could be directly applied to toolmarks if accurate one-dimensional

Gaussian pdfs of toolmark features can be constructed. This would necessitate the designation of well-defined landmarks and features (both subclass and individual) for various classes of toolmarks, which would be difficult, but could be a broad and fertile area for research. Their methods could also be extended to multidimensional feature vectors and non-Gaussian pdfs. This is done by integrating the empirically derived pdf for a population of toolmark patterns from the same class of tools (or at least a very large sample) about some suitably chosen "chance match domain" D that contains the feature vector or vectors of a toolmark of interest **x**:

$$P(\text{error}|\mathbf{x}) = \int_{D} \sum_{i=1}^{n} p(\mathbf{x}'|\text{tool}_i) \, d\mathbf{x}' \text{ with } \mathbf{x}, \mathbf{x}' \in D.$$

Above, the pdf determined from empirical measurements is

$$\sum_{i=1}^{n} p(\mathbf{x}'|\text{tool}_i) = p(\mathbf{x}').$$

The numerical output of this generally difficult procedure is the probability of finding another random toolmark in a population lying in the same patch of feature space as the toolmark of interest. The chance match domain should be large enough to account for a reasonable amount of variation within features for the toolmark of interest. Note that choosing the chance match domain will be difficult for high-dimensional non-Gaussian pdfs because the advantage of visualization of how the feature data spread out in space is lost.

In the case of one-dimensional features (i.e., points) and a Gaussian pdf, a reasonably sized domain is typically taken to be one or two standard deviations about a measurement, x, and the above formula simplifies to[91]

$$P(\text{error}|x) = \frac{1}{\sqrt{2\pi}s_p} \int_{x-\alpha s_i}^{x+\alpha s_i} \exp\left(-\frac{(x'-\bar{x}_p)^2}{2s_p^2}\right) dx'$$

with $\alpha \in \{1,2\}$.

Above, α is the desired number of standard deviations, s_i is the mean feature found in the sample of toolmarks made by the same tool (i.e., number of intrasample standard deviations), $\bar{x}_p$ is the estimated population mean, and s_p is its estimated standard deviation. The chance match domain, D, is $[x - \alpha s_i, x + \alpha s_i]$, and hopefully $s_i \ll s_p$. This random match probability formula is graphically represented by the shaded area in the graph shown in Figure 8.11.

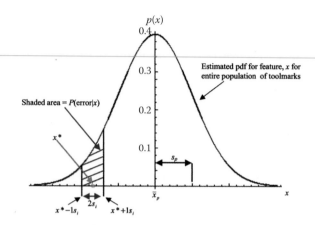

Figure 8.11 Hypothetical Gaussian probability density function for a one-dimensional feature measured from a set of toolmarks. The green star marks the location of a specific value, x^*, for the feature measured from a specific tool. The red line spans two intrasample standard deviations, s_i, for the feature measured from that same tool, and is centered about x^* (i.e., $\alpha = 1$). The blue shaded area represents the probability that another random tool could have left a feature the same as or within two intrasample standard deviations of x^*. s_p is the estimated population variance.

Again, if the features **x** are Gaussian distributed and are transformed to an uncorrelated set of new variables, **z**, then the above random match probabilities, $P(\text{error}|\mathbf{z})$, are statistically independent and can be multiplied together for different features to form a joint random match probability, which will likely be very small.[46,48,91] Note, however, that probabilities for different feature vectors *cannot* be multiplied unless they are statistically independent. While uncorrelated Gaussian distributed features are also statistically independent, this is generally not true for other distributions.

While it is true that one cannot simply multiply probabilities of statistically dependent toolmark features to form a joint random match probability, it may be possible to use a technique called independent component analysis to transform the features into a new set of approximately independent variables.[89] Probability density functions could then be constructed for this new set of approximately independent variables and approximate random match probabilities could be computed. To our knowledge this route has never been explored and could yield groundbreaking results. Again, the drawback here would be collecting enough toolmark feature data across enough tools to build accurate and reliable pdfs.

As for statistically dependent toolmark features, a newly developing area of statistics may be able to help. Copula methods take one-dimensional probability density functions of systems with multiple random variables (i.e., marginal densities) and "glue" them together into a joint probability distribution using what is called a copula function.[92] One-dimensional densities are advantageous to work with because they do not suffer from the curse of dimensionality and are thus much easier to accurately measure. Also, copulas contain adjustable parameters that allow one to study the statistical dependence between the variables that make up the joint distribution. If one-dimensional features that occur with regular enough frequency to be measured accurately can be identified, then copula methods can be tried in order to build joint probability distributions with adjustable degrees of statistical dependence. The dependence parameters could be fit from observed joint frequencies recorded in a database. Also, by varying the amount of dependence, best- and worst-case random match probability plots can be made. Such plots could be helpful to a jury in assessing the reliability of random match probabilities for toolmarks.

Note that it may be difficult to apply this type of error analysis to toolmarks (i.e., computing random match probabilities from pdfs) because there are no well-defined loci or landmarks for inter-tool-mark comparisons. Also, multidimensional probability densities are difficult to construct, and there is no reason to expect that toolmark features follow normal distributions. Next, consider that allelic frequencies at the assorted designated STR loci are in the range of 10%. For toolmarks, there is no reason to expect a particular feature at a point on a set of toolmarks occurs enough times to measure a frequency. That is, of course, if the feature is not a subclass characteristic. Even if the feature is a subclass characteristic, it probably will not be found in a set of tools of the same class enough times to accurately and reliably estimate its frequency. In other words, it is difficult to measure the probability of the rare events that characterize features of toolmarks! Much more research is needed in this direction.

If the probability functions for a toolmark comparison problem are not known or impossible to obtain, all is certainly not lost. In fact, for most applications of statistical pattern recognition to real-world problems, the underlying probability densities or distributions are not known. Still, however, estimates of error rates are needed. In order to address this fact, empirical estimates of error rates can be computed. The simplest method to empirically estimate the error rate is **resubstitution**.[93] This is simply the application of the computed classification rules to the set of data used to derive them. The percentage of misclassifications via the resubstitution method is called the **apparent error rate** and is simply the empirical risk, R_{emp}. This is a biased estimate and tends to be overly optimistic and should be corrected. The first and simplest correction is called **hold-one-out cross-validation**.[46] This method computes the decision rules using all but one of

the toolmark patterns in the data set. Let $\mathbf{x}$ be the held-out toolmark pattern with true identity y, and let $g^{\text{hold-out-x}}(\mathbf{x})$ denote the identity of $\mathbf{x}$ assigned by the hold-one-out decision rules. Misclassifications are assigned a 1 and correct classifications a 0. Symbolically this is written as

$$1 - \delta_{y,g(\mathbf{x})},$$

where the Kronecker delta denotes

$$\delta_{y,g(\mathbf{x})} = \begin{cases} 1 & if\ y=g(\mathbf{x}) \\ 0 & if\ y\neq g(\mathbf{x}) \end{cases}.$$

The hold-one-out procedure is repeated for each toolmark pattern in the data set and the results are averaged to compute an estimated error rate:[94]

$$\text{Err}^{\text{HOO-CV}} = \frac{1}{n}\sum_{i=1}^{n} 1 - \delta_{y_i, g^{\text{hold-out-x}_i}(\mathbf{x}_i)}.$$

If c toolmark patterns are held out, the resulting error rate is called c-fold cross-validation. Another error rate estimate that typically performs better than cross-validation is the **bootstrap**.[94,95] First a set of B bootstrap data, $\mathbf{X}^*$, are generated by randomly selecting (with replacement) n toolmark pattern feature vectors from the original data set, $\mathbf{X}$. Note that each bootstrap data set contains the same number of elements (toolmark pattern feature vectors) as the original data set; thus, some patterns may be repeated. The decision rules are recomputed for each bootstrap sample (g^*) and an average error rate is computed using them on the original data:[94]

$$\text{Err}^{\text{all-data}} = \frac{1}{n}\sum_{i=1}^{n} 1 - \delta_{y_i, g^*(\mathbf{x}_i)}.$$

as well as the bootstrapped data used to compute them:

$$\text{Err}^{\text{boot-data}} = \frac{1}{n}\sum_{i=1}^{n} \#\{\mathbf{x}_i \in \mathbf{X}^*\}\left(1 - \delta_{y_i, g^*(\mathbf{x}_i)}\right).$$

Above, $\#\{\mathbf{x}_i \in \mathbf{X}^*\}$ means the number of times toolmark pattern $\mathbf{x}_i$ occurs in the bootstrapped data set $\mathbf{X}^*$. The difference between these two averages is called the bootstrap estimated optimism.[94,95] Averaging together these optimisms gives the **expected bootstrap estimated optimism** $\hat{\omega}^{\text{boot}}$:

$$\hat{\omega}^{\text{boot}} = \frac{1}{B}\sum_{i=1}^{B} \text{Err}_i^{\text{all-data}} - \text{Err}_i^{\text{boot-data}},$$

which is then added to the apparent error rate to obtain the final error estimate:

$$\mathrm{Err}^{\mathrm{boot}} = R_{\mathrm{emp}} + \hat{\omega}^{\mathrm{boot}}.$$

The jackknife error rate

$$\mathrm{Err}^{\mathrm{jack}} = R_{\mathrm{emp}} + \hat{\omega}^{\mathrm{jack}}$$

is another estimate, which typically yields values between the bootstrap and cross-validation estimates. The **expected jackknife estimated optimism**, $\hat{\omega}^{\mathrm{jack}}$, is computed as[94]

$$\hat{\omega}^{\mathrm{jack}} = \frac{1}{n} \sum_{i=1}^{n} 1 - \delta_{y_i, g^{\mathrm{hold-out-}x_i}(\mathbf{x}_i)}$$

$$- \frac{1}{n^2} \sum_{i=1}^{n} \sum_{j=1}^{n} 1 - \delta_{y_i, g^{\mathrm{hold-out-}x_j}(\mathbf{x}_i)},$$

where the first sum is just the hold-one-out cross-validation error estimate. The jackknife error rate is usually closer in value to the cross-validation estimate. Evidently the expected jackknife estimated optimism is a quadratic approximation to the expected bootstrap estimated optimism, and thus all three methods for error rate estimation (cross-validation, bootstrap, and jackknife) are related.[94]

Most modern statistical pattern comparison algorithms can only produce predictions of pattern identity; they cannot give an indication of how reliable those predictions are. Error rate bounds for many modern machine learning methods do exist; however, they tend to be very conservative and in practice can only give an indication of how well one particular algorithm is performing with respect to another.[8,13,54,96,97] Clearly this is of little or no use to a jury. Recently, a method that gives confidence levels to identification of unknown patterns has arisen from the study of algorithmic randomness. This method, called **conformal prediction**, can be applied to any statistical pattern comparison algorithm and holds a great deal of potential if applied to toolmark analysis.[98] **Prediction regions** produced by conformal prediction can give a judge or jury an easy-to-understand measure of reliability for toolmark pattern identification because the method yields both confidence and credibility values on a scale of 0 to 100%. A reliable identification should have both high confidence and credibility.

The way the method works is actually very simple.[98,99] Given a training set of toolmark patterns with known identities (called a **bag**) and at least one toolmark pattern of unknown identity, an estimate of randomness is computed for the bags containing the unknown toolmark with all possible labels for its identity. The toolmark identity is assigned by the bag with the highest estimated randomness. The higher the estimated randomness of the bag, the less likely the toolmark in question with the identity assigned is an outlier.[98] The only assumption is that the toolmark patterns of the training set are drawn independently from the same, but unknown, probability distribution.

The measure of randomness is arbitrary, but no matter what the choice is, valid predictions of concrete confidence levels are produced. Randomness of the bag is tested in a way analogous to what is done in traditional hypothesis testing.[71,72,98] The null hypothesis is that unknown toolmark pattern $\mathbf{x}$ with assigned identity label y (i.e., the pair $(\mathbf{x}, y)$) belongs in the bag and does not significantly decrease the bag's randomness. The alternative hypothesis is that the pair $(\mathbf{x}, y)$ does not belong in the bag, and thus y must be a different label than the one assigned. Randomness estimates of the bags are computed as p-values, and the null hypothesis is accepted at the $\alpha \times 100\%$ level (α, the level of significance, is a number between 0 and 1) if $p > \alpha$.[98] Note that the null hypothesis can be accepted for multiple labelings of the toolmark's identity. In such cases the identity assignment (i.e., the prediction region) at the $(1 - \alpha) \times 100\%$ confidence level is ambiguous. Hopefully the prediction region will contain only one label with a p-value β 0.5, meaning that the conformal prediction algorithm has produced a prediction region with only one label and a confidence level of at least 95%.

Prediction regions for toolmark pattern identities can be thought of as generalizations of confidence intervals known from textbook hypothesis testing. Traditionally **confidence intervals** are computed for population parameters (e.g., a sample average) to give an indication of regions where their true values may fall. Technically, the Neyman-Pearson interpretation of $(1 - \alpha) \times 100\%$ confidence interval for an estimated population parameter constructed from a random sample of a given sample size will contain the true population parameter $(1 - \alpha) \times 100\%$ of the time.[71,72,99] The parameter α is called the **level of significance** and is the probability that any given confidence interval constructed from a random sample will *not* contain the true population mean. Note that a $1 - \alpha$ confidence interval for a prediction region *does not mean* that there is a $(1 - \alpha) \times 100\%$ chance that the true identity of the toolmark falls within the region. Rather, it means that $(1 - \alpha) \times 100\%$ of the prediction regions computed from random samples drawn from the same population contain the true identity of the toolmark.

The major advantages of conformal prediction is that there is no assumption about the structure of the underlying population distribution (for traditional hypothesis testing the underlying population distribution must be known or assumed), it can be applied to the results of any known statistical pattern comparison algorithm so long as there are sufficient data, and it is a simple idea to implement and interpret.

Results of a Pilot Study on Screwdriver Striation Patterns

In order to assess the feasibility of employing the mathematical machinery described in this chapter to realistic toolmark identification, we performed a pilot study to identify striation patterns of standard slotted screwdrivers. Several high-quality, quarter-inch slotted screwdrivers were purchased at a local hardware store. The screwdrivers were brand new and came in packages of three. Figure 8.12 displays nine of the screwdrivers obtained.

The first six screwdrivers were used to generate multiple reproducible striation pattern standards. Modeling clay was used as the impression medium. Figure 8.13 illustrates the process. Further details of standards generation for striation patterns are available in Petraco et al.[51]

The striation patterns made by each of the six screwdrivers were digitally photographed under the stereomicroscope, and the positions/widths of several of the striations (lines/grooves) were measured with a stage micrometer. Striation line/groove data were recorded for only one side of each screwdriver. The total numbers of patterns recorded for each of the screwdrivers were as follows: screwdriver 1, 8 striation patterns; screwdriver 2, 6 striation patterns; screwdriver 3, 9 striation patterns; screwdriver 4, 8 striation patterns; screwdriver 5, 9 striation patterns; and screwdriver 6, 9 striation patterns; total: 49 striation patterns.

The photographs of all the striation patterns were cropped and stacked for each screwdriver. Striation positions/widths for one pattern from each screwdriver were calibrated with the stage micrometer. The calibrated patterns were used to calibrate the image processing program ImageJ.[100] Distances of each line or grove from the left edge of each striation pattern were measured to the nearest 0.05 mm. For each of the patterns a list of 140 "boxes" long (7×0.05 mm) is created. A 1 is recorded in a box if a line/grove is present or spans the box, and a 0 otherwise. This procedure yields a 140-dimensional binary feature vector for each pattern that is reminiscent of a bar code (cf. Figure 8.14).

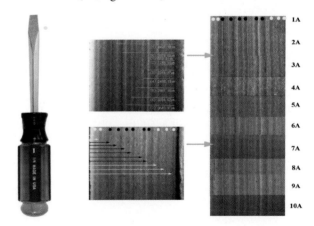

Figure 8.13 Process to generate striation pattern standards. As one can see from the figure, screwdriver 1 was used to make nine striation pattern standards.

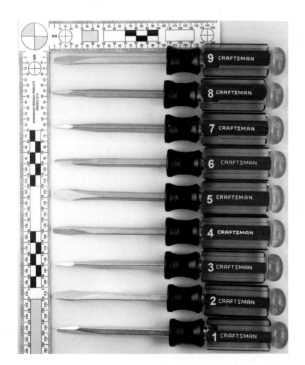

Figure 8.12 Nine quarter-inch standard slotted screwdrivers purchased for pilot study.

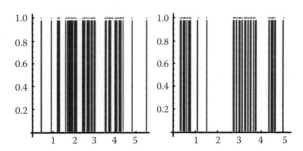

Figure 8.14 Graphical representations of feature vectors for two striation patterns. On the left, screwdriver # and, on the right, screwdriver #3.

Note from the stack of striation patterns in Figure 8.13 (rightmost picture in the figure) that some of the patterns require alignment (registration).

Principal component analysis was used to reduce the data's dimension to 3D for visualization purposes (51% of data's variance retained) and 24D to give a 95% variance representation of the data. Using LDA for classification of the striation patterns, the 3D PCA data set had a hold-one-out error rate of 8%, while the 24D PCA data set had a hold-one-out error rate of only 2%. Figures 8.14 and 8.15 show alternative views of the 3D PCA data set. Note that these plots represent the striation line/groove data for all six screwdrivers, projected from 140D space

to 3D space. In order to do this projection, 48% of the data's variance (i.e., structure) needed to be discarded. Despite this large loss of information, Figures 8.15 and 8.16 clearly show that most of the striation patterns are distinguishable between screwdrivers. The closest sets were screwdrivers 1, 3, and 6, but remember, we have thrown out 48% of the information in this data set to make a 3D picture. In 24D space these striation patterns are likely much farther apart, as inferred from the low hold-one-out error rate.

Finally, conformal prediction theory using a linear three-nearest-neighbor classification rule was used to classify the PCA reduced data and obtain confidence levels and credibility measures for the results. For the 3D PCA data, the classification confidence level was 98%; however, three multilabel confidence intervals were obtained.

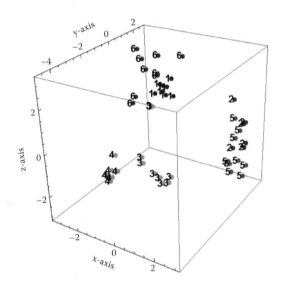

Figure 8.15 3D PCA plot of striation patterns from all six screwdrivers. This plot accounts for 51% of the data's variance. The numbers labeling each point represent the screwdriver number of the striation pattern.

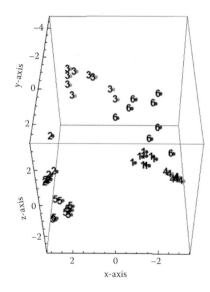

Figure 8.16 Alternative view of 3D PCA plot shown in Figure 8.15.

References

1. Moran, B. A. 2002. Report on the AFTE theory of identification and range of conclusions for toolmark identification and resulting approaches to casework. *AFTE J.* 34:227–35.
2. Bhagat, P. 2005. *Pattern recognition in industry.* 1st ed. Amsterdam: Elsevier.
3. Duda, R. O., Hart, P. E., and Stork, D. G. 2001. *Pattern classification.* 2nd ed. New York: John Wiley & Sons.
4. Theodoridis, S., and Koutroumbas, K. 2006. *Pattern recognition.* 3rd ed. San Diego: Academic Press.
5. Fukunaga, K. 1990. *Statistical pattern recognition.* 2nd ed. San Diego: Academic Press.
6. Bishop, C. M. 2006. *Pattern recognition and machine learning.* 1st ed. New York: Springer.
7. AFTE. 1998. Theory of identification as it relates to toolmarks. *AFTE J.* 30:86–88.
8. Shawe, T. J., and Cristianini, N. 2004. *Kernel methods for pattern analysis.* London: Cambridge University Press.
9. Standards and Training Committee A. 2001. *Glossary of the Association of Firearms and Toolmark Examiners.* Montreal.
10. Butler, J. M. 2005. *Forensic DNA typing.* 2nd ed. New York: Academic Press.
11. Campbell, N. A., and Reece, J. B. 2004. *Biology.* 7th ed. New York: Benjamin Cummings.
12. Mattia, N. 2008. Discussion of what statistical values are important to the AFTE certified toolmark examiner. Personal communication.
13. Vapnik, V. N. 1998. *Statistical learning theory.* New York: John Wiley & Sons.
14. Taroni, F., Champod, C., and Margot, P. 1996. Statistics: A future in toolmarks comparison? *AFTE J.* 28:222–32.
15. Champod, C., Baldwin, D., Taroni, F., and Buckleton, J. S. 2003. Firearm and toolmarks identification: The Bayesian approach. *AFTE J.* 35:307–16.

16. Buckleton, J., Nichols, R., Triggs, C., and Wevers, G. 2005. An exploratory Bayesian model for firearm and toolmark interpretation. *AFTE J.* 37:352–61.

17. Biedermann, A., and Taroni, F. 2006. A probabilistic approach to the joint evaluation of firearm evidence and gunshot residues. *Forensic Sci. Int.* 163:18–33.

18. Katterwe, H., Baldwin, D., van Beest, M., Besler, C., Birkett, J., and Girod, A. 2006. Conclusion scale for shoeprint and toolmark examinations. *J. Forensic Identification* 56:255–81.

19. Neel, M., and Wells, M. 2007. A comprehensive statistical analysis of striated toolmark examinations. 1. Comparing known matches to known non-matches. *AFTE J.* 39:176–98.

20. Biasotti, A. 1959. A statistical study of the individual characteristics of fired bullets. *J. Forensic Sci.* 4:34–50.

21. Miller, J., and Neel, M. 2004. Criteria for identification of toolmarks. III. Supporting the conclusion. *AFTE J.* 37:7–38.

22. Brackett, J. 1970. A study of idealized striated marks and their comparison using models. *J. Forensic Sci. Soc.* 10:27–56.

23. Blackwell, R., and Framan, E. 1980. Automated Firearms Identification Systems AFIDS: Phase I. *AFTE J.* 12:11–37.

24. Deinet, W. 1981. Studies of models of striated marks generated by random processes. *J. Forensic Sci.* 26:35–50.

25. Stone, R. 2003. How unique are impressed toolmarks? *AFTE J.* 35:376–83.

26. Collins, E. 2004. How unique are impressed toolmarks? An empirical study of twenty worn hammer faces. *AFTE J.* 2:252–95.

27. Bunch, S. 2000. Consecutive matching striation criteria: A general critique. *J. Forensic Sci.* 45:955–62.

28. Banno, A. 2004. Estimation of bullet striation similarity using neural networks. *J. Forensic Sci.* 49:1–5.

29. Leon, F. P. 2006. Automated comparison of firearm bullets. *Forensic Sci. Int.* 156:40–50.

30. Bachrach, B. 2002. Development of a 3D-based automated firearms evidence comparison system. *J. Forensic Sci.* 47:1–12.

31. Bachrach, B. 2006. *A statistical validation of the individuality of guns using 3D images of bullets.* Grant Report 97-LB-VX-0008. National Institute of Justice.

32. Geradts, Z., and Keijzer, J. 1996. TRAX for toolmarks. *AFTE J.* 28:183–90.

33. Geradts, Z., Keijzer, J., and Keereweer, I. 1994. A new approach to automatic comparison of striation marks. *J. Forensic Sci.* 39:974–80.

34. Geradts, Z., Bijhold, J., Hermsen, R., and Murtaugh, F. 2001. Image matching algorithms for breech face marks and firing pins in a database of spent cartridges of firearms. *Forensic Sci. Int.* 119:97–106.

35. Senin, N., Groppetti, R., Garofano, L., Fratini, P., and Pierni, M. 2006. Three-dimensional surface topography acquisition and analysis for firearm identification. *J. Forensic Sci.* 51:282–95.

36. Faden, D., Kidd, J., Craft, J., Chumbley, L. S., Morris, M., Genalo, L., et al. 2007. Statistical confirmation of empirical observations concerning toolmark striae. *AFTE J.* 39:205–14.

37. DeKinder, J., Tulleners, F., and Thiebaut, H. 2004. Reference ballistic imaging database performance. *Forensic Sci. Int.* 140:207–15.

38. DeKinder, J., and Bonfanti, M. 1999. Automated comparisons of bullet striations based on 3D topography. *Forensic Sci. Int.* 101:85–93.

39. Song, J., Vorburger, T., Renegar, T., Rhee, H., Zheng, A., Ma, L., et al. 2006. Correlation of topography measurements of NIST SRM 2460 standard bullets by four techniques. *Measure. Sci. Technol.* 17:500–3.

40. Nichols, R. G. 1997. Firearms and toolmark identification criteria: A review of the literature. *J. Forensic Sci.* 42:466–74.

41. Nichols, R. G. 2003. Firearm and toolmark identification criteria: A review of the literature. Part 2. *J. Forensic Sci.* 48:318–27.

42. Nichols, R. G. 2007. Defending the scientific foundations of the firearms and toolmark discipline: Responding to recent challenges. *J. Forensic Sci.* 53:586–94.

43. Gonick, L., and Smith, W. 1993. *The cartoon guide to statistics.* 1st ed. New York: Harper Collins.

44. Donnelly, R. A. 2004. *The complete idiot's guide to statistics.* 1st ed. New York: Alpha.

45. Bertsekas, D. P., and Tsitsiklis, J. N. 2002. *Introduction to probability.* 1st ed. Belmont, MA: Athena Scientific.

46. Rencher, A. C. 2002. *Methods of multivariate analysis.* 2nd ed. Hoboken, NJ: John Wiley & Sons.

47. Morgan, S. L., and Bartick, E. G. 2007. Discrimination of forensic analytical chemical data using multivariate statistics. In *Forensic analysis on the cutting edge: New methods for trace evidence analysis,* ed. R. D. Blackledge, 331–72. New York: Wiley.

48. Schaeffer, R. L., and McClav, J. T. 1986. *Probability and statistics for engineers.* 2nd ed. Boston: Duxbury.

49. Davis, J. E. 1958. *An introduction to toolmarks, firearms and the striagraph.* Springfield, IL: Charles C. Thomas.

50. Petraco, N., Petraco, N. D. K., and Pizzola, P. A. 2005. An ideal material for the preparation of toolmark test prints. *J. Forensic Sci.* 50:1407–10.

51. Petraco, N., Petraco, N. D. K., Faber, L., and Pizzola, P. A. 2009. Preparation of toolmark standards with jewelry modeling waxes. *J. Forensic Sci.* 54:353–58.

52. Vapnik, V. N. 2000. *The nature of statistical learning theory.* New York: Springer.

53. Popper, K. 1968. *The logic of scientific discovery.* 2nd ed. New York: Harper Torch.

54. Scholkopf, B., and Smola, A. J. 2002. *Learning with kernels.* Boston: MIT Press.

55. Chatfield, C., and Collins, A. J. 1980. *Introduction to multivariate analysis.* New York: Chapman & Hall.

56. Hastie, T., Tibshirani, R., and Friedman, J. 2001. *The elements of statistical learning.* New York: Springer.

57. Petraco, N., and Kubic, T. K. 2004. *Color atlas and manual of microscopy for criminalists, chemists and conservators.* 1st ed. Boca Raton, FL: CRC Press.

58. Abbott, J. R. 1964. *Footwear evidence*. Springfield, IL: Charles C. Thomas.

59. Needham, G. H. 1958. *Practical use of the microscope*. Springfield, IL: Charles C. Thomas.

60. Russ, J. C. 2001. *Forensic uses of digital imaging*. 1st ed. Boca Raton, FL: CRC Press.

61. Russ, J. C. 2006. *The image processing handbook*. 5th ed. Boca Raton, FL: CRC Press.

62. Akca, D. 2007. Matching of 3D surfaces and their intensities. *J. Photogrammetry Remote Sensing* 62:112–21.

63. Shammaa, M. H., Suzuki, H., and Michikawa, T. 2007. Registration of CAD mesh models with CT volumetric model of assembly of machine parts. *Vision Computer* 23:965–74.

64. Rabbani, T., Dijkman, S., Heuvel, F., and Vosselman, G. 2007. An integrated approach for modeling and global registration of point clouds. *J. Photogrammetry Remote Sensing* 61:355–70.

65. Wang, S., Wang, Y., Jin, M., Gu, X., and Samaras, D. 2007. Conformal geometry and its applications on 3D shape matching, recognition, and stitching. *Trans. Pattern Anal. Machine Intell.* 29:1209–20.

66. Geradts, Z. 2002. *Content-based information retrieval from forensic image databases*. Utrecht: University of Utrecht.

67. Geradts, Z., Keijzer, J., and Keereweer, I., Eds. 1995. Automatic comparison of striation marks and automatic classification of shoe marks. Paper presented at *Proceedings of SPIE*.

68. Jolliffe, I. T. 2004. *Principal component analysis*. 2nd ed. New York: Springer.

69. Mardia, K. V., Kent, J. T., and Bibby, J. M. 1980. *Multivariate analysis*. 1st ed. Amsterdam: Academic Press.

70. Krzanowski, W. J. 1994. Orthogonal canonical variates for discrimination and classification. *J. Chemometrics* 9:509–20.

71. Dekking, F. M., Kraaikamp, C., Lopuhaa, H. P., and Meester, L. E. 2005. *A modern introduction to probability and statistics: Understanding how and why*. 1st ed. New York: Springer.

72. Lehmann, E. L., and Romano, J. P. 2005. *Testing statistical hypotheses*. 3rd ed. New York: Springer.

73. Kingston, C. 1992. Neural networks in forensic sciences. *J. Forensic Sci.* 37:252–64.

74. Petraco, N. D. K., Gambino, C., Kubic, T. A., Olivo, D., and Petraco, N. 2010. Statistical discrimination of footwear: A method for the comparison of accidentals on shoe outsoles inspired by facial recognition techniques. *J. Forensic Sci*, 55:34–41.

75. Petraco, N. D. K., Gil, M., Pizzola, P. A., and Kubic, T. A. 2008. Statistical discrimination of liquid gasoline samples from casework. *J. Forensic Sci.* 53:1092–101.

76. Sandercock, P. M. L., and Pasquier, E. D. 2003. Chemical fingerprinting of unevaporated automotive gasoline samples. *Forensic Sci. Int.* 134:1–10.

77. Sandercock, P. M. L., and Pasquier, E. D. 2004. Chemical fingerprinting of gasoline. 2. Comparison of unevaporated and evaporated automotive gasoline samples. *Forensic Sci. Int.* 140:43–59.

78. Sandercock, P. M. L., and Pasquier, E. D. 2004. Chemical fingerprinting of gasoline. 3. Comparison of unevaporated automotive gasoline samples from Australia and New Zealand. *Forensic Sci. Int.* 140:71–77.

79. Egan, W., Morgan, S. L., Bartick, E. G., Merrill, R. A., and Taylor, H. J. 2003. Forensic discrimination of photocopy and printer toners. II. Discriminant analysis applied to infrared reflection absorption spectroscopy. *Anal. Bioanal. Chem.* 376:1279–85.

80. Egan, W., Galipo, R. C., Kochanowski, B. K., Morgan, S. L., Bartick, E. G., Miller, M. L., et al. Forensic discrimination of photocopy and printer toners. III. Multivariate statistics applied to scanning electron microscopy and pyrolysis gas chromatography/mass spectrometry. *Anal. Bioanal. Chem.* 2003:1286–97.

81. Platt, J. C., Cristianini, N., and Shawe-Taylor, J. 2000. Large margin DAGs for multiclassification. In *Advances in neural information processing systems*, ed. S. A. Solla, T. K. Leen, K.-R. Muller, 547–53. Cambridge, MA: MIT Press.

82. Abe, S. 2005. *Support vector machines for pattern classification*. London: Springer.

83. Crammer, K., and Singer, Y., Eds. 2000. On the learnability and design of output codes for multiclass problems. Paper presented at *Proceedings of the Thirteenth Annual Conference on Computational Learning Theory*, Palo Alto, CA.

84. Cristianini, N., and Shawe-Taylor, J. 2000. *An introduction to support vector machines and other kernel-based learning methods*. London: Cambridge University Press.

85. Lanckriet, G. R. G., Cristianini, N., Bartlett, P., Ghaoui, L. E., and Jordan, M. I. 2004. Learning the kernel matrix with semidefinite programming. *J. Machine Learning Res.* 5:27–72.

86. Vandenberghe, L., and Boyd, S. 1996. Semidefinite programming. *SIAM Rev.* 38:49–95.

87. Hatcher, J. S., Jury, F. J., and Weller, J. 1957. *Firearms investigation identification and evidence*. 1st ed. Philadelphia: Ray Riling Arms Books. Reprinted.

88. Butler, J. M., Schoske, R., Vallone, P. M., Redman, J. W., and Kline, M. C. 2003. Allele frequencies for 15 autosomal STR loci on U.S. Caucasian, African American and Hispanic populations. *J. Forensic Sci.* 48:1–4.

89. Hyvarinen, A., Karhunen, J., and Oja, E. 2001. *Independent component analysis*. New York: Wiley-Interscience.

90. Kennedy, R. B., Pressmann, I. S., Chen, S., Petersen, P. H., and Pressman, A. E. 2003. Statistical analysis of barefoot impressions. *J. Forensic Sci.* 48:55–63.

91. Kennedy, R. B., Chen, S., Pressmann, I. S., Yamashita, A. B., and Pressman, A. E. 2005. A large-scale statistical analysis of barefoot impressions. *J. Forensic Sci.* 50:1071–79.

92. Nelsen, R. B. 2006. *An introduction to copulas*. 1st ed. New York: Springer.

93. Smith, C. A. B. 1947. Some examples of discrimination. *Ann. Eugen.* 13:272–83.

94. Efron, B., and Tibshirani, R. J. 1993. *An introduction to the bootstrap*. 1st ed. Boca Raton, FL: Chapman & Hall/CRC.

95. Efron, B. 1983. Estimating the error rate of a prediction rule: Improvement on cross-validation. *J. Am. Stat. Assoc.* 78:316–31.

96. Devroye, L., Gyorfi, L., and Lugosi, G. 1996. *A probabilistic theory of pattern recognition.* 1st ed. New York: Springer.

97. Herbrich, R. 2002. *Learning kernel classifiers.* 1st ed. Cambridge, MA: MIT Press.

98. Vovk, M., Gammerman, A., and Shafer, G. 2005. *Algorithmic learning in a random world.* 1st ed. New York: Springer.

99. Shafer, G., and Vovk, V. 2008. A tutorial on conformal prediction. *J. Machine Learning Res.* 9:371–421.

100. Rasband, W., and Image, J. 2008. National Institute of Health. http://rsb.info.nih.gov/ij/.

Atlas of Common Hand Tools

II

Common Hand Tools Seen in Casework

9

A significant form of physical evidence often recovered in the investigation of all types of criminal acts is toolmarks, which can help identify the tool or tools employed in the commission of the crime. The identified tool might be the device used to break into a premise during a burglary, or it may be the weapon used in an assault or homicide.

The identity of the tool is normally deduced by a thorough examination of the scratches, marks, imprints, outlines, or impressions that the questioned tool has left on the outer surface of an object or individual.

Toolmarks are placed into four classes according to how they are produced:

1. Scratch marks such as those made by lock picks, knives, saws, and files when they are repeatedly applied to the same surface
2. Impression marks such as those left by pliers, wrenches, seals, and hammers when they are applied to a softer material's surface
3. Outlines or contours such as those left by a beer can opener, awl, and ream when used to punch metal surfaces
4. Any combination marks, comprised of impressions or shaped outlines and scratches such as those made by drill bits, punches, chisels, crowbars, and screwdrivers, as well as those produced by the improper use of any tool

The variety of hand tools available today that are capable of producing all three classes of toolmarks is staggering. This fact can make the toolmark examiner's primary task seem daunting: to either eliminate a particular tool as not having made the questioned toolmark or demonstrate that a particular tool did make the questioned toolmark to the exclusion of all others. The author believes that a thorough working knowledge of common hand tools, how they work, and their nomenclature is essential to make examiners' challenging charge somewhat easier. To this end, Part 2 of this text will attempt to cover the hand tools commonly encountered in toolmark casework. The first class of tools to be discussed will be the levers or prying tools commonly known as jimmies in law enforcement.[1] This category of hand tools includes screwdrivers, crowbars, and pry bars. The first to be discussed will be screwdrivers.

Levers

Screwdrivers

Arguably the most common hand tool available to the general public is the screwdriver. A screwdriver is an assembly tool that tightens and loosens screws. Screwdrivers contain a handle with a grip on one end attached to a round or square blade with a tip on the other end that corresponds to the head on the screw type it is designed to fasten. Screwdrivers are inexpensive and available to most individuals; these two facts would account for the ubiquitous encountering of screwdrivers in crimes scenes involving breaking and entering, i.e., burglaries. A DNA study conducted at the NYCPD Forensic Investigation Division of unsolved burglaries showed that screwdrivers are also used as weapons to assault, stab, injure, and kill.

The screwdriver is a device designed for the tightening of screws. Screwdrivers are mechanical devices that enable one to fasten, by hand, pieces of materials together with screws. This is accomplished by placing the driver's tip into a screw slot and rotating the device in a clockwise or counterclockwise direction to either tighten or loosen the screw. Screwdrivers are designed and manufactured with various shaped handles and blades or slot-shaped tips. The most common tips are the slotted, Phillips®, Robertson, Torx®, hex, and clutch. Each tip design is intended for a specific purpose. Figure 9.1 shows two familiar screwdrivers with their parts and nomenclature, while Figure 9.2 depicts the most common tip shapes in use today.

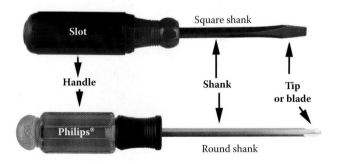

Figure 9.1 Shown are two common screwdrivers with their various parts and nomenclature. The standard screwdriver, which has a handle or head, square or round shaft and tip on the end.

111

The standard slot screwdriver has a flattened, wedge-shaped tip with a round or square shaft that ranges in length from 2 to 16 in. The Phillips type screwdrivers are typically used by sheet metal workers and tin smiths. The Phillips screwdriver has a round shaft and a tip with four simple slots or grooves forming a cross-shaped point. Five normal sizes of Phillips screwdrivers are the #0 to #4, with #2 being the most used (see Figure 9.4). Standard slotted and Phillips screwdrivers are typically used by metal smiths, carpenters, and electricians (see Figures 9.3 and 9.4).

Screwdrivers designed for specialized industrial applications are generally available to anyone on the Internet.

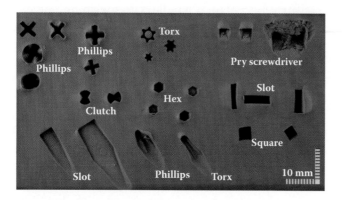

Figure 9.2 Impressions in sculpting clay of the various screwdriver tip types available in most hardware or tool stores. Many tip or blade shapes are available for specific applications.

Figure 9.3 A standard slot screwdriver; close-up enlargements of the slot or blade impressions of the tip made in No. 2 Roma Plastilina sculpting clay.

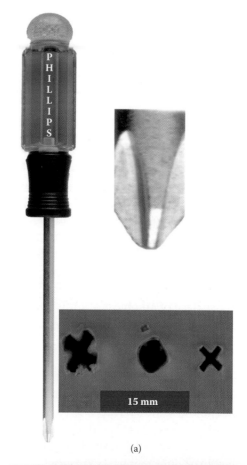

(a)

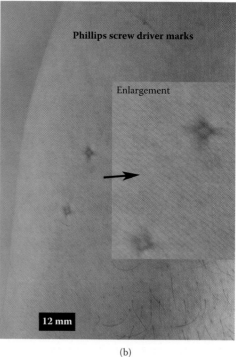

(b)

Figure 9.4 (a) The Phillips screwdriver has a round shaft and a tip with four simple slots cut into a cross-shaped point. Close-up impressions of the Phillips head tip made in No. 2 Roma Plastilina sculpting clay is shown along with an enlargement of the Phillips tip. (b) The Phillips screwdriver marks on human skin.

Square tip, hex tip, clutch head, Pozidriv®, and Torx are just a few of the types of screwdrivers made for use in the security, aerospace, electronic, appliance, and automotive industries. Allen or hex (hexagonal) tips are used in repair work in the electronics field, particularly in radio and television repair. They are used to tighten socket-set screws and usually come in sets. Hex keys are tools used to drive screws and bolts that have a hexagonal-shaped socket in their head. When used in combination with screwdrivers, hex-shaped tips are typically encountered with multibit interchangeable-tip screwdrivers. Examples of some of the specialty screwdriver tip configurations and their overall appearance are seen in Figures 9.2 and 9.5 to 9.7. An awl used to punch holes into tough materials such as leather is shown in Figure 9.8, while a mechanical handheld screwdriver is depicted in Figure 9.9.

If a screwdriver's tip is too big or too small for the screw it is being applied to, the screw's head and screwdriver's tip can be easily damaged. Additionally, screwdrivers are often misused as a pry bar or chisel. The use of over- or undersized tips and the misuse of a screwdriver can often cause damage to a tool. This damage can help one determine the manner in which the screwdriver was used by an intruder or burglar.

In casework involving the need to prepare known standard toolmark striation patterns, the known screwdriver's blade is placed at the desired angle to the surface of the chosen test material—sheet of lead, block of clay, sheet or block of wax, wood. Each side of the blade working surface is scraped along the surface of the test material as shown in Figure 9.10. The amount of pressure exerted on the screwdriver depends on the desired depth of the resulting toolmark, which will usually vary from case to case. This process is repeated for each side of the blade. At least three reproducible standards must be made for each of the tip's or blade's working surfaces before they are usable as known standards. This is essential because one cannot possibly determine if a questioned toolmark was produced by a known tool if one cannot make reproducible standards with that tool. The use of tool jigs to hold the subject tool while preparing known standards, as first

Figure 9.5 Torx is a type of screw head characterized by a six-point, star-shaped pattern. A variant of the Torx screw head is the Torx plus, an impression of which can be seen at the top right of this figure. Torx screws are commonly found on automobiles, computer systems, and consumer electronics, and are also becoming increasingly popular in construction. Close-up impressions of the Torx tip made in No. 2 Roma Plastilina sculpting clay are shown along with an enlargement of the Torx tip.

Figure 9.6 A Robertson screwdriver (also called a square drive screwdriver) is a type of screwdriver with a square-shaped tip. These screwdrivers are used mainly in Canada, but are growing in popularity around the world, because they are one of the most reliable screwdrivers. Close-up impressions of the square tip made in No. 2 Roma Plastilina sculpting clay are shown along with an enlargement of the Robertson tip.

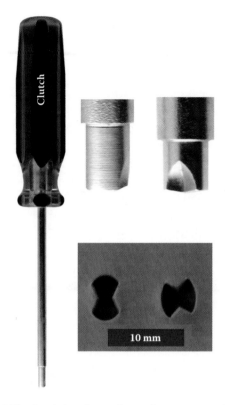

Figure 9.7 Clutch-head tips have four points of contact. They lock into the screw head when turned counterclockwise. The driver is unlocked by turning it in the opposite direction. Because of the many contact points, the tip will normally not damage the screw's head. Close-up impressions of the clutch tip made in No. 2 Roma Plastilina sculpting clay are shown along with an enlargement of the clutch tip.

Figure 9.8 An awl for punching holes. Awls produce toolmarks that are very similar to ice pick marks.

suggested by Burd and Kirk, can sometimes be helpful.[2] In Figure 9.11 a Graver's sharpening jig is employed to hold the subject tool at the desired angle while the known toolmarks are being prepared. Figure 9.12 depicts three "Husky" ¼ in. slot blade screwdrivers purchased from the same store, on the same day, from the same rack. Each of these screwdrivers was used to prepare known striation pattern standards for use in a pending research project, as seen in Figure 9.13.

Finally, Figure 9.14 depicts a small tack puller having a screwdriver-like handle and shaft. The blade is shaped like a pry bar end or small, bifurcated claw. This device is normally employed to remove small nails and tacks. However, it is appropriate to present this device prior to

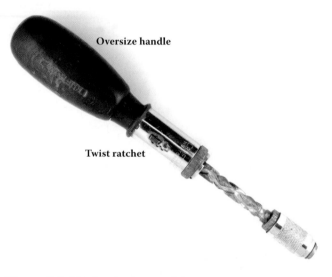

Figure 9.9 Mechanical screwdriver.

Figure 9.10 One process that can be used to prepare striation patterns with screwdrivers and other scraping tools.

a discussion of pry bars and crowbars because it can also be utilized as a prying tool.

Crowbars/Pry Bars

A crowbar, also called pry bar, or more informally known in law enforcement for nearly a century as a

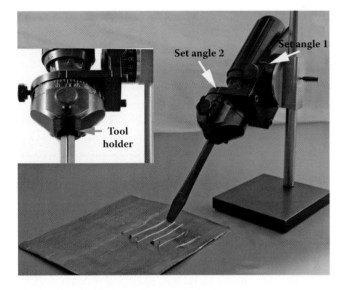

Figure 9.11 Use of a Graver's sharpening jig to hold the subject tool at the desired angles during the preparation of known standards.

Figure 9.13 Standard striation patterns made in No. 2 Plastilina sculpting clay of both sides of the three screwdrivers depicted in Figure 9.12. The striation pattern for each side of each screwdriver is reproduced at least ten times before it is eligible to be used in the author's research study. Note that each striation pattern is different for each side of the three study screwdrivers. To date the author has prepared and examined both striation patterns for fifty ¼ in. slot screwdrivers and has yet to observe the same pattern for any two sides. Further study and statistical analysis are currently under way.

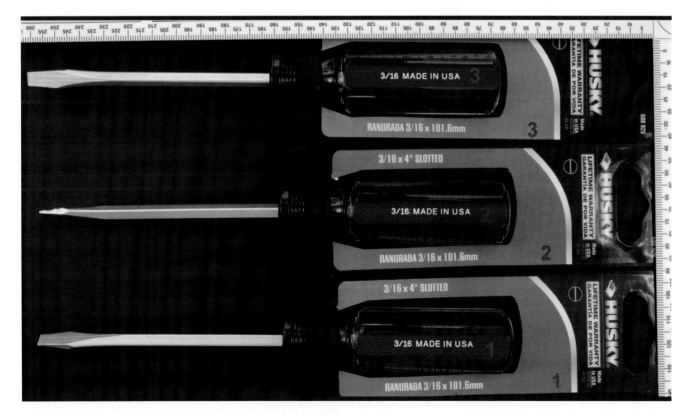

Figure 9.12 Three new Husky ¼ in. slot blade screwdrivers purchased from the same store on the same day from the same rack.

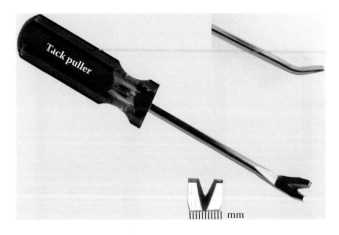

Figure 9.14 A tack puller with a screwdriver's handle and shaft. The blade is shaped like a pry bar end or small, bifurcated claw. This device is use to remove small nails and tacks.

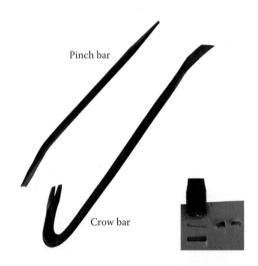

Figure 9.15 Classic crowbars and some of their marks.

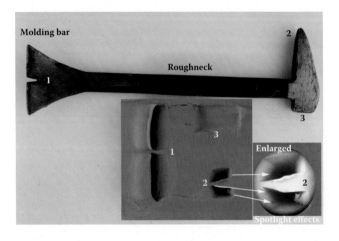

Figure 9.16 A Roughneck® pry bar; the numbers about the tool correspond to the numbered toolmarks made on clay. The Adobe® spotlight effects command was used to light up toolmarks #2 on the clay block (bottom right).

jimmy,[1] is a tool consisting of a metal bar with one curved end and one flattened end, often with small clefts on the ends for removing nails. A crowbar or pry bar is a type of tool used to pry and pull objects apart, take out nails, and for general demolition purposes. Crowbars and pry bars can be found in most construction tool kits because they can be used in a wide variety of applications. Crowbars and pry bars come in a number of different sizes and weights, depending on how the tool will be used, and some construction workers have more than one style so that they can use the right tool for the job.

Crowbars as construction tools date back to the 1400s, when the tool was known as a crow. The name of the tool referenced directly to the forked end of the crowbar, which resembles the foot of a crow. In the mid 1700s, the tool came to be known as a crowbar, presumably to eliminate confusion between the animal and the construction tool. In the 1800s, the terms *crow-bar* and *crowbar* began to emerge.[3]

There are several varieties of crowbars, but the basic shape is a long, heavy metal bar with one end shaped like a wedge, while the other end is slightly forked or split. The wedge end can be squeezed under various objects while the bar is used as a lever to separate them, and the forked end can be used to pull out nails. Some crowbars are curved at the forked end to provide more leverage; this type of crowbar is known as a wrecking bar because it is designed for demolition. Pry bars just tend to be smaller versions of their cousin crowbars, and thus are used in lighter applications.

Crowbars are typically used to force heavy doors or windows open. Since these tools are used to demolish heavy wood and metal objects, it is not unusual to find large impression marks in combination with scratches

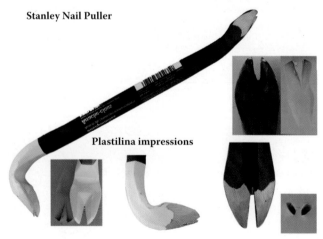

Figure 9.17 Nail puller with the resultant toolmarks.

and other telltale damage and scars left on the items with which they interact. Often these marks can be used to help quickly characterize the class of tool used in the event, as well as to associate a known tool to the questioned marks. A variety of crowbars and pry bars are shown in Figures 9.15 to 9.22. Figures 9.23 to 9.26 demonstrate the appearance of trace debris on a screwdriver's and pry bar's blade, along with some common toolmarks made by these tools, as well as how to determine the direction a tool was applied to a surface. Figure 9.25 is a close-up of a scratch on the door lock plate showing the starting and termination points along with the direction the tool was applied to the plate's surface. Figure 9.26a and b depicts crowbar marks on wooden doors and frames, and metal lock parts.

Handsaws

Crosscut Saw

The crosscut saw is made to cut wood across its grain. Crosscut saws have teeth that cut wood at a right angle

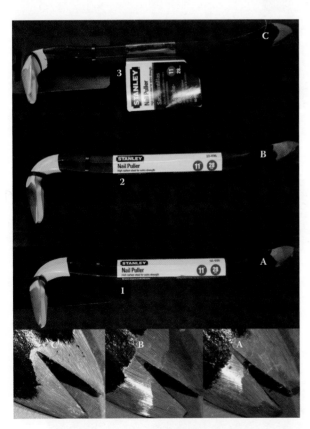

Figure 9.18 Three nail pullers. Note the obvious difference in the finish of designated claws due to the finishing process (grinding). All six claws on these tools have different shapes and striation patterns.

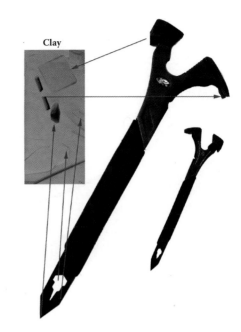

Figure 9.19 Ultimate® wrecking bar.

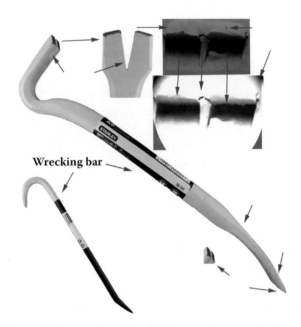

Figure 9.20 Wrecking bar with some class marks demonstrated in clay.

Figure 9.21 Wrecking bar.

to the direction of the wood grain. Crosscut saws normally have six to ten triangular-shaped teeth per inch, each with two knife-blade-like edges on both sides of each tooth. The teeth are set far apart and parallel to one another. A typical blade length is 26 in., although

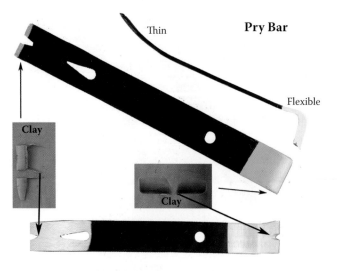

Figure 9.22 A pry bar and its common toolmarks in clay.

they can vary from 20 to 28 in. long. A crosscut saw cuts on both the downstroke and upstroke. Several styles of crosscut saws are depicted in Figures 9.27 to 9.32.

Crosscut saws have fine teeth, usually numbering between fourteen and eighteen per inch. The blade of a backsaw or miter saw is thin—hence the need for the top metal support to stiffen the blade. The average blade length is between 12 and 14 in. The teeth are set similarly to those of a crosscut saw, and they are normally used to make fine cuts across the grain of interior moldings (see Figure 9.32). Figures 9.33 and 9.34 depict toolmarks made in human bone by a crosscut saw blade.

Rip Saw

Rip saws are used to cut along the grain of a piece of wood. Rip saws have fewer teeth than crosscut saws, typically having five to seven per inch set, and a blade length between 20 and 28 in. long. Unlike the crosscut saw, rip saws have chisel-like teeth; each tooth has a flat front edge and it is not angled forward or backward, which allows

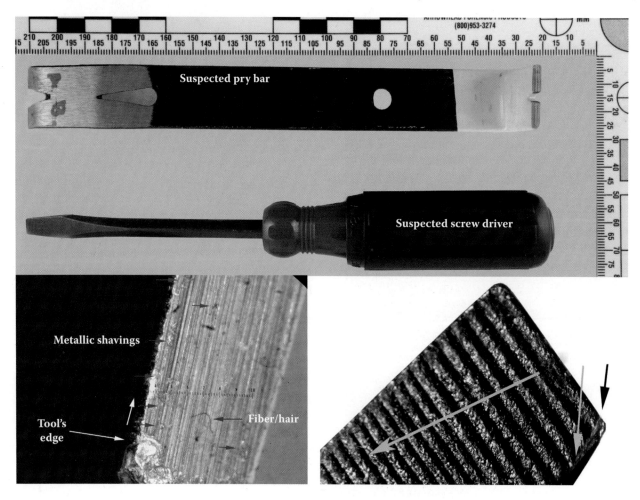

Figure 9.23 Pry bar and screwdriver with trace material (brass shavings) on their blades.

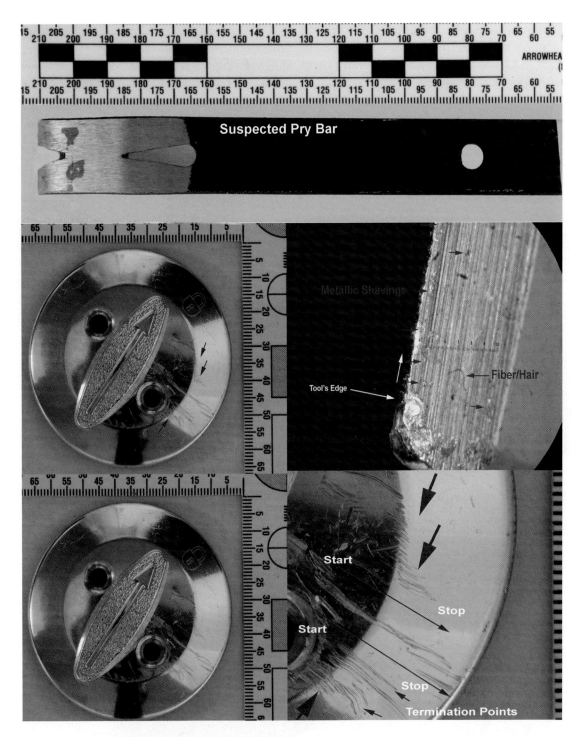

Figure 9.24 Brass trace on pry bar examined with other trace evidence to determine if this pry was used in this event. Scratch marks on the lock cover plate were examined and the direction of the tool's application is reconstructed (see Figure 9.25).

the saw to easily cut along grain lines, in order to achieve a straight cut. Figure 9.35 depicts a rip saw.

Miscellaneous Handsaws

The compass or keyhole saw is used to saw inside curves and to cut holes or keyholes into pieces of lumber. A compass saw blade is typically 12 in. long, tapers to a point, and has eight teeth per inch. Its shape allows it to be used to cut inside curves, holes, and keyholes (when a small blade is used) readily into lumber (see Figure 9.36).

Coping saws are very versatile handsaws and are typically utilized to cut complex, asymmetric shapes in wood. A coping saw's blade is mounted with its teeth facing the handle, which causes it to cut on the downward stroke. The kerf produced by a coping saw's blade is narrow. A coping saw is depicted in Figure 9.37.

A drywall saw has a short blade (7 in.) with large teeth for cutting through paper facings, backings, and the gypsum core. Some types of drywall saws have a pointed end on the saw blade that allows them to pierce sheets of drywall and cut openings in panels of sheetrock. A drywall saw is depicted in Figure 9.38.

Standard hacksaws utilize blades with fine teeth that are placed under tension when mounted in a rectangular-shaped frame. Hacksaw frames have a set of prongs for attaching the blade to the frame. A wing nut

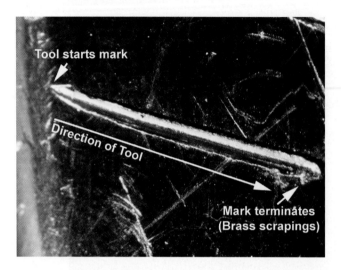

Figure 9.25 Close-up of a scratch on the door lock plate showing the starting and termination points along with the direction the tool was applied to the plate's surface.

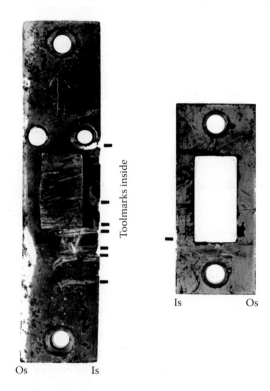

Figure 9.26 The appearance of common toolmarks caused by a crowbar on metal lock and door frame components.

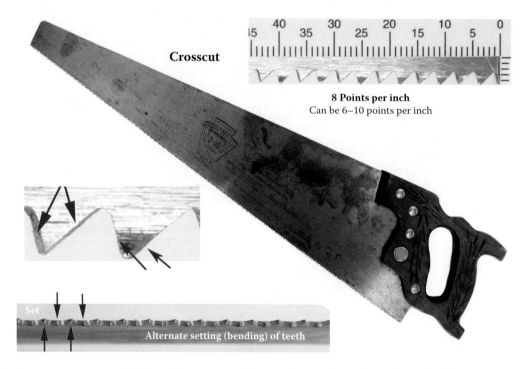

Figure 9.27 Crosscut saws normally have six to ten teeth (points) per inch, each with two knife-blade-like edges on both sides of each tooth. A crosscut saw cuts on both the downstroke and upstroke, and across the wood's grain. A popular blade length is 26 inches, although the blades's length can vary from 20 to 28 inches.

screw is then turned to place the blade under tension. When properly mounted, a hacksaw blade's teeth point toward its handle. Blades are available in standardized lengths, with typically eighteen to thirty-two teeth per inch (tpi). Blades with 28 tpi are normally used to cut copper pipe, while blades with 24 tpi are recommended

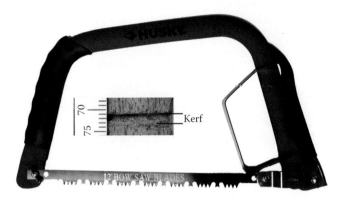

Figure 9.28 Bow saw. The kerf is the width of the channel or notch the saw's blade makes when used to cut materials such as wood, bone, and so on.

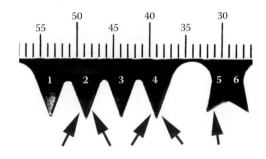

Figure 9.29 Crosscut-shaped teeth with knife edges on teeth 2, 3, and 5 facing the reader, and teeth 1, 3, and 6 facing the opposite side of the saw blade.

Figure 9.30 Coarse cut saw with twelve teeth per inch on the blade's front portion, and nine teeth per inch on the back portion of the 14 in. blade. Gullets are positioned for waste (sawdust) to escape.

for general use. Figures 9.39 to 9.41 show a hacksaw and its nomenclature, three standard hacksaw blades, and different blade sets.

Striking Tools

Hammers, Hatchets, and Axes

Claw hammers are used to drive nails and remove nails. There are several types of claw hammers; the curved claw and the straight claw are the most common. Some claw hammers have smooth faces, while other models have checkered pattern faces to minimize slipping (see Figures 9.42 to 9.44).

Ball-peen and cross-peen hammers are commonly used in all-purpose metal work and for working with

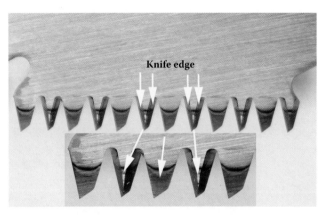

Figure 9.31 Crosscut saw with twelve teeth per inch on the blade's front portion, and nine teeth per inch on the back portion of the 14 in. blade. Gullets are positioned for waste (sawdust) to escape. The blade has alternating teeth, with one set facing the right side and one facing the left side, parallel to each other. Each tooth has two knife sharp cutting edges on adjacent sides.

Figure 9.32 Backsaw with twelve teeth per inch on the blade's front portion, and nine teeth per inch on the back portion of the 14 in. blade. Gullets are positioned for waste (sawdust) to escape. The blade has alternating teeth, with one set facing the right side and one facing the left side, parallel to each other. Each tooth has two knife sharp cutting edges on adjacent sides. The backsaw or miter saw is a tool used to make accurate crosscuts.

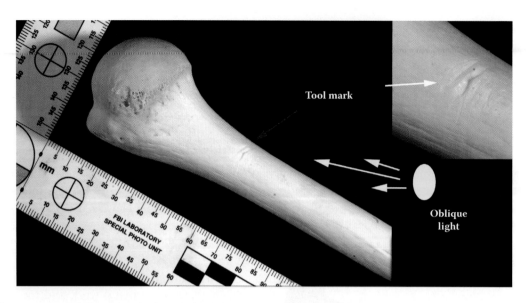

Figure 9.33 Crosscut saw marks in human bone viewed with oblique light.

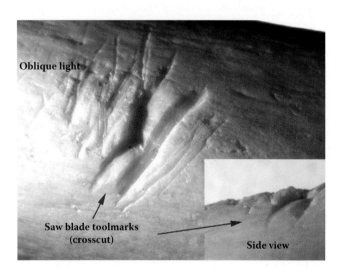

Figure 9.34 Close-up and side view of crosscut saw marks.

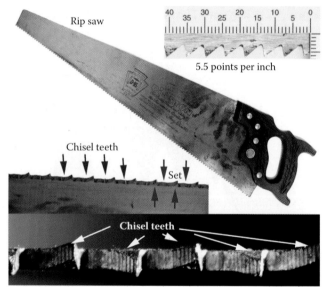

Figure 9.35 Rip saws are used to cut along the grain of a piece of wood. Rip saws have fewer teeth than crosscut saws, typically having five to seven teeth per inch set, and a blade length between 20 and 28 in. long. Unlike the crosscut saw, rip saws have chisel-like teeth, each tooth has a flat front edge, and it is not angled forward or backward, which allows the saw to easily cut along grain lines, in order to achieve a straight cut.

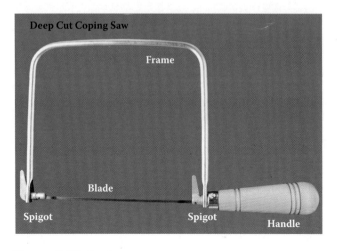

Figure 9.37 Coping saw.

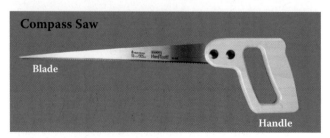

Figure 9.36 Compass or keyhole saw.

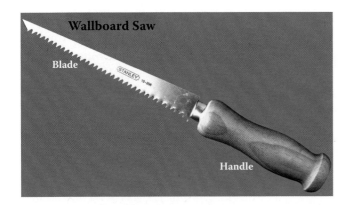

Figure 9.38 Drywall or sheetrock saw.

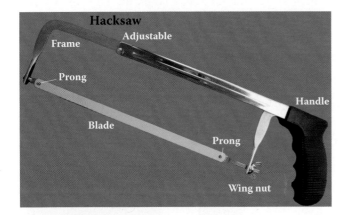

Figure 9.39 A typical hacksaw with its component parts: a bow-shaped adjustable frame, a pistol grip, and two prongs to hold the blade, with one prong incorporating a wing nut mechanism to place the blade under tension.

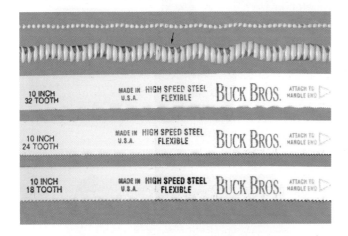

Figure 9.40 Three standard hacksaw blades.

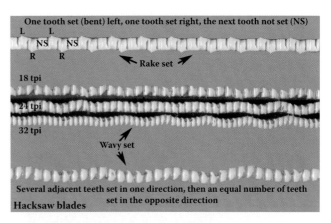

Figure 9.41 Three hacksaw blades with 18, 24, and 32 tpi. The top blade's teeth have a rake set and the bottom blade's teeth have a wavy set.

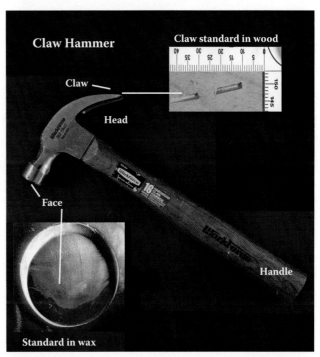

Figure 9.42 A common carpentry curved claw hammer with typical toolmarks in wood and wax.

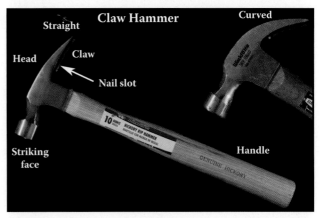

Figure 9.43 Two claw hammers, one straight and one curved.

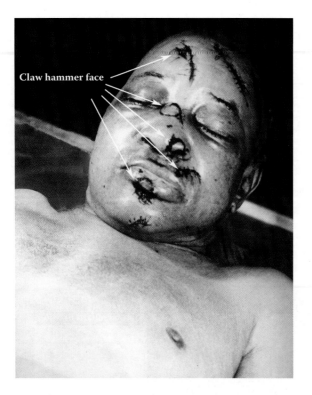

Figure 9.44 Homicide of an adult male struck and killed with a claw hammer.

striking chisels and punches. They are available in a large variety of weights, from 1 oz. to 30 oz. The ball-peen hammer's face is flat and the peen rounded, while the cross peen hammer's face is flat and the peen wedge shaped, designed for shaping metal (see Figures 9.45, 9.46, and 9.50).

The sledge hammer is designed for general heavy-duty applications like driving in large nails or spikes, breaking up concrete, and striking large cold chisels. Slug hammer heads are typically slightly convex, and the head can weigh from 1 to 5 lb (see Figures 9.47 to 9.49).

Another type of sledge hammer, used by blacksmiths, has a long handle, a large, flat face on one end, and a forming wedge on the other. Figure 9.50a depicts a common 4 lb forming hammer, while Figure 9.50b shows two standard toolmarks made on a lead sheet.

The mason's hammer is made to cut and shape bricks, stones, and concrete blocks. It has a flat face on one end of the head and a tapered chisel-like edge on the other end, as depicted in Figure 9.51.

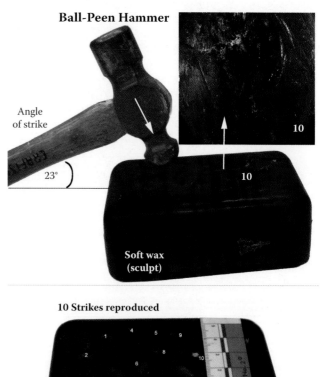

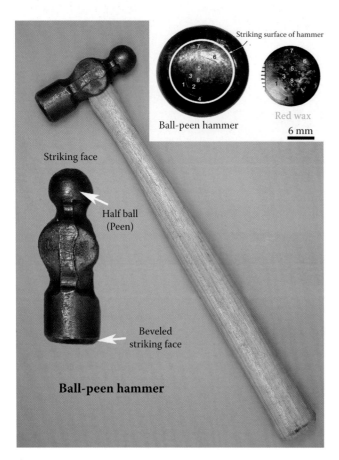

Figure 9.45 Ball-peen hammer with wax standard.

Figure 9.46 Making ball-peen hammer standards with a block of red sculpture wax.

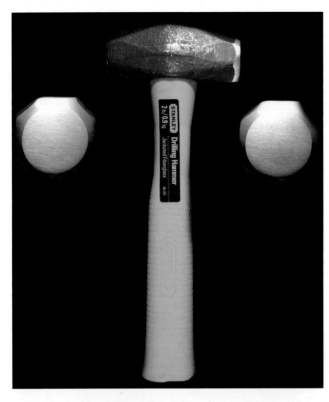

Figure 9.47 The sledge hammer is designed for general heavy-duty applications such as driving in large nails or spikes, breaking up concrete, and striking large cold chisels. Slug hammer heads typically are slightly convex.

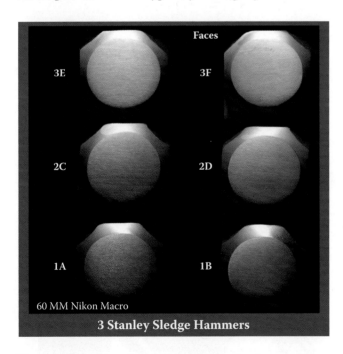

Figure 9.48 Three 2½ lb Stanley® sledge hammers purchased at a tool store off the shelf at the same time. Each was numbered (1–3), and each face was labeled (1A to 3F). All six faces were photographed to show their different striation patterns (see Figure 9.49).

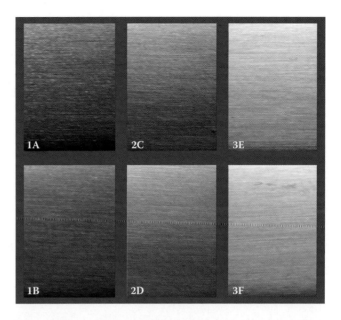

Figure 9.49 Three 2½ lb Stanley sledge hammers showing different striation patterns. These differences are due to the grinding during the finishing process.

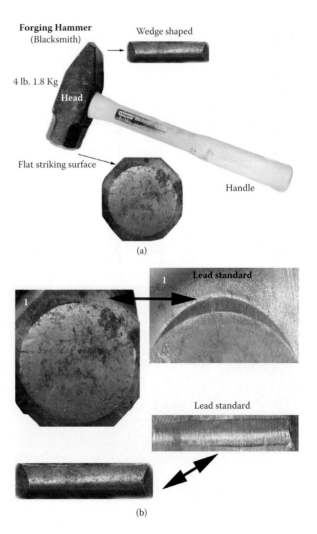

Figure 9.50 (a) A blacksmith or forging hammer. (b) Standard toolmarks made in lead with a blacksmith hammer.

Mallets are normally employed when a softer blow is required. Mallets have various round and cylinder-shaped heads used for driving dowels, small stakes, and wooden-handled chisels, and for forming and shaping sheet metal. Their heads are typically constructed

from a variety of hard woods, polymers, rubber, metal, and leather or rawhide. Several mallets are shown in Figure 9.52a and b.

The axe is used to shape, carve, split, and cut wood, and as a weapon. An axe is wedge shaped and thus splits wood by the application of pressure concentrated at the blade. Its handle is a lever that allows its user to increase the force at the cutting edge. Cutting axes have a thin wedge angle, while axes used to split wood have a deeper angle. A hatchet typically is a small, single-edged blade that integrates a hammer on its opposite side. Examples of axes, mauls, hatchets, and the marks they make are given in Figures 9.53 to 9.57. Figure 9.58 depicts a setup often used by the author to make axe, hatchet, and hammer toolmark standards.

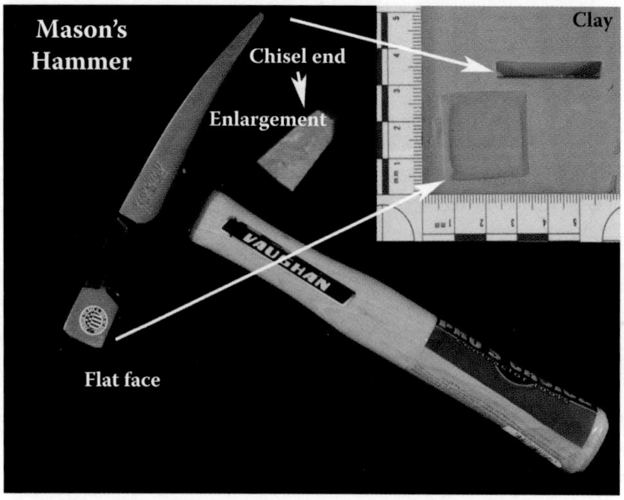

Figure 9.51 A mason's hammer is made to cut and shape bricks, stones, and concrete blocks. It has a flat face on one end of the head and a tapered chisel-like edge on the other end. Standard toolmarks are shown in clay.

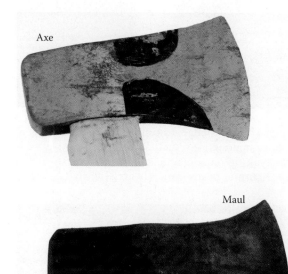

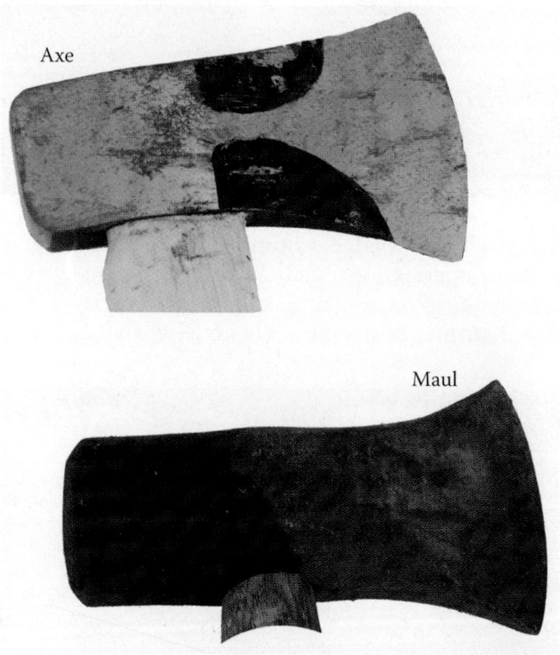

Figure 9.53 An axe and a maul.

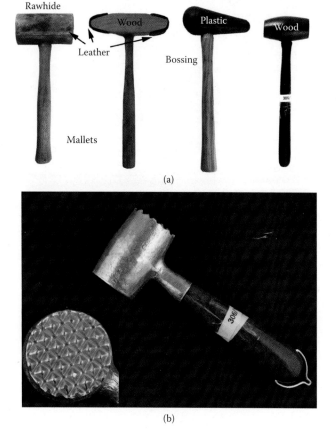

Figure 9.52 (a) Four different types of mallets. (b) Meat mallet made of aluminum.

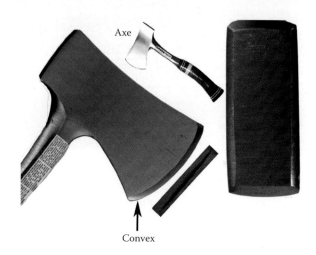

Figure 9.54 A hand axe.

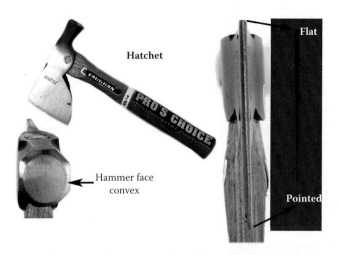

Figure 9.55 A typical modern hatchet.

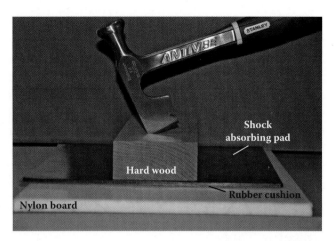

Figure 9.58 Setup often used to make toolmark standards.

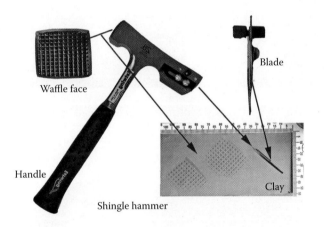

Figure 9.56 A shingling hatchet is to drive the nails that hold shingles in place. The hatchet side of the tool can be used to mark the exposure on the shingle courses.

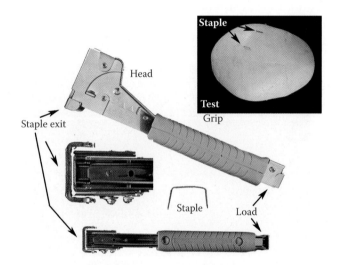

Figure 9.59 A hammer stapler.

Figure 9.57 A drywall hammer.

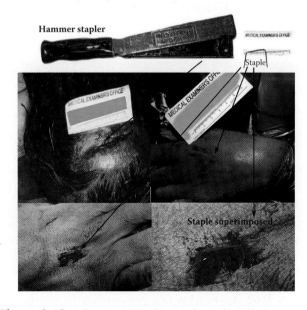

Figure 9.60 A hammer stapler used in a homicide.

The hammer stapler (Figure 9.59) is a tool used in construction to attach building paper and roofing felt to the underlayment wood surface. It is used with one hand, one would employ a hammer. It releases a staple when it is struck against the surface. This device is very efficient for affixing light-weight materials to building surfaces. The staples can be selected in different lengths and gauges, from ¼ to ½ in. long. Figure 9.60 shows the type of damage that can be made by a hammer staple on a human body.

Grasping Tools

Wrenches

The pipe or Stillson wrench is used by plumbers to attach and take apart soft iron pipes. The size of pipe wrenches typically varies from 10 to 48 in. The pipe wrench is an adjustable wrench used for turning soft iron pipes and pipe fittings with a rounded surface. The wrench's adjustable jaw allows it to move back and forth in the frame, such that any forward pressure on the handle tends to pull the jaws tighter together. Teeth angled in the direction of turn dig into the soft pipe. The teeth contained within the jaws of a pipe wrench typically cut into the pipe to get a grip and thus leave toolmarks in the shape of the pipe's teeth embedded into the pipe's outer surface. Figures 9.61 to 9.66 illustrate two types of pipe wrenches and some of the marks they can leave.

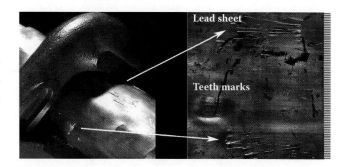

Figure 9.63 Standard toolmarks made in lead by a Stillson wrench.

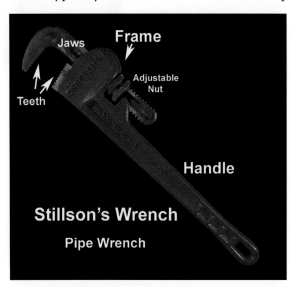

Figure 9.61 An 18 in. Stillson wrench.

Figure 9.62 Application of a pipe wrench to an iron gas pipe.

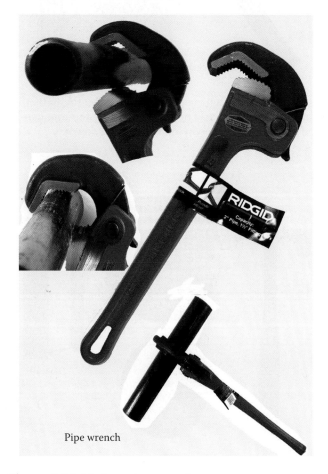

Figure 9.64 Modern pipe wrench.

Vise-Grips

Vise-grips are pliers that can be locked into position. To use, the pliers' jaws are set to a size slightly smaller than the diameter of the object to be gripped by turning the bolt in one handle with the jaws closed. When the jaws are opened and the handles squeezed together, they move a lever over its center point and lock the jaw of the pliers onto the gripped object. One side of the handle includes a bolt that is used to adjust the spacing of the

jaws; the other side of the handle usually includes a lever to push the two sides of the handles apart to unlock the pliers. The term *vise-grip* is an industry name for many different brands and types of locking pliers. These pliers are available in many different configurations, such as needle-nose locking pliers, locking wrenches, and locking clamps, and various shapes to fix metal parts for welding. Several locking pliers are shown in Figures 9.67 to 9.71. Figures 9.72 to 9.74 depict class features and individual features of a curve-jaw vise-grip made in lead and PVC pipe primer.

Figure 9.65 A pipe wrench's tooth marks being prepared on a sheet of ¹⁄₃₂ in. lead, wrapped around a 1½ in. cast iron pipe. Note the movement of the teeth (left to right) within the jaws when pressure is applied to the handle.

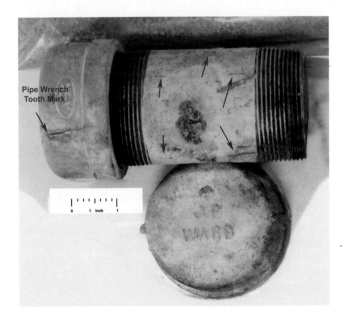

Figure 9.66 A pipe bomb with pipe wrench tooth marks designated with a blue arrow.

Pliers

Pliers are a class of hand tool used to grip and hold objects securely. Pliers are typically used to remove nuts from bolts; hold wood, plastic, or metal stock while cutting with a saw or knife; hold tubing or wire while bending; and so on. Pliers are constructed of a pair of metal or polymer handles, each of which has a jaw fashioned at one end. The two handles are connected at a pivot

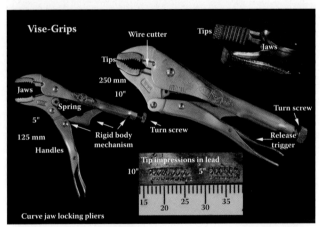

Figure 9.67 Curve jaw vise-grip with nomenclature and standard teeth marks made in lead.

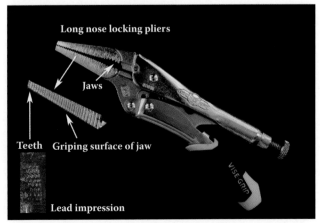

Figure 9.68 Needle- or long-nose vise-grip with teeth marks made in lead.

point and act as levers allowing the opening and closing movement of the two opposing jaws. The assemblage of two handles, two opposing jaws, and a pivot point allows for the gripping and manipulating of objects. There are many types of pliers; some are designed for grasping objects and others for doing specific jobs. Figures 9 75 to 9.81 depict a number of commonly encountered types of pliers and some of the toolmarks they can produce.

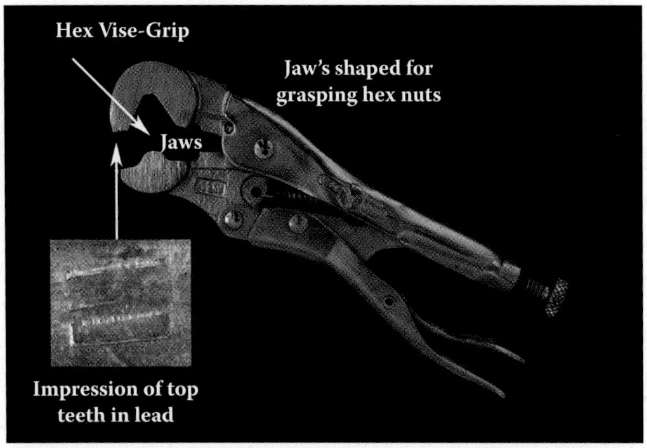

Cutting Tools

Metal Snips

Metal snips are tools used to cut thin sheets of metal. Metal tin snips work like common scissors by cutting in a shearing action. They separate metal and other materials by moving two sharp, angled, opposing blades in opposite directions (one descending and one ascending),

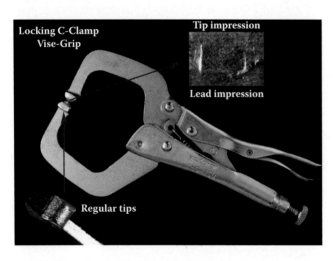

Figure 9.69 Hex nut vise-grip with teeth impressions in lead.

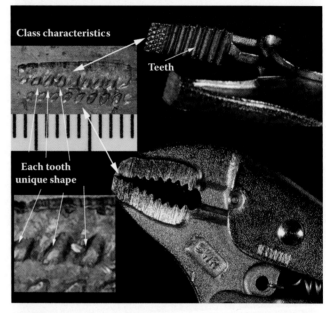

Figure 9.72 Curved jaw vise-grip with teeth impression in lead.

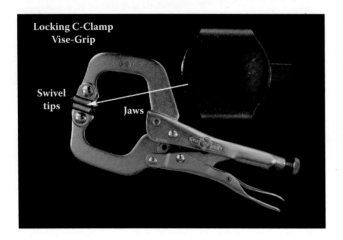

Figure 9.70 Locking C-clamp vise-grip with foot impression in lead.

Figure 9.71 Locking C-clamp vise-grip with foot impression in lead.

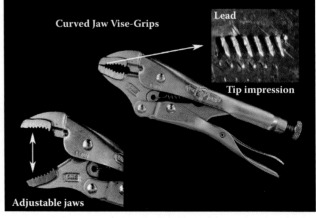

Figure 9.73 Curved jaw vise-grip with teeth impression in lead.

thus scoring and pushing the material apart as depicted in Figure 9.84.

There are three styles of aviation snips in common use: straight cutting, left cutting, and right cutting. The straight-blade variety cut sheet metal in a straight line, left-cutting blades will cut in a tight curve to the left, and right-cutting blades will cut in a tight curve to the right. Figure 9.82 depicts all three cutting blade patterns: straight cut (yellow handles), left cut (red handles), and right cut (green handles). Aviation snips also come in a variety of blade patterns for cutting angles, long straight cuts, and unusual shapes. Bulldog or short-jaw aviation snips are shown in Figure 9.83; they are used to make

Figure 9.74 Curved jaw vise-grip with teeth impression in PVC pipe coated with PVC pipe primer.

Figure 9.75 Common combination or slip-joint pliers.

Figure 9.76 A side cutting or linemen pliers.

Figure 9.77 Long-nose or needle-nose pliers with toolmark patterns in wax. The top sheet of wax is illuminated with reflected light, while the bottom wax sheet is illuminated at an oblique angle held underneath the sheet of wax.

Figure 9.78 An assortment of channel-lock pliers.

short cuts in thick metal sheets or sheets made of several layers of metal. Right angle and offset snips are designed to make 45 and 90 degree angle cuts in sheets of metal (see Figures 9.84 and 9.85).

Another type of metal snip used by tin smiths to cut sheet metal is the duckbill snip, which is used to cuts curves, circles, and odd shapes in metal sheeting. These tools also cut metal and other materials by utilizing a shearing action (see Figures 9.86 and 9.87). An assortment of duckbill metal snips is shown in Figure 9.88.

All-purpose metal shears also have the same cutting action as metal snips. The cutting blades are typically straight and at least 2 in. long. These multipurpose shears are used to make angular, straight, and curved cuts in all types of materials. A pair of these shears is shown in Figure 9.89.

Wire Cutters

Wire cutters are pliers designed for the cutting of wire; they are not used to grasp, hold, or tighten anything. These implements are also referred to as diagonal cutters. Both cutting edges of each jaw are ground to an

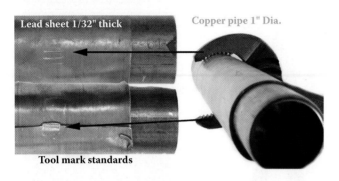

Figure 9.79 Toolmarks made by curved jaw channel-lock pliers on a lead sheet wrapped around a 1 in. copper pipe.

Figure 9.80 Groove-lock pliers with nomenclature.

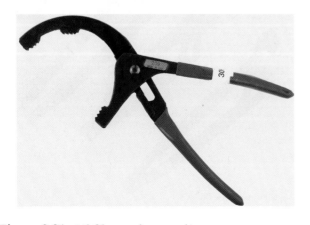

Figure 9.81 Oil filter and water pliers.

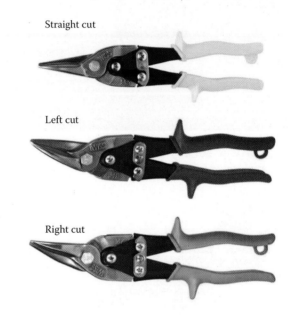

Figure 9.82 Aviation snips with all three cutting blade patterns: straight cut (traditionally yellow handles), left cut (traditionally red handles), and right cut (traditionally green handles).

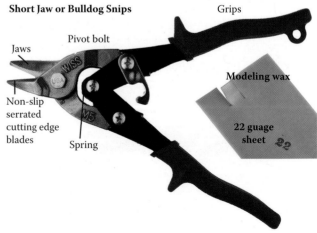

Figure 9.83 Bulldog or short-jaw aviation snips are used to make short cuts in thick metal sheets and multiple layers of metal.

angle, thus forming a wedge or shaped edge. Unlike scissors, which cut by a shearing action, the wire cutter's jaws cut wire by scoring the wire on opposite sides, then wedging both sides of the wire apart. The action of wire cutters is illustrated in Figures 9.90 through 9.93.

Diagonal wire cutters are used for cutting copper, brass, iron, aluminum, and steel wire.

Bolt and Cable Cutters

Bolt and cable cutters are used for cutting bolts, lock shackles, chain links, fencing mesh wire, and thick-diameter solid and multistrand cables. Bolt and cable cutters

Figure 9.84 Right angle aviation snips make cuts in metal at a 90 degree angle.

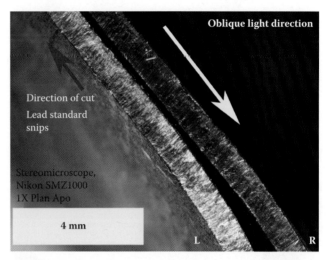

Figure 9.87 Oblique lighting being utilized to observe striations in lead sheet.

Figure 9.85 Offset aviation snips make cuts in metal at a 45 degree angle.

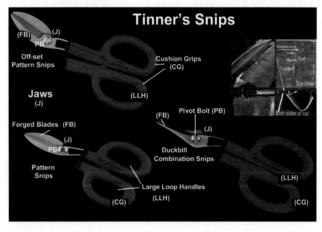

Figure 9.88 An assortment of tinner's metal snips: offset, straight, and duckbill.

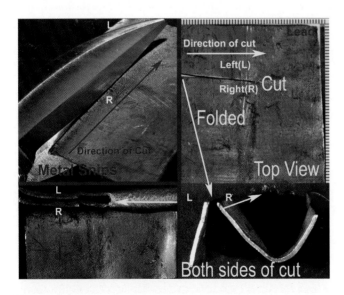

Figure 9.86 Duckbill metal snips being used to prepare a toolmark standard by cutting a 1/32 in. lead sheet.

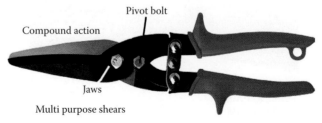

Figure 9.89 A pair of multipurpose shears used to make all types of cuts in a large variety of materials.

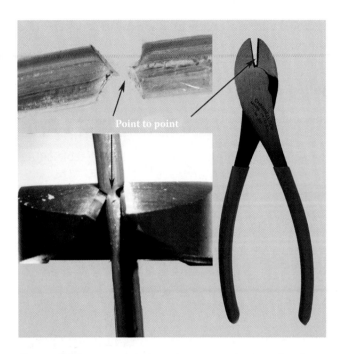

Figure 9.90 Diagonal-shaped jaws cut both ends of wire into wedge shapes.

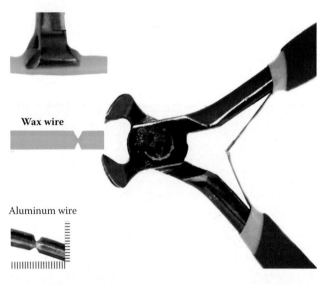

Figure 9.91 End-cut wire cutters cut both ends of wire into wedge shapes.

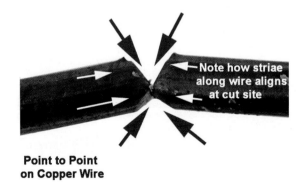

Figure 9.92 Copper that was wire cut with a point-to-point wire cutter.

are normally made with long handles and short blades. Most types have compound hinges to maximize leverage and cutting strength. These tools can have different types of blades, including angular cutting blades, center cutting blades (point-to-point), clipper cutting blades, which have one angled sharp blade and one flat surface blade to cut against, and shearing cutting blades (scissors). Bolt and cable cutters typically range in length from 10 to 36 in.; however, many variations of these versatile tools are manufactured today. In Figure 9.94 a typical bolt cutter and its nomenclature are shown. Figure 9.95 depicts the cutting action of a center cutting blades (point-to-point) bolt

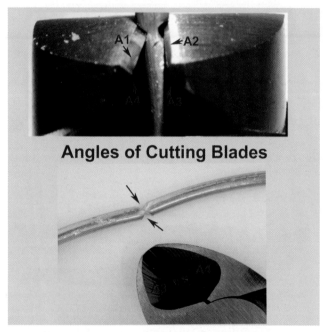

Figure 9.93 Diagonal-shaped jaws cut both ends of wire into wedge shapes. Jaw sides A1 and A2 score and then push metal upwards, whereas jaw sides A4 and A3 score and push metal downwards (top). Note the trace metal residue left on the cutting surface A3–A4 (bottom).

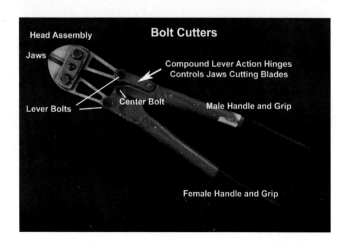

Figure 9.94 A common type of bolt cutter and its parts.

cutter. Shown in Figure 9.96 is a lock that was cut using a bolt cutter while open in a staged burglary. Figure 9.97a and b illustrates the cutting action of a shearing action cable cutter in which blade A pushes the metal in one direction while blade B pushes the metal in the opposite direction until the cable fatigues (C). Figure 9.98a and b portrays the working action of a specialized copper cable cutter. Figure 9.99a and b demonstrates another specialized copper cable cutter with both a shearing action set of cutting blades and a set of clipper cutting blades.

Crimping Tools

Crimping tools join two pieces of metal by bending and stretching one or both pieces of metal in order to form a joint that will hold or affix them to each other. The joint that is produced is known as a crimp. Crimping is

Figure 9.95 The cutting action of a center cutting blades (point-to-point) bolt cutter is depicted.

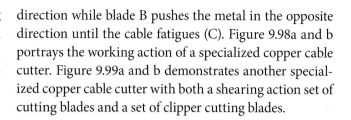

Figure 9.96 A staged burglary in which the lock's shackle was cut while opened with a shearing action bolt cutter.

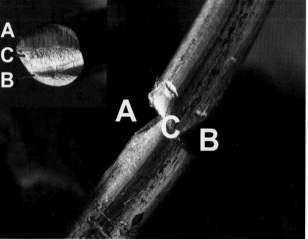

Figure 9.97 The shearing cutting action of a cable cutter blade (A) pushes the metal in one direction while blade B pushes the metal in the opposite direction until the cable fatigues (C).

used most often by metal smiths and metal duct workers. Figures 9.100 through 9.102 illustrate several crimping tools.

Knives, Scissors, and Shears

Knives

Knives are any sharp cutting edge or blade held in the hand or in some other manner, or otherwise used to cut wood, flesh, soft tissue, or some other pliable substance. Knives can be made from any material that can hold a sharp edge. The first knives were made from obsidian, a naturally occurring igneous rock (volcanic glass), and flint, a form of mineral quartz having a fine

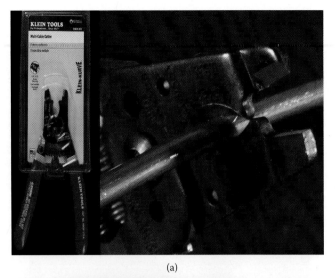

(a)

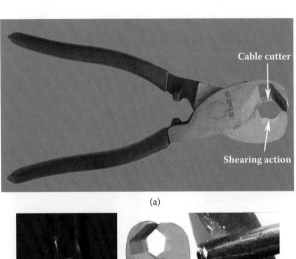

(a)

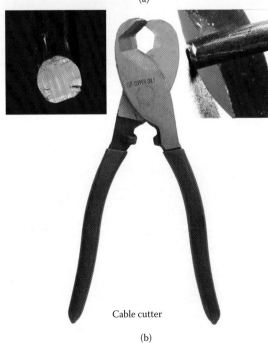

Cable cutter

(b)

Figure 9.98 (a) A cable cutter designed to cut only copper cable. (b) The shearing action of two highly angled, very sharp, opposing blades to cut copper cable.

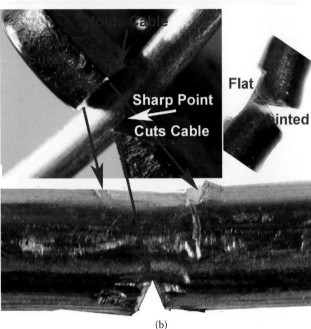

(b)

Figure 9.99 Copper cable cutter. (a) Shearing action set of blades. (b) Cutting action of clipper cutting blades. One side has a sharp, centered, pointed blade that cuts the cable, while a flat-surfaced blade holds it in place as force is applied to the lever action jaws by squeezing both handles.

Multi-blade crimp

Figure 9.100 A typical multiblade tool used to crimp metal together with cold joints without the need for welding or soldering.

microcrystalline structure and formed as a sedimentary rock. Other early knives were made from pieces of copper metal, iron metal, or alloys such as bronze.

Modern knives have many forms but generally fall into one of two very large classifications: fixed-blade knives and folding knives. Knives typically have a blade with a sharp edge, and a handle needed to hold and manipulate the knife. The tip of a knife is generally the first third of the blade, while the point is at the end of the blade opposite the handle. The point is used for piercing.

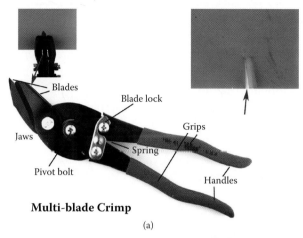

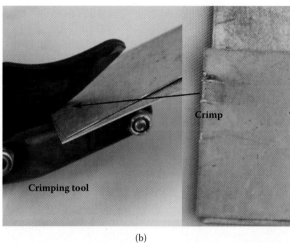

Figure 9.101 (a) The action of a crimping tool is demonstrated on a sheet of wax. (b) The action of a crimping tool is demonstrated on two sheets of metal.

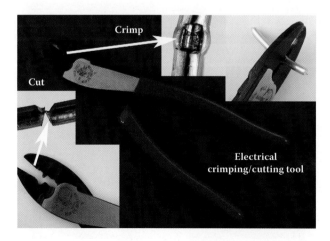

Figure 9.102 A crimping and cutting tool used by electricians.

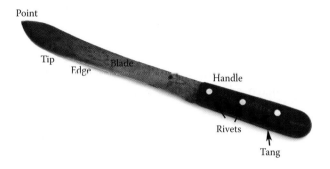

Figure 9.103 A typical kitchen knife and its major components.

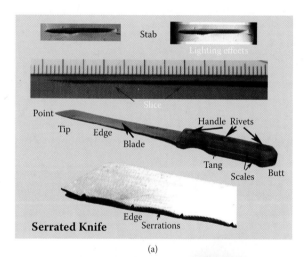

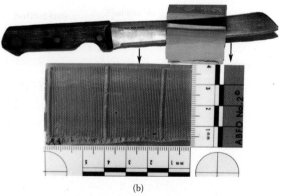

Figure 9.104 (a) A serrated edge knife with its components. Several toolmarks made by this knife were prepared in Plastilina clay and wood. (b) The serrated knife was used to slice Plastilina clay to demonstrate its blade's class characteristics.

The handle can include rivets to affix it to the blade, a tang or extension of the metal blade that is secured to the handle, a counterweight or bolster, and a guard that separates the blade from the handle. Several knives and their components are illustrated in Figures 9.103 to 9.108. Figures 9.109 and 9.110 depict some common knife toolmarks often seen on human remains. A common household kitchen cleaver is seen in Figure 9.142. Much larger cleavers are used in the food preparation industry. Cleaver toolmarks often mimic those of hand axes.

Scissors and Shears

Scissors are a cutting tool used to cut paper, fabric, string, and other thin sheets of pliable material by hand. A pair of scissors denotes a single tool composed of two pieces of metal fashioned into blades with sharp edges joined together in a way that allows the sharp edges to slide back and forth against one another. Scissors are also commonly used to cut food items, and for personal hygiene (cutting hair, toenails, and fingernails).

Scissors are made in a wide variety of forms depending on their intended use. The term *shears* describes instruments that are similar in structure and purpose, but are larger than 6 in. An assortment of scissors is illustrated in Figure 9.111. Figure 9.112 depicts cuts made in fabric by two different pairs of scissors.

Figure 9.113 depicts two pieces of wire examined during a homicide investigation. One end of the Q1 wire

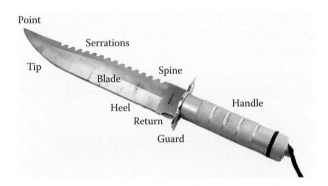

Figure 9.105 A Bowie type knife with its components.

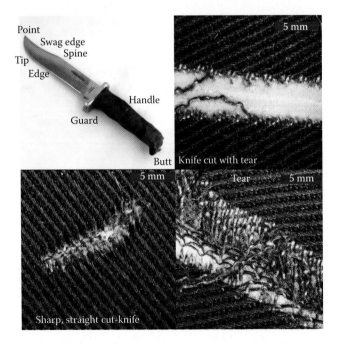

Figure 9.106 Top left: A common hunting knife and its components. Top right: A tear of black denim cloth initially started with a small knife cut. Bottom left: A cut made by a stabbing motion into a piece of denim with a sharp knife. Bottom right: A piece of torn blue denim.

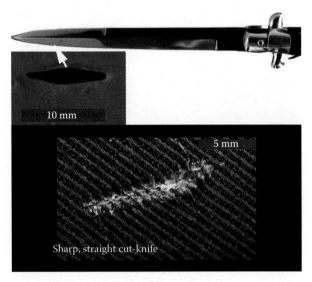

Figure 9.107 A stiletto folding switchblade knife with a stab mark in clay and in a piece of denim.

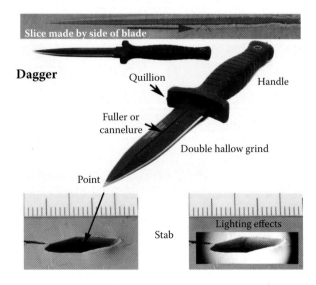

Figure 9.108 A dagger with component parts, a stab mark, and a slice mark prepared in Plastilina clay.

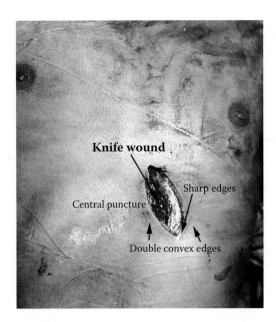

Figure 9.109 Appearance of a large dagger type stab wound in a human body.

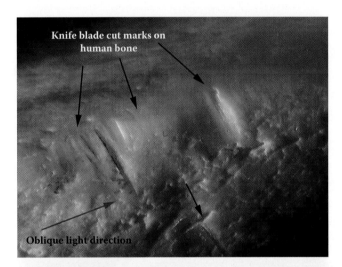

Figure 9.110 Knife marks made on human bone. These marks can be easily cast with Mikrosil®.

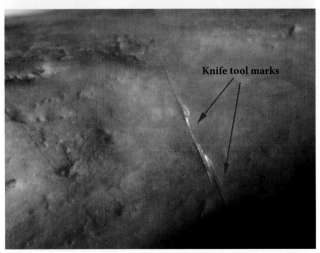

removed from the victim's neck at autopsy jigsawed into one end of the K1 piece of wire obtained from the suspect's apartment during a warrant-authorized search. Both ends showed signs of being cut with a knife (never recovered). Figures 9.114 and 9.115 depict two case

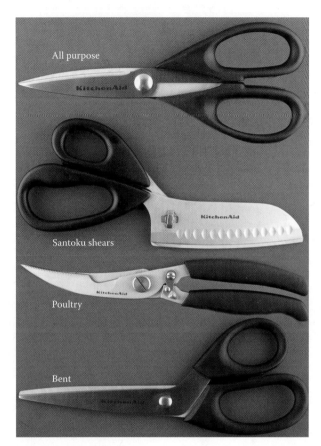

Figure 9.111 An assortment of scissors.

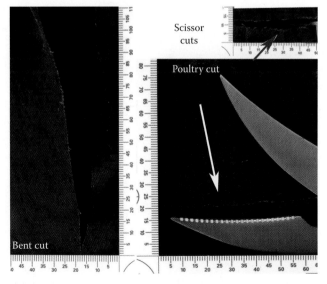

Figure 9.112 On the left, a cut made in cloth with a pair of bent scissors. On the right, a cut made with a pair of poultry scissors.

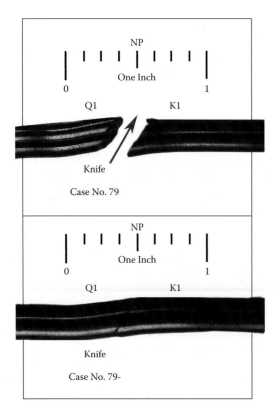

Figure 9.113 A homicide by strangulation with the Q1 piece of multistrand appliance wire. One end of the Q1 wire removed from the victim's neck at autopsy jigsawed into the K1 piece of wire obtained from the suspect's apartment. Both ends show signs of being cut with a knife (never recovered).

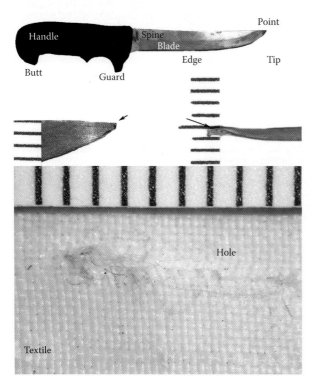

Figure 9.114 A case involving the assault of a police officer with a knife. Note the damage and hole in the Kevlar® vest's insert holder made with the above knife, which bent on impact.

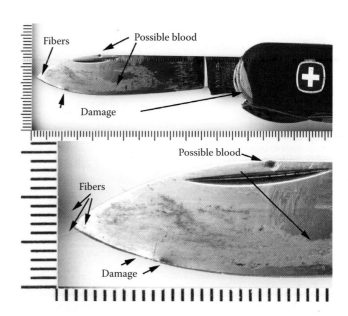

Figure 9.115 Pocketknife from suspect with blood and fibers from victim of an assault.

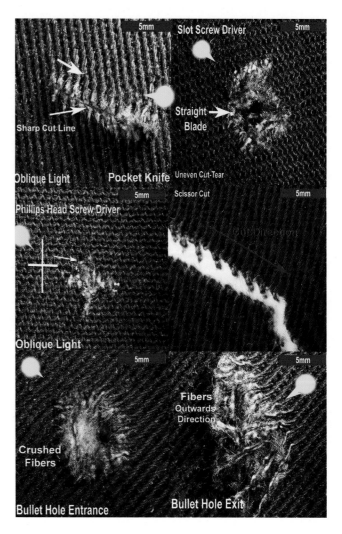

Figure 9.116 Assorted cuts and holes in denim. The yellow spots indicate the illuminator's position.

involving knives used during two different assaults. Both knives were damaged during the commission of the assaults, and the pocketknife in Figure 9.115 has blood and trace fibers from the victim on its blade.

The appearance of damage caused to textiles by various objects and weapons has been a topic of research for many years in the forensic community. Taupin has published a series of articles on textiles damage and its forensic significance; the articles are a great source of information on this topic.[4–7] Figure 9.116 illustrates marks made by cutting and stabbing denim with various implements. The interested reader is referred to the literature for a complete discussion of this topic.

Chisels and Punches

A chisel is a tool with a shaped cutting edge used to chip and cut stone, tiles, bricks, concrete, and other masonry

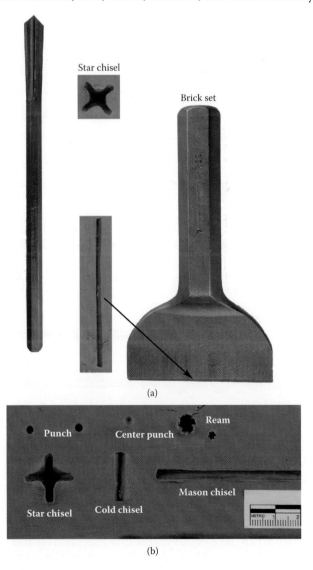

Figure 9.117 (a) Masonry chisels. (b) Characteristic chisel and punch marks made in modeling clay.

Figure 9.118 An assortment of common punches and chisels with their marks.

Figure 9.119 Mason's chisel used to break bricks, cinder blocks, and concrete.

materials, as well as cut, carve, gouge, sculpt, and shape wood. Chisels can be made from single pieces of cast or forged metal or metal blades fashioned with wood, polymer, or plastic handles. Chisels are used by striking the tops of their handles with a mallet or hammer, thus driving the chisel's cutting edge into the material being worked. Figures 9.117 to 9.120 show a variety of chisels and some of their characteristic toolmarks.

Figure 9.120 A wood chisel used to cut and shape lumber.

Figure 9.121 A common hand crank drill with its parts.

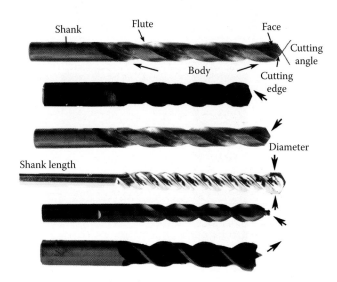

Figure 9.122 Five different twist drill bits with nomenclature.

Drill Bits

Drill bits are tools used to cut cylindrically shaped holes into blocks of metal, lumber, plastic, and many other materials. Drill bits are held in a tool called a drill. Two common hand drills are illustrated in Figures 9.121 and 9.123. Drill bits are secured into a drill by means of a chuck, which has jaws that, when tightened, hold the bit secure as the drill is caused to rotate by mechanical means.

Today, a large variety of drill bits are manufactured. The geometric shape of a drill bit will determine how effective it is in producing holes. Several features, such as the drill's twist or number of spirals per inch, point

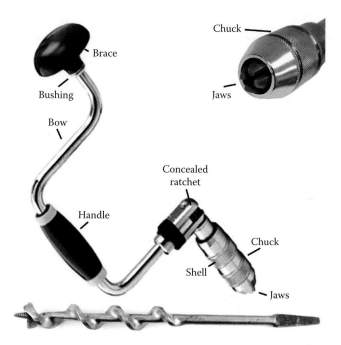

Figure 9.123 A bit brace holds auger bits.

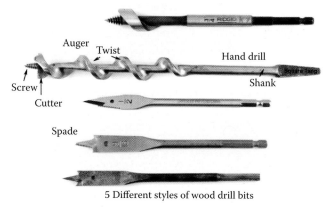

5 Different styles of wood drill bits

Figure 9.124 Five wood bits; the long auger bit is normally used with a brace, while the remaining four bits are used with electric drills.

angle, lip angle, length, and diameter, all affect its performance and efficiency. A selection of popular drill bits, their nomenclatures, geometric features, and the holes they cut are depicted in Figures 9.122 and 9.124 to 9.132.

Finally, the wounds of a woman killed by stabbing with a drill are seen in Figures 9.133 and 9.134. Chuck marks from the drill were found cut into the victim's body and on a bathroom wall as blood patterns. The victim's hair and blood were also on the drill, chuck, bit holder, and screwdriver bit. Some less commonly seen tools are depicted in Figures 9.135 through 9.147. Figures 9.148 and 9.149 illustrate a cataloged standards hand tool collection.

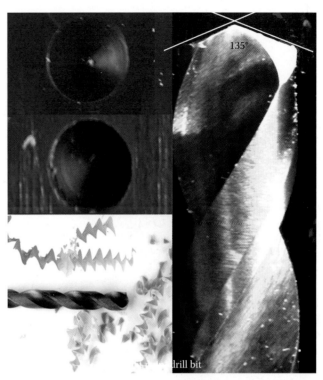

Figure 9.127 Twist split point drill bit with standard made in wax. Twist drill bit angles can vary from 118 to 150 degrees. Shallower cutting angles are used to drill into harder materials such as steel.

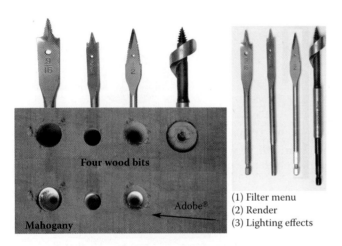

(1) Filter menu
(2) Render
(3) Lighting effects

Figure 9.125 Four wood bits with standards made in hard wood. Adobe lighting effects in render menu used to look down into holes.

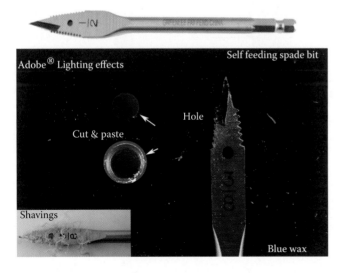

Figure 9.126 Self-taping spade bit with standards in wax. Adobe lighting effects in render menu used to look down into hole.

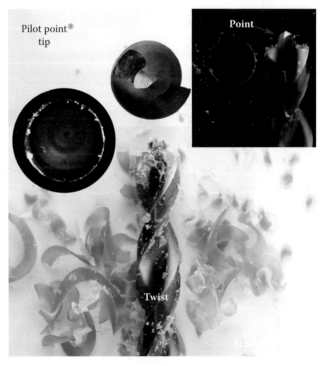

Figure 9.128 Pilot drill bit; the tip starts a pilot hole in the material being cut.

Figure 9.129 Countersink bits cut holes into material in order that screws and bolts can sit flush with or below the surface of a finished piece.

Figure 9.131 An electric drill auger bit with standard holes drilled in wax and scarf or waste shavings of wax shown on the tip of the blade.

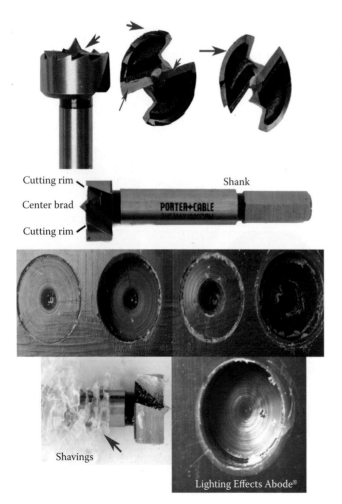

Figure 9.130 Forstner bits cut very precise flat-bottom holes in wood and other soft materials. Some Forstner bits have teeth on their cutting rims. Adobe lighting effects in render menu used to look down into hole.

Figure 9.132 Hole saw. Used for cutting holes in doors for lock cylinders and/or door knob apparatus.

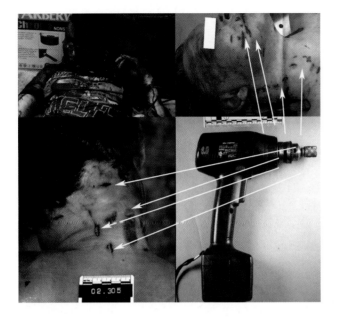

Figure 9.133 Chuck marks and drill bit holder marks on homicide victim.

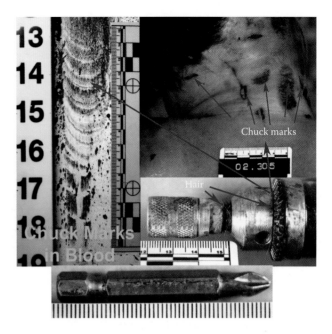

Figure 9.134 Chuck marks found on the victim's body and chuck mark blood patterns found on the bathroom wall. Victim's blood and hair found on drill bit.

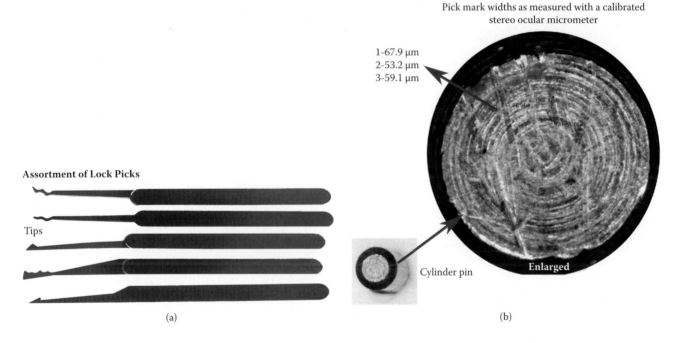

(a)   (b)

Figure 9.135 (a) Lock picks are made of thin, hardened steel, and they come in a large array of tip shapes. (b) A lock pin displaying pick marks indicating the lock cylinder it was removed from was picked.

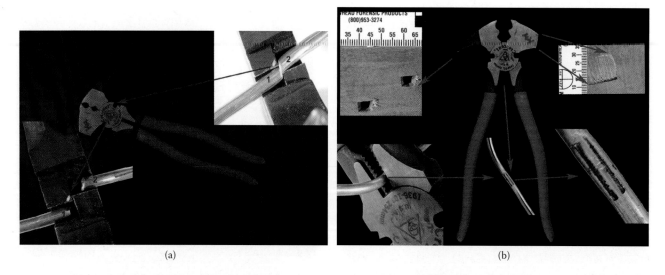

(a)   (b)

Figure 9.136 (a) Fence pliers are a multifacetted tool designed to do most tasks involved in putting up fences. They can be used as a wire or cable cutter; a hammer to drive nails; or pliers to grasp, bend, and shape wire or remove nails or staples; to make holes with the spiked end; and many other tasks involved in fence repair and construction. They are shown here cutting thick wire. (b) Several possible toolmarks made in wood and on metal wire by fence pliers.

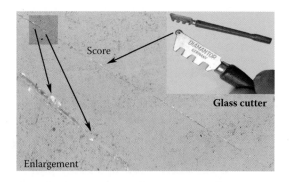

Figure 9.137 Glass scored by a glass cutter, sometimes seen in staged and real burglaries.

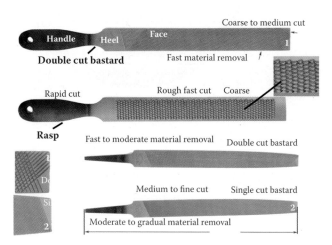

Figure 9.138 Several common files and a rasp with their nomenclature.

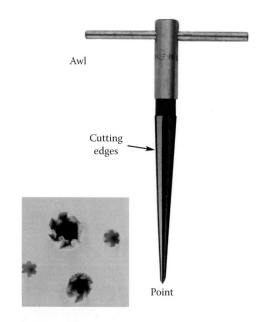

Figure 9.139 An awl with sharp cutting edges that enable it to be used to make holes in metal, wood, and other, larger materials. Several toolmarks made by an awl are displayed in clay.

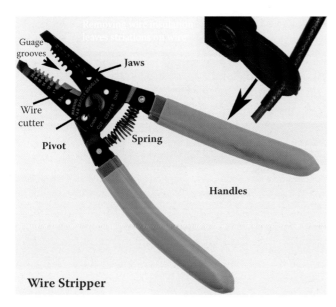

Wire Stripper

Figure 9.140 Common wire stripper used to cut various gauges of wire, as well as, crimp, and remove the insulation from electrical wires.

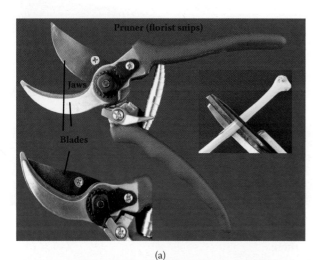

(a)

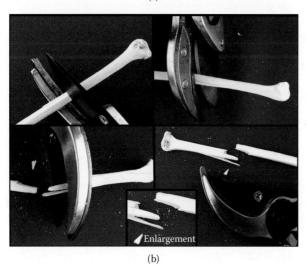

(b)

Figure 9.141 (a) A plant pruner sometimes used to cut fingers to remove valuable rings. (b) Fracture made by a pruner on thin, dried bone.

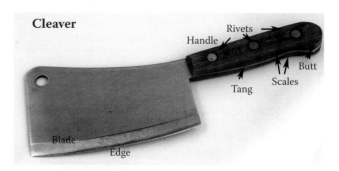

Figure 9.142 A cleaver, with its nomenclature, is often used in violent assaults. It makes toolmarks in skin and bone similar to those made by an axe.

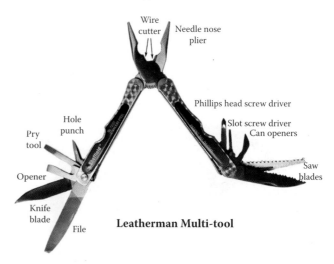

Leatherman Multi-tool

Figure 9.143 A Leatherman is a multi-tool capable of making many different types of toolmarks. This tool is becoming a favorite for criminals because of its small size and versatility.

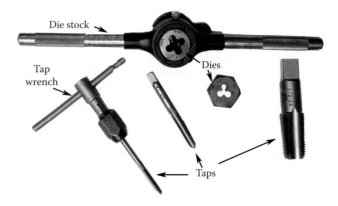

Figure 9.144 (a) Taps and dies used to make thread screws and bolts, as well as thread holes in metal, plastics, and other materials.

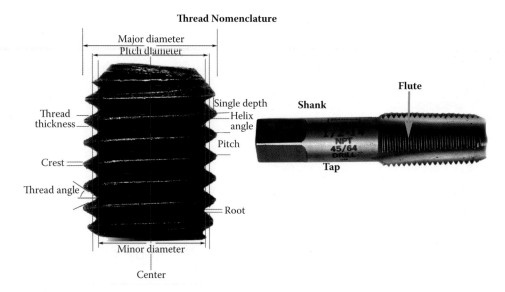

Figure 9.144 (b) Thread and tape nomenclature.

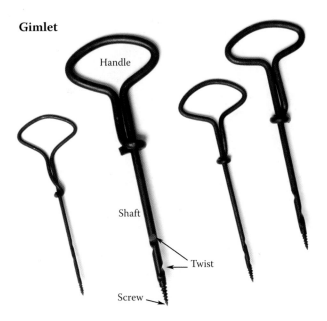

Figure 9.145 Various size gimlets are used to make small holes in wood.

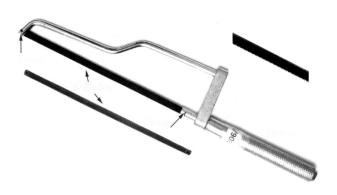

Figure 9.146 Small type of hacksaw, with its nomenclature, used to cut metal.

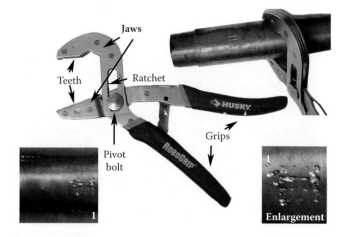

Figure 9.147 Robo grasping wrench, one of many kinds out there.

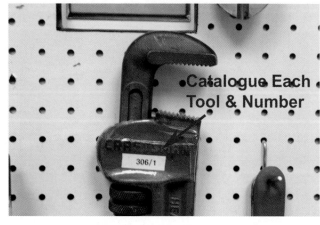

Figure 9.148 A pipe wrench with its catalogue number.

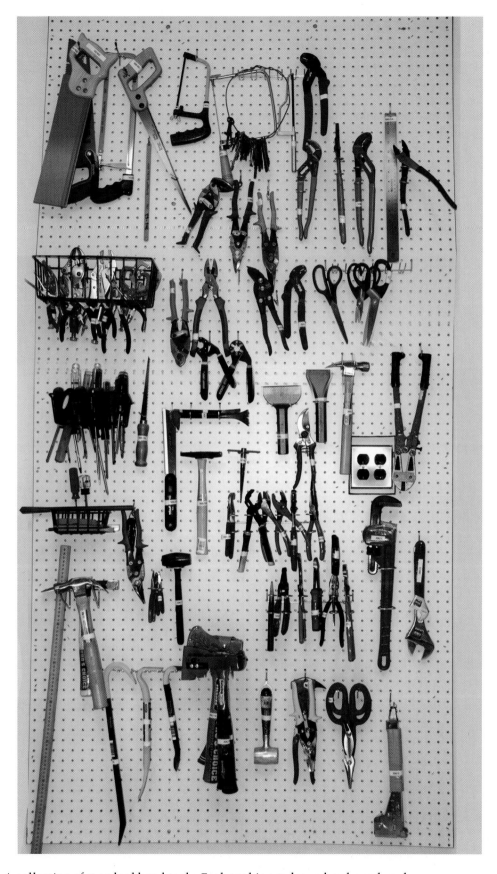

Figure 9.148 A collection of standard hand tools. Each tool is catalogued and numbered.

References

1. O'Hara and J.W. Osterburg, *An Introduction to Criminalistics: The Application of the Physical Sciences to the Detection of Crime*, 2nd edition, pp. 121–30, The MacMillan Co., NY 1952.
2. Burd, D.Q. and Kirk, P.L., "Tool marks—Factors involved in their comparison and use as evidence," *Journal of Criminal Law and Criminology, 32*, 1942, pp. 681.
3. http://www.wisegeek.com/what-is-a-crowbar.htm. Written by S. E. Smith, copyright © 2008.
4. Taupin, J.M., Damage to a wire security screen: Adapting the principles of clothing damage analysis. *J Forensic Sci* 1998, 43, 4, pp. 897–900.
5. Taupin, J.M., Testing conflicting scenarios: A role for simulation experiments in damage analysis of clothing. *J Forensic Sci* 1998, 43, 4, pp. 891–96.
6. Taupin, J.M., Comparing the alleged weapon with damage to clothing, *J Forensic Sci* 1999, 44, 1, pp. 205–07.
7. Taupin, J.M., Arrow damage to textiles: Analysis of clothing and bedding in two cases of crossbow deaths. *J Forensic Sci* 1998, 43, 1, pp. 205–07.1-C.E.

Bibliography

Abbott, J. R. 1964. *Footwear evidence*. Springfield, IL: Charles C. Thomas.

Abramowitz, M. 1988. *Microscope basics and beyond*. Vol. 1. Melville, NY: Olympus America.

Abramowitz, M. 1990. *Reflected light microscopy: An overview*. Vol. 3. Melville, NY: Olympus America.

Abe, S. 2005. *Support vector machines for pattern classification*. Springer: London.

Ahlhorn, T., Katterwe, H., Braune, M., Schreck, G., and Drews, F. 1999. Computerized comparison of toolmarks [Abstract]. In *3rd SPTM Meeting*, Sweden.

Akca, D. 2007. Matching of 3D surfaces and their intensities. *J. Photogram. Remote Sensing* 62:112–21.

Allen, T. J., and Scnetz, B. 1991. The removal of paint smears from tools and clothing for microscopical examination and analysis. *Forensic Sci. Int.* 52:101–5.

Andahl. 1978. The examination of saw marks. *J. Forensic Sci. Soc.* 18:31–46.

Arrowood, M. C., and Berglund, J. S. 1983. Examination of toolmarks from a hit and run. *AFTE J.* 15:100–1.

Aschoff, W. W., Kobilinsky, L., Loveland, R. P., McCrone, W. C., and Rochow, T. G. 1989. *Glossary of microscopical terms and definitions*. Chicago: McCrone Research Institute.

Bachrach, B. 2002. Development of a 3D-based automated firearms evidence comparison system. *J. Forensic Sci.* 47:1–12.

Bachrach, B. 2006. *A statistical validation of the individuality of guns using 3D images of bullets*. Grant Report 97-LB-VX-0008. National Institute of Justice.

Baldwin, D., Birkett, J., and Gibbins, B. 1995. Tool mark and shoe mark evidence. *MPFSL* 23:52–60.

Banno, A. 2004. Estimation of bullet striation similarity using neural networks. *J. Forensic Sci.* 49:1–5.

Bertsekas, D. P., and Tsitsiklis, J. N. 2002. *Introduction to probability*. 1st ed. Belmont, MA: Athena Scientific.

Bhagat, P. 2005. *Pattern recognition in industry*. 1st ed. Amsterdam: Elsevier.

Bellavic, H. 1934. Identifikation von Sägesspuren. *Arch. Kriminol.* B94:139–46.

Bessemans, A. 1955. Die Identifizierung der Spuren von Schneide- und Hackwerkzeugen. *Arch. Kriminol.* B115-116:61–72.

Biasotti, A. 1959. A statistical study of the individual characteristics of fired bullets. *J. Forensic Sci.* 4:34–50.

Biasotti, A., and Murdoch, J. 1984. Criteria for identification in firearms and toolmark identification. *AFTE J.* 16:16–24.

Biasotti, A., and Murdoch, J. 1987. Criteria for identification in firearms and toolmark identification—Progress since Oxford 1984 [Abstract]. In *IAFS Meeting*, Vancouver.

Blackwell, R., and Framan, E. 1980. Automated firearms identification systems AFIDS: Phase I. *AFTE J.* 12:11–37.

Bishop, M. 2006. *Pattern recognition and machine learning*. 1st ed. New York: Springer.

Bonfanti, M., Vicario, A., Gallusser, C., Baur, C., and Margot, P. 1995. Development of a 3-D automatic comparison system for toolmarks [Abstract]. In *European Meeting for SP/TM Examiners*, Finland.

Bonte, W. 1972. Gesichtspunkte zur Schartenspurenidentifizierung bei Stichverletzungen. *Arch. Kriminol.* B149:77–96.

Bonte, W. 1975. Tool marks in bones and cartilage. *J. Forensic Sci.* 20:315–25.

Bonte, W. 1974. Zur Differentialdiagnose von Mord und Selbstmord bei Stichverletzungen des Halses. *Arch. Kriminol.* B154:9–24.

Brackett, J. W. 1965. A study of idealized striated marks and their comparisons using models. Paper presented at the *26th Seminar of the CAC*.

Brackett, J. 1970. A study of idealized striated marks and their comparison using models. *J. Forensic Sci. Soc.* 10:27–56.

Buckleton, J., Nichols, R., Triggs, C., and Wevers, G. 2005. An exploratory Bayesian model for firearm and tool mark interpretation. *AFTE J.* 37:352–61.

Bunch, S. 2000. Consecutive matching striation criteria: A general critique. *J. Forensic Sci.* 45:955–62.

Burd, D. Q., and Gilmore, A. E. 1968. Individual and class characteristics of tools. *J. Forensic Sci.* 13:380–96.

Burd, D. Q., and Kirk, P. L. 1942. Tool marks: Factors involved and their comparison and use as evidence. *J. Crim. Law Criminol.* 32:679–86.

Burd, D. Q., and Greene, R. S. 1948. Tool mark comparisons in criminal investigations. *J. Crim. Law Criminol.* 39:379–91.

Burd, D. Q., and Greene, R. S. 1957. Tool mark examination techniques. *J. Forensic Sci.* 2:297–306.

Butcher, S. J., and Pugh, P. D. 1975. A study of marks made by bolt cutters. *J. Forensic Sci. Soc.* 15:115–26.

Butler, J. M., Schoske, R., Vallone, P. M., Redman, J. W., and Kline, M. C. 2003. Allele frequencies for 15 autosomal STR loci on U.S. Caucasian, African American and Hispanic populations. *J. Forensic Sci.* 48:1–4.

Butler, J. M. 2005. *Forensic DNA typing*. 2nd ed. New York: Academic Press.

Campbell, N. A., and Reece, J. B. 2004. *Biology*. 7th ed. New York: Benjamin Cummings.

Canibano, T., Miguel, A., Estrada, A., and Jose, I. 1995. Identification of dies used to forge registration plates [Abstract]. In *European Meeting for SP/TM Examiners*, Finland.

Carlson, C. J. 1983. Use of Coe-Flex for test toolmarks. *AFTE J.* 15:87.

Carlsson, K. 1997. Some techniques used in Sweden for comparison of shoeprint and for toolmark identification [Abstract]. In *First European Meeting of Forensic Sciences, Switzerland*.

Cassidy, F. H. 1980. Examination of tool marks from sequentially manufactured tongue-and-groove pliers. *J. Forensic Sci.* 25:796–809.

Cassidy, F. H. 1996. New colours of 'Mikrosil' casting rubber help in toolmark identification. *Tieline* 20:15–18.

Cassidy, F. H. 1997. Bolt cutter tool marks. *J. Assoc. Firearm Toolmark Exam.* 29:484–86.

Catterick, T., and Taylor, M. C. 1987. A photometric method for the quantitative mapping of parallel striated marks. *Forensic Sci. Int.* 33:197–207.

Chamot, E. M., and Mason, C. W. 1930. *Handbook of chemical microscopy*, 4–50. Vol. I. New York: John Wiley & Sons.

Clark, E. G. I., and Sperry, K. L. 1992. Distinctive blunt force injuries caused by a crescent wrench. *J. Forensic Sci.* 37:1172–78.

Clow, C. M. 2005. Cartilage stabbing with consecutively manufactured knives: A response to *Ramirez v. State of Florida*. *AFTE J.* 37:86–116.

Cochrane, D. W. 1985. Class characteristics of cutting tools and surface designation. *AFTE J.* 17:73–82.

Cook, C. W. 1979. The firearms/toolmark investigator: An excursion into the realm of the weird and wonderful. *AFTE J.* 11:35–43.

Costello, P. A., and Lawton, M. E. 1990. Do stab-cuts reflect the weapon which made them? *J. Forensic Sci. Soc.* 30:89–95.

Crammer, K., and Singer, Y., Eds. 2000. On the learnability and design of output codes for multiclass problems. In *Proceedings of the Thirteenth Annual Conference on Computational Learning Theory*, Palo Alto, CA.

Cristianini, N., and Shawe-Taylor, J. 2000. *An introduction to support vector machines and other kernel-based learning methods*. London: Cambridge University Press.

Cowles, D. L., and Dodge, J. K. 1948. A method for comparison of tool marks. *J. Crim. Law Criminol.* 39:262–64.

Davies, D. 1996. A case involving a drill bit with an unusual profile [Abstract]. *FSS Note*, No. 4, pp. 1–2.

Davis, J. E. 1958. *An introduction to tool marks, firearms and the striagraph*. Springfield, IL: Charles C. Thomas.

Davis, R. J. 1981. An intelligence approach to footwear marks and toolmarks. *J. Forensic Sci. Soc.* 21:183–93.

Dean, W. L. 1987. A case involving the physical matching of telephone wires [Abstract]. In: *IAFS Meeting*, Vancouver.

DeForest, P. R. 1982. Foundations of forensic microscopy. In *Forensic science handbook*, ed. R. Saferstein, 416–528. Vol. 1. Englewood Cliffs, NJ: Regents/Prentice Hall.

De Forest, P. R., Gaensslen, R. E., and Lee, H. C. 1983. *Forensic science: An introduction to criminalistics*, 383–88. New York: McGraw-Hill.

Deinet, W. 1981. Studies of models of striated marks generated by random processes. *J. Forensic Sci.* 26:35–50.

DeKinder, J., Tulleners, F., and Thiebaut, H. 2004. Reference ballistic imaging database performance. *Forensic Sci. Int.* 140:207–15.

DeKinder, J., and Bonfanti, M. 1999. Automated comparisons of bullet striations based on 3D topography. *Forensic Sci. Int.* 101:85–93.

Dekking, F. M., Kraaikamp, C., Lopuhaa, H. P., and Meester, L. E. 2005. *A modern introduction to probability and statistics: Understanding how and why*. 1st ed. New York: Springer.

Delly, J. G. 1980. *Photography through the microscope*. 8th ed. New York: Eastman Kodak Co.

Devroye, L., Gyorfi, L., and Lugosi, G. 1996. *A probabilistic theory of pattern recognition*. 1st ed. New York: Springer.

Dijk van, T. M. 1985. Steel marking stamps—Their individuality at the time of manufacture. *J. Forensic Sci. Soc.* 25:243–53.

Donnelly, R. A. 2004. *The complete idiot's guide to statistics*. 1st ed. New York: Alpha.

Duda, R. O., Hart, P. E., and Stork, D. G. 2001. *Pattern classification*. 2nd ed. New York: John Wiley & Sons.

Egan, W., Morgan, S. L., Bartick, E. G., Merrill, R. A., and Taylor, H. J. 2003. Forensic discrimination of photocopy and printer toners. II. Discriminant analysis applied to infrared reflection absorption spectroscopy. *Anal. Bioanal. Chem.* 376:1279–85.

Egan, W., Galipo, R. C., Kochanowski, B. K., Morgan, S. L., Bartick, E. G., Miller, M. L., et al. 2003. Forensic discrimination of photocopy and printer toners. III. Multivariate statistics applied to scanning electron microscopy and pyrolysis gas chromatography/mass spectrometry. *Anal. Bioanal. Chem.* 376:1286–97.

Efron, B. 1983. Estimating the error rate of a prediction rule: Improvement on cross-validation. *J. Am. Stat. Assoc.* 78:316–31.

Efron, B., and Tibshirani, R. J. 1993. *An introduction to the bootstrap*. 1st ed. Boca Raton, FL: Chapman & Hall/CRC.

Faden, D., Kidd, J., Craft, J., Chumbley, L. S., Morris, M., Genalo, L., et al. 2007. Statistical confirmation of empirical observations concerning tool mark striae. *AFTE J.* 39:205–14.

Fekete, J. F., and Fox, A. D. 1980. Successful suicide by self-inflicted multible stab wounds of the skull, abdomen and chest. *J. Forensic Sci.* 25:634–37.

Frazier, R. A. 1975. Toolmark test material. *AFTE J.* 7:25.

Gallusser, A., and Bonfanti, M. 1996. A particular case of toolmark examination. *Information Bull. Shoeprint/Toolmark Exam.* 3:8–18.

Geradts, Z., Bijhold, J., Hermsen, R., and Murtaugh, F. 2001. Image matching algorithms for breech face marks and firing pins in a database of spent cartridges of firearms. *Forensic Sci. Int.* 119:97–106.

Geradts, Z., and Keijzer, J. 1996. TRAX for tool marks. *AFTE J.* 28:183–90.

Geradts, Z., Keijzer, J., and Keereweer, I. 1994. A new approach to automatic comparison of striation marks. *J. Forensic Sci.* 39:974–80.

Gonick, L., and Smith, W. 1993. *The cartoon guide to statistics*. 1st ed. New York: HarperCollins.

Good, R. R. 1979. Tool mark identification in a gambling case (identification of illegally manufactured slugs). *AFTE J.* 11:49–50.

Green, M. A. 1978. Stab wound dynamics—A recording technique for use in medico-legal investigations. *J. Forensic Sci. Soc.* 18:161–63.

Greene, R. S., and Burd, D. Q. 1950, Special techniques useful in tool mark comparisons. *J. Crim. Law Criminol.* 41:523–27.

Hatcher, J. S., Jury, F. J., and Weller, J. 1957. *Firearms investigation identification and evidence.* 2nd ed. 438–41. Harrisburg, PA: The Stackpole Company.

Hatcher, J. S., Jury, F. J., and Weller, J. 1957. *Firearms investigation identification and evidence.* 1st ed. Philadelphia: Ray Riling Arms Books.

Hall, J. M. 1992. Consecutive cuts by bolt cutters and their effect on identifications. *AFTE J.* 24:260–71.

Heard, B. J. 1986. A new approach to the examination of stria on transparent and translucent materials. *AFTE J.* 18:25–34.

Hinsch, J. 1995. Shortcuts to teaching polarized light microscopy. *Microscope* 43:193–94.

Herbrich, R. 2002. *Learning kernel classifiers.* 1st ed. Cambridge, MA: MIT Press.

Hofmeister, A. G. 1981. Examination of stapler toolmarks. *AFTE J.* 13, 4:76.

Hoole, R., and Facey, O. 1990. A prototype automatic tool mark comparison [Abstract]. In *IAFS.*

Huelke. 1958. *Zentrale Werkzeugsperensammlung,* 89–92 [Centralized toolmark collection]. Bundekriminalamt Wiesbaden: Grundfragen der Kriminaltechnik.

Hunt, A. C., and Cowling, R. J. 1991. Murder by stabbing. *Forensic Sci. Int.* 52:107–12.

Hyvarinen, A., Karhunen, J., and Oja, E. 2001. *Independent component analysis.* New York: Wiley-Interscience.

Johnson, N. A. G., Pailthorpe, M. T., van Tets, K. F., and Robertson, J. 1995. Interpreting forensic evidence from stabbed knitwear. In *Advances in Forensic Sciences—Proceedings of the 13th Meeting of the IAFS,* Düsseldorf, 1993, pp. 255–64.

Jones, S. P. 1993. Specialized tools for forensic investigations: The trace mark microstamp. *J. Forensic Identification* 43:449–56.

Krzanowski, W. J. 1994. Orthogonal canonical variates for discrimination and classification. *J. Chemometrics* 9:509–20.

Kennedy, R. B., Pressmann, I. S., Chen, S., Petersen, P. H., and Pressman, A. E. 2003. Statistical analysis of barefoot impressions. *J. Forensic Sci.* 48:55–63.

Kenny, R. L. 1978. Identification of insulating material surrounding wires. *AFTE J.* 10:64.

Kingston, C. 1992. Neural networks in forensic sciences. *J. Forensic Sci.* 37:252–64.

Kirk, P. L. 1953. *Crime investigation,* 311–27. New York: John Wiley & Sons.

Koehler, A. 1937. Techniques used in tracing the Lindbergh kidnapping ladder. *J. Crim. Law Criminol.* 27:712–24.

Knight, B. 1975. The dynamics of stab wounds. *Forensic Sci.* 6:249–55.

Kockel, R. 1980. About the appearance of clues or marks from knife blades. *AFTE J.* 12:16–28.

Komar, S. M., and Scala, G. E. 1993. Examiner beware: New bolt cutter blades—Class or individual. *AFTE J.* 25:298–300.

Kubic, T., and Petraco, N. 2009. *Forensic science laboratory manual and workbook,* 1–15, 23–29, 111–18, 141–47, 307–34. 3rd ed. Boca Raton, FL: CRC Press.

Lapierre, J. A. G. 1978. Two interesting and unusual tool mark cases. *AFTE J.* 10:57–58.

Lehmann, E. L., and Romano, J. P. 2005. *Testing statistical hypotheses.* 3rd ed. New York: Springer.

Leon, F. P. 2006. Automated comparison of firearm bullets. *Forensic Sci. Int.* 156:40–50.

Lesko, J., Torpey, W. F., and Kelly, J. P. 1977. *Crime scene technician's manual.* New York: City of New York Police Department.

Liukkonen, M., Majamaa, H., and Virtanen, J. 1996. The role and the duties of the shoeprint/toolmark examiners in forensic laboratories. *Forensic Sci. Int.* 82:99–108.

Lucas, A. 1935. *Forensic chemistry and scientific criminal investigation.* New York: Longmans, Green.

Luna, A., Solano, C., Gomez, M., and Banon, R. 1989. Incised wound margins caused by steel blades—Scanning electron microscopy to determine wound direction. *Forensic Sci. Int.* 43:21–26.

Maheswari, H. S. 1981. Influence of vertical angle of tool on its tool mark. *Forensic Sci. Int.* 18:5–12.

Majamaa, H., and Ytti, A. 1996. Experiences of using the technique of "double casting." *Information Bull. Shoeprint/Toolmark Exam.* 2:9–12.

Majamaa, H. 1995. Knifemarks in cartilage. In *Advances in Forensic Sciences—Proceedings of the 13th Meeting of the IAFS,* Düsseldorf, 1993, pp. 270–72.

Majamaa, H. 1997. Toolmarks on staples: A case report [Abstract]. In *First European Meeting of Forensic Science,* Switzerland.

Majamaa, H. 1998. Toolmarks on staples: A case report. *Information Bull. SP/TM Examiners* 4:18–23.

Margot, P., Baur, C., Gallusser, A., Bonfanti, M., and Vicario, A., 1995. Development of a 3-D automatic comparison system for toolmarks. In *Proceedings of the 11th Interpol Forensic Science Symposium,* November 21–24.

Mason, J. J., and Grose, W. P. 1987. The individuality of toolmarks produced by a label marker used to write extortion notes. *J. Forensic Sci.* 32:137–47.

May, L. S. 1930. The identification of knives, tools, and instruments: A positive science. *Am. J. Police Sci.* 1:246–59.

Mayer, R. M. 1933. Kann man Sägen aus der Sägesspur wiederer-kennen? *Arch. Kriminol.* B92:157–60.

McGraw, A. C. 1984. Casting, another means of identification. *J. Forensic Sci.* 29:1212–22.

McGuire, D. L., and Brodie, T. G. 1975. Standard toolmark production device. *AFTE J.* 7:33–37.

McGuire, D., and Kennington, R. H. 1977. Comparative micrography techniques. *AFTE J.* 9:7–14.

The Merriam-Webster dictionary, 429. 1997. Springfield, MA.

Meyers, C. 1977. Tool marks on paper matches. *AFTE J.* 9:131.

Mezger, O., Hasslacher, F., and Frankle, P. 1930. Identification of marks made on trees. *Am. J. Police Sci.* 1:358–65.

Miller, S. A., and Jones, M. D. 1996. Kinematics of four methods of stabbing: A preliminary study. *Forensic Sci. Int.* 82:183 90.

Miller, J., and McLean, M. 1998. Criteria for identification of toolmarks. *AFTE J.* 30:15–61.

Miller, J., ed. 1998. Theory of identification as it relates to toolmarks. *AFTE J.* 30(1).

Miller, J. 2000. Criteria for identification of toolmarks. II. Single land comparisons. *AFTE J.* 32:116–30.

Miller, J., and Neel, M. 2004. Criteria for identification of tool marks. III. Supporting the conclusion. *AFTE J.* 37:7–38.

Mittleman, R. E., and Wetli, C. V. 1982. The threaded bolt injury pattern. *J. Forensic Sci.* 27:567–71.

Moenssens, A. A., Inbau, F. E., and Starrs, J. E. 1986. *Scientific evidence in criminal cases*, 236–40. 3rd ed. Mineola, NY: Foundation Press.

Molnar, S. 1970. Techniques for making test tool marks involving a vise and C-clamp. *AFTE J.* 2:26–30.

Molnar, S. 1970. Unusual tool mark impression identification. *AFTE J.* 2:32–33.

Molnar, S., and Nicholcon, T. V. 1976. Tool mark adapter for comparison microscope. *AFTE J.* 8:14.

Monahan, D. L., and Harding, H. W. J. 1990. Damage to clothing—Cuts and tears. *J. Forensic Sci.* 35:901–12.

Moran, B. A. 2002. Report on the AFTE theory of identification and range of conclusions for tool mark identification and resulting approaches to casework. *AFTE J.* 34:227–35.

Morgan, S. L., and Bartick, E. G. 2007. Discrimination of forensic analytical chemical data using multivariate statistics. In *Forensic analysis on the cutting edge: New methods for trace evidence analysis*, ed. R. D. Blackledge, 331–72. New York: John Wiley & Sons.

Murdock, J. E. 1970. Silicone rubber replicas of tool marks. *AFTE J.* 2:22–23.

Murdock, J. E. 1974. The individuality of tool marks produced by desk staplers. *AFTE J.* 6:23–29.

Needham, G. H. 1958. *The practical use of the microscope*, 225–29. Springfield, IL: Charles C. Thomas.

Neel, M., and Wells, M. 2007. A comprehensive statistical analysis of striated tool mark examinations. 1: Comparing known matches to known non-matches. *AFTE J.* 39:176–98.

Neel, M., and Wells, M. 2007. Errata: Correction to the article: Comprehensive statistical analysis of striated tool mark examinations. 1. Comparing known matches to known non-matches [AFTE J. 39 (2007): 176–98]. *AFTE J.* 39:264.

Nelsen, R. B. 2006. *An introduction to copulas.* 1st ed. New York: Springer.

Nichols, R. G. 1997. Firearms and toolmark identification criteria: A review of the literature. *J. Forensic Sci.* 42:466–74.

Nichols, R. G. 2003. Firearm and tool mark identification criteria: A review of the literature. 2. *J. Forensic Sci.* 48:318–27.

Nichols, R. G. 2007. Defending the scientific foundations of the firearms and tool mark discipline: Responding to recent challenges. *J. Forensic Sci.* 53:586–94.

O'Hara, C. E., and Osterburg, J. W. 1952. *An introduction to criminalistics*, 121–30. 2nd ed. New York: Macmillan Co.

O'Hara, C. E. 1974. *Fundamentals of criminal investigation*, 705–11. 3rd ed. Springfield, IL: Charles C. Thomas.

Paholke, A. R. 1978. The identification of class characteristics of tool marks: The evidence receipt/activity report. *AFTE J.* 10:59–62.

Pasquie, D. E., Hebrard, J., Margot, P., and Ineichen, M. 1996. Evaluation and comparison of casting materials in forensic sciences: Applications to tool marks and foot/shoe impressions. *Forensic Sci. Int.* 82:33–43.

Pasescu, G. 1995. Identification of tools for breaking door bolts open. Paper presented at *European Meeting for Shoeprint/Toolmark Examiners*, Finland.

Pelton, W. R. 1995. Distinguishing the cause of textile fiber damage using the scanning electron microscope (SEM). *J. Forensic Sci.* 40:874–82.

Pelton, W., and Ukpabi, P. 1995. Using the scanning electron microscope to identify the cause of fibre damage. II. An exploratory study. *J. Can. Soc. Forensic Sci.* 28:89–200.

Petraco, N., Petraco, N. D. K., and Pizzola, P. A. 2005. An ideal material for the preparation of tool mark test prints. *J. Forensic Sci.* 50:1407–10.

Petraco, N., Petraco, N. D. K., Faber, L., and Pizzola, P. A. 2009. Preparation of tool mark standards with jewelry modeling waxes. *J. Forensic Sci.* 54:353–58.

Petraco, N., and Sherman, H. 2006. *Illustrated guide to crime scene investigation.* Boca Raton, FL: CRC Press.

Petraco, N., and Kubic, T. 2002. *Microscopy for criminalists, chemists, and conservators.* Boca Raton, FL: CRC.

Petraco, N. D. K., Gil, M., Pizzola, P. A., and Kubic, T. A. 2008. Statistical discrimination of liquid gasoline samples from casework. *J. Forensic Sci.* 53:1092–101.

Petraco, N. D. K., Gambino, C., Kubic, T. A., Olivo, D., and Petraco, N. 2010. Statistical discrimination of footwear: A method for the comparison of accidentals on shoe outsoles inspired by facial recognition techniques. *J. Forensic Sci.*, 55:34–41.

Piper, A. G. 1985. The matching of secateurs to a harvested marijuana crop—A case report. *J. Forensic Sci. Soc.* 25:281–83.

Platt, J. C., Cristianini, N., and Shawe-Taylor, J. 2000. Large margin DAGs for multiclassification. In *Advances in neural information processing systems*, ed. S. A. Solla, T. K. Leen, and K.-R. Muller. Cambridge, MA: MIT Press.

Plumtree, W. G. 1978. Everything is not as it appears to be. *AFTE J.* 10:66–67.

Plumtree, W. G. 1982. Examination techniques for picked locks. *AFTE J.* 14:23–24.

Pollak, S., and La Harpe, R. 1936. Geformte Kontusionsmarken durch das Messerheft. *Arch. Kriminol.* B190:1–8.

Rasband, W. 2008. Image J. National Institute of Health. http://rsb.info.nih.gov/ij/.

Rao, V. J. 1986. Patterned injury and its evidentiary value. *J. Forensic Sci.* 31:768–72.

Rao, V. J., and Hart, R. 1983. Tool mark determination in cartilage of stabbing victim. *J. Forensic Sci.* 28:794–99.

Rathman, G. A. 1992. Tires and toolmarks. *AFTE J.* 24:146–59.

Reitz, J. A. 1975. An unusual tool mark identification case. *AFTE J.* 7:40–43.

Russ, J. C. 2001. *Forensic uses of digital imaging.* 1st ed. Boca Raton, FL: CRC Press.

Russ, J. C. 2006. *The image processing handbook.* 5th ed. Boca Raton, FL: CRC Press.

Sandercock, P. M. L., and Pasquier, E. D. 2003. Chemical fingerprinting of unevaporated automotive gasoline samples. *Forensic Sci. Int.* 134:1–10.

Sandercock, P. M. L., and Pasquier, E. D. 2004. Chemical fingerprinting of gasoline. 2. Comparison of unevaporated and evaporated automotive gasoline samples. *Forensic Sci. Int.* 140:43–59.

Sandercock, P. M. L., and Pasquier, E. D. 2004. Chemical fingerprinting of gasoline. 3. Comparison of unevaporated automotive gasoline samples from Australia and New Zealand. *Forensic Sci. Int.* 140:71–77.

Sansone, S. J. 1977. *Police photography.* Cincinnati, OH: Anderson, Inc.

Scott, C. C. 1969. *Photographic evidence.* 2nd ed., 3 vols. St. Paul, MN: West Publishing Co.

Schubert, K. D. 1985. Toolmarks link bomb components with suspects. *AFTE J.* 17:122–23.

Seghal, V. N., Singh, S. R., Dey, A., Kumar, M. R., Jain, C. K., and Grover, S. K. 1988. Tool marks comparison of a wire cut ends by scanning electron microscopy—A forensic study. *Forensic Sci. Int.* 36:21–29.

Senin, N., Groppetti, R., Garofano, L., Fratini, P., and Pierni, M. 2006. Three-dimensional surface topography acquisition and analysis for firearm identification. *J. Forensic Sci.* 51:282–95.

Shafer, G., and Vovk, V. 2008. A tutorial on conformal prediction. *J. Machine Learning Res.* 9:371–421.

Shillaber, C. P. 1944. *Photomicrography in theory and practice*, 198–99. New York: John Wiley & Sons.

Singh, R. P., and Aggarwal, H. R. 1984. Identification of wires and the cutting tool by scanning electron microscope. *Forensic Sci. Int.* 26:115–21.

Sivaram, S. 1977. Unusual instrument marks on bones. *Forensic Sci.* 9:109–10.

Smith, C. A. B. 1947. Some examples of discrimination, *Ann. Eugenics* 18:272–83.

Sobolewski, W. 1934. Über die Identifizierung von Werkzeugschartenspuren. *Arch. Kriminol.* B94:210–15.

Söderman, H., and O'Connell, J. J. 1936. *Modern criminal investigation.* New York: Funk and Wagnalls.

Song, J., Vorburger, T., Renegar, T., Rhee, H., Zheng, A., Ma, L., et al. 2006. Correlation of topography measurements of NIST SRM 2460 standard bullets by four techniques. *Measure. Sci. Technol.* 17:500–3.

Springer, E. 1995. Toolmark examinations—A review of its development in the literature. *J. Forensic Sci.* 40:964–68.

Starrs, J. E. 1983. The judicial firing line. *AFTE J.* 15:7–10.

Start, R. D., Milroy, C. M., and Green, M. A. 1992. Suicide by self-stabbing. *Forensic Sci. Int.* 56:89–94.

Stone, R. 2003. How unique are impressed tool marks? *AFTE J.* 35:376–83.

Stowell, L. I., and Card, K. A. 1990. Use of scanning electron microscopy (SEM) to identify cuts and tears in a nylon fabric. *J. Forensic Sci.* 35:947–50.

Svensson, A., and Wendel, O. 1971. *Techniques of crime scene investigation*, 98–116. 2nd ed. New York: Elsevier.

Takizawa, H., Nakamura, I., Hashimoto, M., Maekawa, N., and Yamamura, M. 1989. Toolmarks and peculiar blunt force injuries related to an adjustable wrench. *J. Forensic Sci.* 34:258–62.

Templin, R. H. 1980. A safe tool mark. *AFTE J.* 12:20.

Thomas, F. 2007. Reprint: Homicide by blows dealt to the head by means of an axe and identification of the weapon—A 1947 article on toolmarks in bone. *AFTE J.* 39:88–96.

Townshend, D. G. 1976. Photographing and casting toolmarks. *FBI Law Enforcement Bulletin*, April, pp. 9–11.

Taupin, J. M. 1998. Damage to a wire security screen: Adapting the principles of clothing damage analysis. *J. Forensic Sci.* 43:897–900.

Taupin, J. M. 1998. Testing conflicting scenarios: A role for simulation experiments in damage analysis of clothing. *J. Forensic Sci.* 43:891–96.

Taupin, J. M. 1999. Comparing the alleged weapon with damage to clothing. *Forensic Sci.* 44:205–7.

Taupin, J. M. 1998. Arrow damage to textiles: Analysis of clothing and bedding in two cases of crossbow deaths. *J. Forensic Sci.* 43:205–7.

Ukpabi, P., and Pelton, W. 1995. Using the scanning electron microscope to identify the cause of fibre damage. I. A review of related literature. *J. Can. Soc. Forensic Sci.* 28:181–87.

Walker, J. R. 2000. *Modern metalworking.* Tinley Park, IL: The Goodheart-Willcox.

Wang, S., Wang, Y., Jin, M., Gu, X., and Samaras, D. 2007. Conformal geometry and its applications on 3D shape matching, recognition, and stitching. *Trans. Pattern Anal. Machine Intell.* 7:1209–20.

Ward, D. C., and Sibert, R. W. 1986. The use of vacuum evaporation of metals for surface feature enhancement. *AFTE J.* 18:76–77.

Warren, G. 1991. Glass cutter impression identification. *AFTE J.* 23:925–27.

Watson, D. J. 1978. The identification of consecutively manufactured crimping dies. *AFTE J.* 10:43–45.

Vapnik, V. N. 2000. *The nature of statistical learning theory.* New York: Springer.

Verbeke, D. J. 1975. Tool mark on a bullet. *AFTE J.* 7:86–90.

Versailles, J. 1971. Tool marks—Striated vs. impressed. *AFTE J.* 3:13.

Versailles, J. 1973. Toolmarks on painted metal. *AFTE J.* 5:22.

Voorhees, R. 1990. Toolmark and indicia imprint examinations relative to the investigation of suspected postage meter abuses [Abstract]. In *IAFS*.

Vovk, M., Gammerman, A., and Shafer, G. 2005. *Algorithmic learning in a random world.* 1st ed. New York: Springer.

Zieler, H. W. 1972, 1974. *The optical performance of the light microscope.* Parts I and Part II. Chicago: Microscope Publications Ltd.

Zonjee, J. 1995. Some new developments in products for toolmark casting, shoeprint lifting and photographing [Abstract]. In *European Meeting for SP/TM Examiners*, Finland.

Index